MG SportsCars

An illustrated history of the world-famous sporting marque

Malcolm Green

Bramley
Books

CLB 4899
©1997 CLB International,
Godalming Business
Centre,
Woolsack Way,
Godalming,
Surrey GU7 1XW,
UK

This edition published by
Bramley Books.

ISBN 1-85833-606-6

Credits

Studio photography:
Andrew Dee
(with the exception of
pages 14-15 and 18-19:
Stuart McAllister)

Editor
Philip de Ste. Croix

Designer
Roger Hyde

The Author

Malcolm Green is the Southern Correspondent of the monthly "MG Enthusiast Magazine" and the author of two guides to restoring M.G.s, one on the T-types and the other on the MGA. He is also the librarian of the Triple-M Register of The M.G. Car Club and in that capacity has written and published books on the pre-war cars, with the assistance of other members of the Register committee. He is also a regular contributor to other magazines such as "The Automobile", "M.G. Magazine" in America and "Enjoying MG".

His involvement with the marque started in the 1950s, when he gazed longingly through the showroom windows at each new model as it appeared. In 1962, aged eighteen, he at last realized his ambition and bought his first M.G. – a new M.G. Midget. Since then he has always had at least one example of the marque in the garage and has carried out numerous complete rebuilds of models as diverse as a 1932 F-type and 1969 M.G. Midget.

Author's Acknowledgements

The most rewarding thing about being involved with M.G.s are the people you meet. Over the last 35 years I have been privileged to talk to many of those instrumental in making the marque so successful. I must thank Dick Knudson, long-standing chairman of The New England M.G. T Register in the United States, for some of these introductions, and for stimulating my interest in M.G. history all those years ago.

I have many M.G.-owning friends and I have drawn heavily upon their friendship while writing this book. I cannot list here everyone who helped, but would like to single out the particular efforts of both Phil Jennings and Michael Hannigan for their assistance with the vintage cars. To all those owners who spent many boring hours in the studio while their cars were photographed I can only say "Thank you". Who knows, they may even speak to me again one day!

Lastly I want to thank my wife, Andrea. Over the last 30 years she has shared my interest in M.G.s, and assisted with the dirtiest parts of every rebuild! It is largely due to her help and encouragement that this book has been written.

Production
Ruth Arthur
Sally Connolly
Neil Randles
Paul Randles
Karen Staff

Director of production
Gerald Hughes

Page make-up
M.A.T.S.

Colour reproduction
Pixel Tech Prepress PTE
Ltd, Singapore

**Printed and bound in
Singapore**
KHL Printing

CONTENTS

Picture credits

With the exception of the studio photography of the cars detailed in the contents list and the photographs listed below, all the pictures in this book were either taken by the author or are from the author's collection.

Neill Bruce:
114-115 bottom, 115 bottom right, 133 top left and centre, 134 centre, 135 top, 145 all

John Finch:
92 top

Rod Martin:
66 top left and centre left

Jon Mazu:
68, 69, 97 top

Andrew Roberts:
149 all, 156 all, 157 all

Rover Group:
152 bottom, 153 top, 154 centre left

Pete Thelander:
66-67 top

WO 9320

Can anyone explain the appeal of an M.G.? Why is it that millions of people from all over the world recognize that those two letters have come to symbolize the very essence of a sports car? Why in 1995, some 15 years after the final cars were built at Abingdon and 33 years after the last completely new M.G. sports car had been launched, did the announcement of the MGF cause such huge interest? The appeal of the marque for both the enthusiast and the general public was evidently undiminished and a phenomenal amount of publicity was generated in the motoring press, daily newspapers and on television all around the world.

Exotic, high-performance cars have always had enthusiastic devotees and marques like Ferrari and Aston Martin are known worldwide. It is easy to see why the ultimate in performance and beauty should attract a large following but, because the cars themselves are both rare and expensive, ownership is limited to the wealthy few, with the majority of enthusiasts able only to admire the cars from a distance. M.G.s are different. The majority are neither fast nor expensive and anyone who can afford to run a car at all can afford an M.G. – they are the sports car for the ordinary man. Perhaps this, then, is the appeal of an M.G.

Advertising agencies are not averse to using M.G.s to sell other products and for some years old cars, particularly old sports cars, have been seen as a fashionable accessory to help when selling everything from cosmetics to beer. This exposure promotes the cars and must have tempted a few to consider owning one. Ever since the 1930s film makers have understood their appeal and have used them wherever possible. Once they began being exported in large numbers to the United States, especially to the West Coast in the late 1940s and early 1950s, Hollywood producers fell over themselves to include M.G.s in their productions. Many of the most famous actors and actresses shared star billing with TCs, TDs and MGAs, and no story about the wartime exploits of dashing young R.A.F. officers was complete without an M.G., usually painted red, in the picture.

There have been many M.G. saloon cars, and in the 1980s all such cars produced were re-badged and tuned versions of standard saloons and hatchbacks, built to capitalize on the M.G. name. However, to most people an M.G. is quin-tessentially an open two-seater. Explaining the appeal of such cars to the uninitiated is not always easy. Unless you have enjoyed driving a responsive open car through winding country lanes on a summer's day, or experienced the pleasure to be gained from travelling in convoy with other enthusiasts in similar cars on a club outing, then such explanations will be meaningless. Fortunately, there are still many converts made each year to the joys of M.G. motoring and still some uncluttered roads to enjoy.

Fortunately, the pleasure of owning an M.G. isn't just about using it for special occasions and when the weather is fine. It is remarkable just how many of the older models still provide everyday transport, and it is just this everyday use of the MGB, for example, that sustained a thriving parts and restoration industry long after the original dealers ceased to provide spares support. The spares situation now is so good that almost every part of the car, from the bodyshell to a wiper blade, is available "off the shelf". Those who drive their M.G.s every day

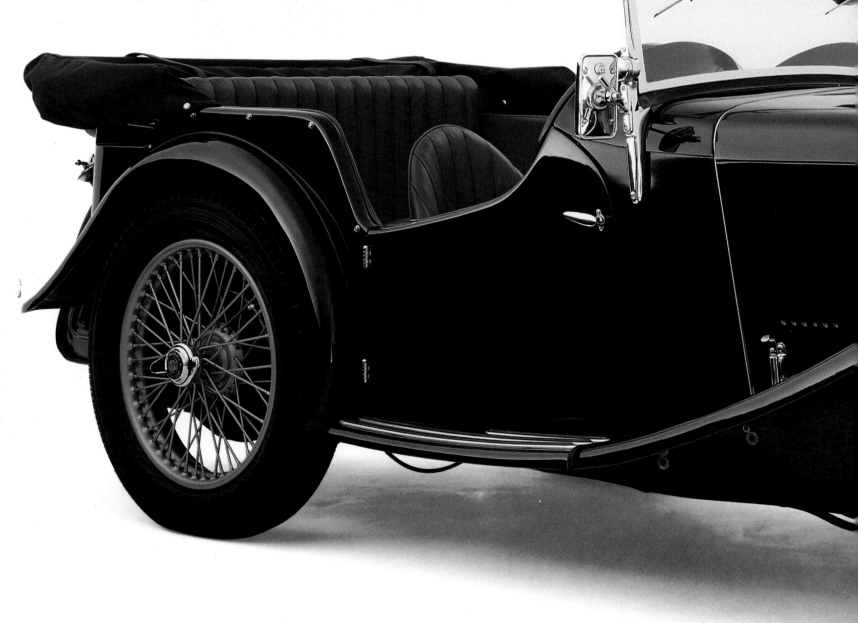

both have the pleasure of using something a little different from the average modern car and can also benefit from driving a car that depreciates little, and one which is often cheaper to run than something newer.

There are certainly many people returning to M.G. ownership after years of driving other cars. Increasing affluence has led some to buy one in later years when they can afford to run it purely as a hobby car. Now that a lot of people in middle age have to take early retirement, many are bought to restore as retirement projects and the models chosen are frequently either those owned many years previously, or ones that - satisfy a long-held ambition. Ownership of such a car brings the M.G. enthusiast into contact with others of like mind, and husbands or wives can also join in the enjoyment of the M.G. I can think of no better way to spend any spare time.

The nice thing about owning an M.G. is that an equivalent degree of pleasure is available from even the cheapest examples. Any two-seater open car in good condition can provide the same

The **MG** Two-Litre "Tickford"
Folding Head Foursome Drop-Head Coupe.
COACHWORK BY SALMONS & SONS.

Above: Not all M.G.s are small sports cars, as this picture of a page of the sales brochure for the SA saloon shows. The Tickford-bodied M.G.s are among the most elegant cars ever built.

EA 5704

measure of enjoyment. Sitting behind the wheel of a Midget or MGA brings all the delight and excitement of which only this type of motoring is capable. Modern sports coupés, or even ordinary family saloons, can provide vastly more speed and roadholding than an old M.G., and soft-top versions will give open-air motoring, but cars like these are only interesting to drive when travelling at high speeds. The lower standards of roadholding and greater wind resistance of the older sports car combine to increase the sensation of speed, thus providing large doses of motoring pleasure without danger to life and limb. The M.G. company slogan that appeared in advertisements from 1930 was *"Safety Fast!"* and this still holds good today.

The M.G. enthusiast has luckily chosen a marque of car that is available in many diverse models. The out-and-out sports car enthusiast, craving fresh air and a lack of basic creature comforts, can be more than happy behind the wheel of one of the more spartan prewar offerings from Abingdon, whilst the performance car enthusiast can spend much of his spare time trying to extract ever more power from his V8-engined MGB. The family man, or indeed

anyone not so keen on such close contact with either the vagaries of the climate or the ultimate in rapid acceleration, can take his pick from a large range of saloons.

So M.G. then adds up to a sports car produced in sufficient quantity to be readily available at affordable prices and in enough diverse styles to appeal to widely differing tastes. The cars are economical to own and run – even when compared to the modern alternatives. So are these the reasons for their popularity? Probably, but I don't think they are by any means the only reasons. They certainly cannot account for the degree of affection displayed by anyone recalling their ownership of examples which were often well worn and often unreliable. A letter I received from an elderly lady recalling a car she owned in the late 1930s described it as "the nicest car I ever owned". Perhaps it is the very simplicity of most models that makes them attractive. Someone once described his MGA as being "a friendly sort of car" which may sound odd to the average reader but will strike a chord with every enthusiast who has tried to find that once-loved and long remembered car they sold many years previously.

Above: Power and beauty go hand in hand. The polished camshaft covers dominate the MGA Twin Cam engine.

My ownership of M.G.s started in 1962 when I bought a new Midget. The model had just been revised for the 1962 London Motor Show and had been fitted with an enlarged engine – all of 1098cc – and disc front brakes. This, the first of a succession of Midgets, was the car that really gave me some idea of the magic of sports car driving. With its modest power output, but superb handling, gear change and steering, it introduced me to the art of steering a car on the throttle on wet roads, taking part in club competitions and generally behaving as if I was the next Stirling Moss – which I certainly was not! The standard cross-ply tyres fitted allowed me to take tremendous liberties at what would now seem ridiculously low speeds. Luckily it would have needed a really stupid driver to get himself into much trouble with that car.

Looked at now, the performance I enjoyed then seems barely adequate, but it must be remembered that traffic speeds in the early 1960s were much lower and there were fewer high-speed roads. I well remember trips of over 100 miles (160km) when I would pass dozens of cars quite safely, without being overtaken once. The combination of a light and agile car, good visibility and excellent handling was more than adequate in those days. Only on the few motorways would the lack of high-speed cruising ability be a disadvantage and I would be passed by Jaguars and their ilk. On winding roads only the Mini-Cooper S was a real competitor amongst the standard production cars. These days almost every vehicle on the road is faster than a 1962 Midget – such is progress!

In spite of owning a wide variety of M.G.s over the intervening years I still recall journeys in that first M.G. with pleasure. That fast cross-country drive on a bright, but cold, winter morning muffled up against the chill, with the tonneau cover over the passenger seat and the heater blasting hot air round my legs. Drives in the open car down quiet country roads on mild nights with the bark of the exhaust reflecting back from banks and brick walls. The attempts at climbing hills using narrow winding roads marked "unsuitable for motors". To be fair, I should also recall the days when the sliding side screens froze up and the times running costs left one short of money to pay the landlady, but I would rather forget those! Yes, owning an M.G., any M.G., is something special.

Malcolm Green

THE START OF IT ALL

None of the cars bearing the famous M.G. badge celebrated in this book would have existed had it not been for the genius of just two men – William Morris, later Lord Nuffield, and Cecil Kimber. Men of vastly differing outlooks and personalities, of the two Morris was probably the more important. Without him there would have been no Morris Garages to employ Cecil Kimber, or Morris cars for Kimber to modify and sell as "M.G. Super Sports", and I would have had nothing to write about years later! Anyway, let us start at the beginning.

The story of personal wheeled transport and of the motor car really starts with the bicycle. Like many other pioneer motor manufacturers, William Morris began his working life in the bicycle business and only later became involved with motor cars. Born in 1877, he showed early technical ability when he constantly dismantled and re-assembled his first bicycle and this expertise was to stand him in good stead when he was forced, by his father's illness, to give up his ambition to study medicine in favour of employment in a local cycle repair shop. This job was to last but a short while. Ambition led him to start his own business trading as a bicycle repairer from a building behind his father's house, with the front room converted to use as shop premises and as a showroom.

Left: William Morris aged eighteen. By this time he had already started out in business on his own as a bicycle repairer.

Above: Cecil Kimber in his office at Abingdon. The silver model of the "Magic Midget" on the desk is a cigarette lighter.

Below: 1924 M.G. Saloon de Luxe built on the standard Morris Oxford chassis. These cars were exceptionally well equipped and had such luxuries as silk blinds on all windows. The model in this picture was Cecil Kimber's first wife, Rene, who took a keen interest in the business.

It was not long before the energetic Morris started to produce his own bicycles, prompted by an order for a special machine from a local rector, Mr. Pilcher. As his reputation grew, he built machines to order and also acted as agent for other company's products. Having outgrown his parent's house, he rented shop premises at 48 High Street, Oxford, a much more convenient position to serve the customers in the town, and a workshop and storage area just around the corner at 1 Queen Street. In addition to building, selling and repairing bicycles, William Morris was also an accomplished racing cyclist. He won innumerable medals and was cycling champion of Oxfordshire, Buckinghamshire and Berkshire, tackling the necessary training regimes with as much determination as he was to exhibit in business later in life.

By 1902 William Morris had made his first moves towards motorized transport by con-

structing a motorcycle using an engine he had built himself from castings he had purchased. This machine was successful and, drawing upon the experience he had gained building and developing it, Morris decided to go into partnership with a friend, Joseph Cooper, to build motorcycles for sale. Additional premises were acquired in Holywell Street and machines built up around 2.75hp de Dion engines were offered for sale. The venture was successful, although the partnership was short lived because of a difference of opinion between the two men. The Holywell Street/Longwall premises were also useful for storing customers' cars and by 1903 he was offering a "repair service for motors".

A Hard Lesson

Another partnership followed, this time with a wealthy undergraduate and an Oxford businessman, trading as "The Oxford Automobile and Cycle Agency". Unfortunately this venture was something of a disaster and after just over one year of trading the business was wound up. Morris had debts of £50 and little else to show for all his efforts. Lack of experience had led the other partners to spend more on promotion than had been justified by sales, and this was a lesson that he was to remember in later years. He was determined to avoid partnerships in future. Back in business on his own, Morris concentrated on servicing, repairing and selling various makes of cars, as well as operating a car hire and taxi business serving the local area.

Above: This specially built M.G. has become known as "Old Number One". Although by no means the first car bearing the famous badge, this is certainly the first M.G. built specifically for use in competition.

Right: Kimber entered the special in the 1925 Land's End Trial and won a Gold Medal. The car was very much a "one off" although many modified Morris components were used in its construction. Today, "Old Number One" can usually be seen in the British Motor Industry Heritage Trust Museum at Gaydon in Warwickshire.

In 1910, increasing amounts of work necessitated the rebuilding of the Longwall premises. The business was now formally called "The Morris Garage", a title later changed to "The Morris Garages" as additional premises were acquired. Morris had become agent for a number of different car makers, such as Humber, Singer, Standard and Wolseley, as well as for some motor cycle manufacturers. By 1912 he was ready to try his hand at producing his own motor car and the first Morris Oxford appeared in 1913. Designed by Morris, the car embodied features that his considerable experience servicing customers' cars had taught him were practical. Although not the cheapest car on sale,

the Morris Oxford was well built and well engineered using components purchased from outside suppliers, and it immediately attracted sufficient orders to justify him acquiring new premises at a disused military training college at Cowley, just east of Oxford.

The cars soon established a reputation for strength and gained some successes in reliability trials. Each of the entrants driving Morris Oxford cars in the 1914 London-Edinburgh Trial was awarded a gold medal. Other models followed, but the First World War saw production at Cowley switching to munitions, with volume car production only returning with peace in 1918. Morris Motors was now a separate entity

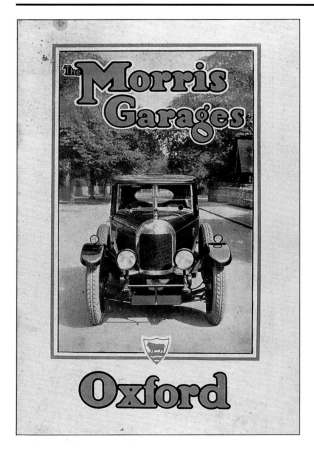

and for the component suppliers E.G. Wrigley of Birmingham, before being taken on as Sales Manager of Morris Garages. Although he could not have anticipated it, this move was to give him the chance to stamp his name on the British motor industry in a way that was to make him known to successive generations of sports car enthusiasts.

As well as running the business, Cecil Kimber designed and marketed special bodywork for the Morris Cowley to sell alongside the standard range of cars. This model was called the Morris Garages Chummy and the cars were assembled at the Longwall Street premises along with the usual repair and servicing work. They sold extremely well, necessitating a move of production to a mews garage in Alfred Lane. Here a small workforce under Cecil Cousins (who was later to become a key element behind the success of M.G.s) collected chassis from Cowley, modified them and took them to the coachbuilders – Carbodies of Coventry – to be fitted with their special bodies. Later they collected them and fitted the final details before preparing the cars for sale. A more sporting version fitted with a two-seater body made by the local coachbuilding firm, Charles Raworth, was also sold in small numbers and it was this model that many considered to be the first M.G. A Morris Garages' advertisement in the November 1923 issue of the Oxford magazine "The Isis" described the Super Sports Morris as an M.G. – using the initials set within the, now, familiar octagon. This is the earliest use of the logo that I can trace.

A new car fitted with a Kimber-designed saloon body, with a "V" shaped windscreen, was advertised in the March 1924 issue of "The Morris Owner" as "our popular M.G. Saloon" on the 14/28 Morris Oxford Chassis, priced at £460. The advertisement went on to point out that in addition to the saloon there was also a Landaulette, Vee front coupé and two or four-seater sports models in the M.G. range. In the following issues of the same magazine the other body styles were illustrated. In common with many other manufacturers, for a time M.G. used confusing model designations. The "14" of the 14/28 refers to the rated horsepower for taxation purposes and the "28" is often taken to be the actual power output. However, these figures often bore more relationship to the company's sales aspirations than to reality and are best taken as merely a way of identifying one model from another.

from Morris Garages, which continued in business selling and repairing cars under Morris' ownership. It was as Sales Manager of Morris Garages that William Morris appointed Cecil Kimber in 1921. The following year, the sudden suicide of Edward Armstead, the General Manager of the business, led to Kimber being promoted to fill the vacancy.

A Man Called Kimber

Cecil Kimber was born in London in 1888, but brought up and educated in the North of England. From his mother he inherited a talent for drawing and painting which was to serve him well in later years when he was able to use this skill to impart his ideas graphically to those working on designs for new M.G. models. There is no doubt that he had a considerable ability to judge if the appearance of a car looked right and it is a tribute to his talent that M.G. never built an ugly or ungainly car whilst he was in charge.

Like most young men at that time, Kimber's first motorized transport was two-wheeled and he bought his Rex motorcycle after he had been working in his father's printing firm for a couple of years. Unfortunately, when riding a borrowed motorcycle, he was involved in a very serious accident with a car that so badly damaged his right leg that it took many months and a number of operations before he could use it again. The injury left his leg a couple of inches shorter than it had been and prompted a transfer from two to four wheels with the purchase of a Singer in 1913, which he used in connection with his father's business.

Having decided that a career in the motor industry was preferable to one in printing, Kimber worked for A.C. Cars at Thames Ditton

Left: A two-seater 14/28 M.G. exhibiting the style that enabled Cecil Kimber to sell these cars at a much higher price than a standard Morris.

Above: 1927 14/28 Salonette. The flat radiator is less attractive than the distinctive bullnose design that was a Morris trademark.

Below: A four-seater 14/28 alongside a First World War tank. The aluminium body sides are engine-turned and lacquered.

The Morris Oxford chassis was modified late in 1924, with the changes including better brakes and a longer chassis. These improvements were incorporated in the chassis used for the 14/28 M.G. with these cars receiving further improvements to the steering, suspension and controls at Alfred Lane before being fitted with their smart coachwork. The M.G. Super Sports range comprised an open four-seater, an open two-seater and a two-door salonette at prices from £350 to

£475 – quite expensive cars in 1924. However, the Morris Garages continued to offer special bodywork on unmodified Morris chassis at lower prices.

Kimber entered a modified Chummy in the 1923 Land's End Trial and won a gold medal, so he decided to enter a specially-built car in the 1925 event. An OHV (overhead valve) Hotchkiss engine was obtained, stripped and modified. He made drawings of a special chassis which was

constructed, using just a few hand tools, from modified Morris Cowley components. The engine was installed in the chassis, which was fitted with a modified braking system constructed from many special parts made in the little machine shop at Longwall Street. Fitted with a purposeful looking two-seater body manufactured by Carbodies, the car was reputed to have been capable of reaching a top speed of 82mph (132kph) when tested by Kimber. With

Described in a contemporary sales brochure as "A true sporting car with amazing performance coupled with extreme comfort", the Bullnose M.G.s are amongst the most elegant of vintage cars. The changes made by Cecil Kimber to the specification of the standard chassis, and the addition of lightweight and attractive coachwork, transformed the humble Morris Oxford into a car that appealed to quite a different sort of owner. Certainly, just the sort of car to tempt a wealthy 1920s' sportsman.

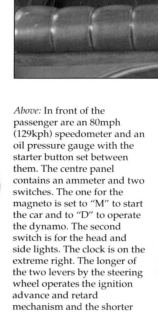

Above: In front of the passenger are an 80mph (129kph) speedometer and an oil pressure gauge with the starter button set between them. The centre panel contains an ammeter and two switches. The one for the magneto is set to "M" to start the car and to "D" to operate the dynamo. The second switch is for the head and side lights. The clock is on the extreme right. The longer of the two levers by the steering wheel operates the ignition advance and retard mechanism and the shorter the choke.

Right: The artillery wheels are fitted with aluminium wheel discs. Wire wheels were the more usual wear for this model. The windscreen wiper is vacuum operated.

Above and below: This beautiful two-seater 14/28 has been owned by Jersey resident, Michael Hannigan, since 1984, and is one of only two surviving running examples of these very early M.G.s. Originally the car carried the registration number WL1940, this being changed to J1926 when Michael bought the car. The headlights have mechanical Barker dipping which is operated by the driver using a lever on the right-hand side of the cockpit, located near the handbrake.

Left: A popular period accessory for cars with four-wheel braking, which were fitted to all M.G.s, to warn drivers of lesser cars that if the car in front stopped suddenly, they might not be able to avoid hitting it!

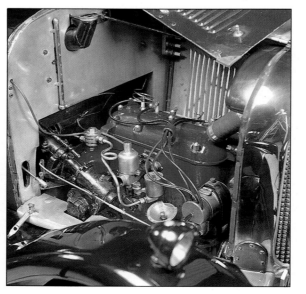

Left: The side valve, 1802cc Morris Oxford engine was modified by fitting aluminium pistons, duralumin connecting rods, polishing the head and raising the compression ratio. This car has an SU carburettor in place of the more usual Solex. A scuttle-mounted fuel tank holds seven gallons (32 litres) of fuel which gravity feeds the carburettor float chamber. A magneto provides ignition. Once modified by M.G. to increase power output, this engine gives the car good performance and a high degree of reliability.

Left: The four-seater 14/28 is mechanically identical to the two-seater. The aluminium covered body has only two doors, one at the front on the left-hand side and one at the rear on the driver's side. The passenger's front bucket seat tips up to allow access from that side for the rear-seat passengers. The driver either uses the front passenger's door, or climbs in over the side of the body!

Right: This 1926 four-seater car has led an interesting life. Built in 1926, by 1931 it was in the hands of Eric Fernihough, a motor-cycle racer of some repute, and he used it right up to 1938 to take his machines to Brooklands. He held the record for travelling at the fastest speed at that track on a two-wheeler – 143.39mph (230.76kph).

SPECIFICATION

Model: 14/28 "Bullnose" two-seater/four-seater

Engine: Four-cylinder in line, side valve, water cooled. 75 x 102mm, 1802cc

Gearbox: Three-speed non-synchromesh

Final drive: 4.42:1. Top gear 20mph/1000rpm (32kph/1000rpm)

Suspension: Solic axles mounted on leaf springs

Dimensions: Wheelbase 8ft 10.5in (2705mm). Track 4ft (1219mm). Overall length 12ft 6in (3810mm)

Unladen weight: 18cwt (915kg)

Cost when new: £345 (two-seater); £360 (four-seater)

Performance: (From contemporary reports): Top speed 65mph (105kph)

Owners: Michael Hannigan (two-seater); Alan Binnington (four-seater)

Above: The sales brochure for the 14/40hp M.G. Mark IV. All the body styles are illustrated by photographs in the brochure, but there are also a number of amusing cartoon drawings showing the perils of buying various other types of car rather than an M.G. 14/40!

Right: A 14/40 four-seater tourer owned by historian Robin Barraclough. These cars are solid and reliable vintage transport.

less than 48 hours to go before the start of the Land's End Trial, it was found to have a cracked chassis frame. Immediate repairs were carried out with some hand-cut strengthening plates being welded in place and the car was ready for action. Cecil Kimber, accompanied by Oxford insurance broker Wilfred Mathews, had a trouble free run, gaining a gold medal.

Soon after the trial Kimber sold the car for £300 to a friend, Stockport businessman Harry Turner, and it passed through the hands of several owners before being rescued by the M.G. Car Company in 1932 for use in publicity as "Old Number One" or "The First M.G." – a title which it most certainly does not deserve, although it was certainly the first purpose-built M.G. com-

petition car. This historic vehicle still survives and can usually be seen on display at the British Motor Industry Heritage Trust museum at Gaydon in Warwickshire.

By September 1925, the space available at Alfred Lane was proving insufficient to cope with the numbers of cars being built there. A section of the newly-completed Morris Radiators'

factory in Bainton Road, Oxford was rented by Morris Garages with M.G. production being transferred there. As there were now 25 employees working on car production, a works manager was appointed and installed in a separate, glass-sided office from where he could oversee operations.

The catalogue of 1926 M.G. models was a much more professional affair than those previously issued by The Morris Garages. Inside the front cover was the proud statement that "Such is the popularity of the various M.G. models that a special factory has been erected to cope with the ever-increasing demand". At that time every new Morris car was sold with one year's free comprehensive insurance and this cover was also available for new M.G.s. The "Super Sports" models were available as two- and four-seaters and also as a salonette which was a small, two-door saloon. This model was fitted with steel disc wheels in place of the wire wheels now standard for the other two models. The basic Morris chassis with solid-spoked artillery wheels was used for the four-door saloon and the Weymann Sedan, although the latter body could be fitted to the "Super Sports" chassis for an additional £30.

Weymann bodies were popular in the late 1920s as their flexible wooden framework construction and fabric covering was thought to give a quieter and more rattle-free ride on poorly surfaced roads. However, a look at contemporary service records reveals that the bodies were, perhaps, sometimes rather too flexible and there were frequent complaints from customers about cracked windows and door pillars, and of bodies almost literally falling apart! To be fair, some of the blame for these difficulties should fall on the flexible chassis fitted to the early cars.

A New Morris Chassis

The M.G. had now established a place in the market as a product that differed distinctly from the Morris cars on which they were based. A combination of some simple chassis modifications and more attractive bodywork had transformed the mundane Morris Oxford into a much better machine that could compete on equal terms with other makes of sporting cars. Around 400 examples of the bullnose 14/28 M.G.s had been built before a radical re-design of the parent car was announced in September 1926, bringing production of this most elegant of vintage cars to a close.

The new Morris Oxford chassis was wider, shorter and much heavier than its predecessor and was now fitted with a wider, flat radiator in place of the familiar rounded bullnose design that had been a distinctive Morris trademark, and one that had blended well with the elegant M.G. body styles. Modifying the chassis and designing new bodies to fit caused Kimber a number of problems and he resorted to asking for assistance from a young engineering gradu-

Right: The amount of labour involved in assembling an M.G. in the 1920s should not be underestimated. Engines were carefully modified to improve performance, and then run-in on coal gas for the equivalent of 750 miles (1200km). The rear wheels of the chassis drive drums connected to air-fans, to simulate normal road conditions, and circulating water cooled the radiators.

Below: Once the running-in was done, the cylinder head was de-coked and re-fitted, and the bulkhead, wings, fuel tank, etc. were then installed on the chassis. With a makeshift seat in place, it was time for a road test and a trip to the coachbuilder where the body was fitted. The picture shows the purpose-built M.G. factory at Edmund Road, Oxford.

ate, H.N. Charles. He persuaded Charles to join his team at Bainton Road at the weekends to sort out what was necessary to get the M.G. range back into production and they spent long periods working on sketches trying to adapt the body styles to suit the flat radiator.

The new models that were eventually put into production featured a number of chassis and brake modifications in an effort to improve on the Morris chassis. The range of body styles for the "Super Sports" was essentially as previously available – two- and four-seater open tourers. The closed cars shown in the catalogue issued for the 1926 Motor Show were limited to two- and four-seater two-door salonettes while the heavy four-door cars were no longer listed. In truth, all the new models were heavier than the previous cars and did not look as good, although the company tried to point out in an advertisement in "The Motor" that they were "more attractive in appearance and specification . . . the

new radiator with larger cooling area giving better body lines". These first cars on the new chassis are now known as 14/28 Flat-nose, to distinguish them from the earlier 14/28s. Development work continued, resulting in various modifications being incorporated into the car which was eventually called the 14/40 Mark lV. Trying to identify the differences between the 14/28 and 14/40 is something of a teaser and this is not helped by the use of the "Mark IV" designation which seems to have signified little beyond the need to make the car appear more up-to-date. One clue is that, visually, the earlier flat-radiator cars lack the apron between the front ends of the chassis rails, or dumb irons, that was fitted to the 14/40s in place of the extension to the bottom of the radiator, and they have an additional set of louvres on the scuttle.

Early in 1927 the M.G. lines were moved to a new section of the works as radiator production was growing apace, matching the increasing

Left: This two-seater 14/40 is owned by Cyril Mellor, who has used the car to undertake many journeys, including one around part of New England in the United States. In spite of its age, the car quite happily covers long distances without causing the owner too many problems.

In September 1926 the Morris Oxford was substantially re-designed, and given a wider and much heavier chassis frame. More noticeable to the layman was the replacement of the familiar bullnose radiator by one of more conventional design. Assisted by a young engineering graduate, H.N. Charles, Cecil Kimber adapted his chassis modifications and bodywork designs to suit the new chassis and launched the revised M.G.s at the London Motor Show. Heavier than the earlier cars, the performance was inferior.

Above: The speedometer and clock flank an oil pressure gauge and an ammeter. At the bottom of the panel are two switches, one is for the lights and the second for the magneto. The horn button is to the right of the steering wheel. Levers on the wheel are for the hand throttle and ignition.

Above and below: The changed radiator shape gives this late 1926 car a quite different appearance. Like the bullnose, the headlamps were dipped by operating a mechanical linkage that was connected to a lever placed alongside the handbrake. A tool kit is stored in the compartment above the rear number plate.

Above: The pattern on the unpainted aluminium side panels is called "engine turning" and is produced by the overlapping application of rotating polishing mops. Once the surface of the aluminium sheet has been polished, it is protected by the application of clear lacquer. Standard colours for the wings and upper surfaces of the body were Saxe Blue or Claret, variations in colour of car or upholstery were available at extra cost.

Below: The rear dickey seat was a popular fitting for two-seaters. It was intended for agile passengers who climbed in aided by one of the two steps alongside the rear wings. There was no wet weather protection.

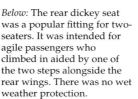

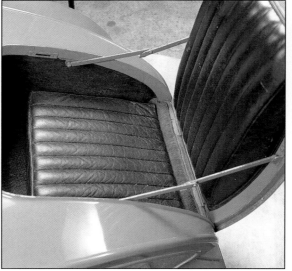

Above: An attractive side lamp on the 14/28. Unlike some of its contemporaries, the M.G. had a twelve-volt lighting system. When built, this car would have had a single tail lamp. Clearly this is insufficient today and it now has extra lamps.

Below: The scuttle vents, reminiscent of nautical practice, were a feature of these early M.G.s. Cecil Kimber was a very keen yachtsman, and he went sailing regularly, which possibly influenced some of the design details on his cars. The windscreen frame design was said to give the minimum of wind resistance and the maximum of protection. The triangular side panels made it stronger than a simple flat screen would have been.

Above: The special, winged, M.G. "calormeter" radiator-cap temperature gauge was a standard fitting.

Above: 27 inch by 4.4 inch tyres on Dunlop bolt-on wire wheels were standard on the 1927 model year cars.

Right: The scuttle-mounted fuel tank has a built-in fuel gauge and feeds the Solex 30 MHD carburettor by gravity. The pipe leading from the carburettor mounting flange provides vacuum for the Dewandre servo mechanism that assists the driver operate the heavy brakes. The dished aluminium disc below the carburettor float chamber is the oil filler cap which incorporates a dip stick. A magneto provides ignition, and this must be turned on, using the dashboard switch, before the car is started. Turning that switch to the "off" position earths the magneto and stops the engine.

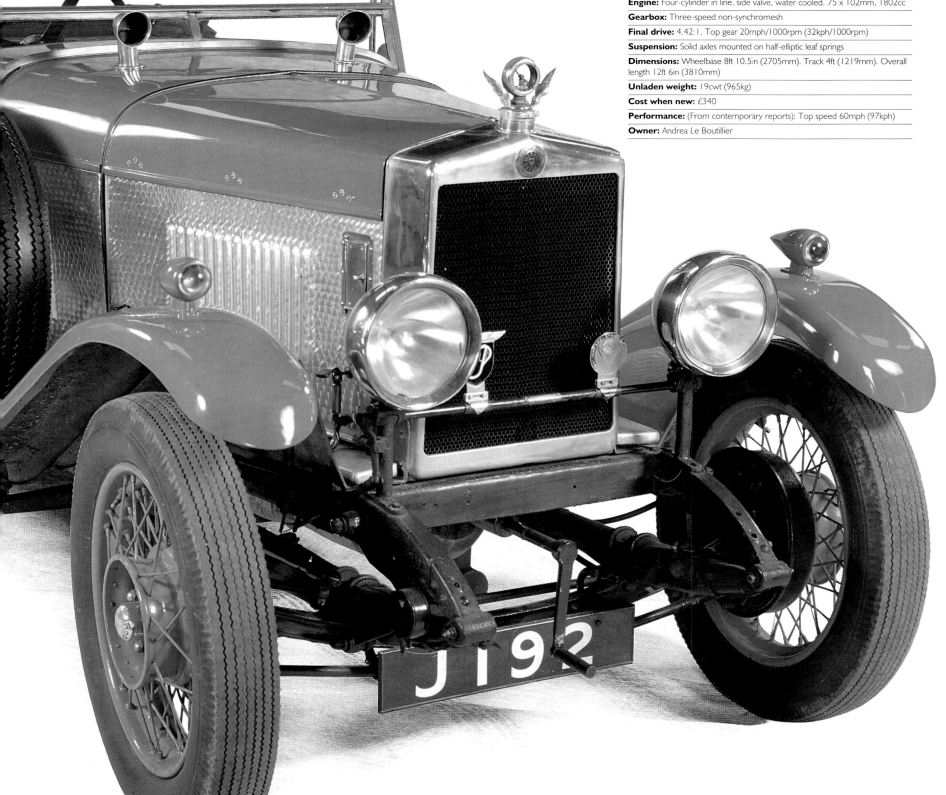

SPECIFICATION

Model: 14/28 "Flat radiator" two-seater

Engine: Four-cylinder in line, side valve, water cooled. 75 x 102mm, 1802cc

Gearbox: Three-speed non-synchromesh

Final drive: 4.42:1. Top gear 20mph/1000rpm (32kph/1000rpm)

Suspension: Solid axles mounted on half-elliptic leaf springs

Dimensions: Wheelbase 8ft 10.5in (2705mm). Track 4ft (1219mm). Overall length 12ft 6in (3810mm)

Unladen weight: 19cwt (965kg)

Cost when new: £340

Performance: (From contemporary reports): Top speed 60mph (97kph)

Owner: Andrea Le Boutillier

sales of Morris cars. It was obvious that new premises would eventually be needed to accommodate the car assembly work, so Cecil Kimber approached William Morris for permission to have a separate factory built especially for M.G. production. The go-ahead was given, and work commenced on new buildings in Edmund Road, Cowley where they were close to the Morris works with easy access to the greater proportion of the components they needed.

The new factory had an eight-bay assembly area and the only real problem Kimber encountered during construction was with the electricity suppliers who were proving unhelpful. Kimber told them he would install his own plant if necessary so, when a public supply was not forthcoming, he fitted a 45 Kilowatt Crompton generator, belt driven by a Rushton engine, with lighting and power cables run into the assembly areas. The factory also had its own boiler house to provide steam heating. The entire job was carried out very quickly and production was moved from Bainton Road to Edmund Road in September 1927.

A Purpose-Designed Factory

M.G. now had a proper factory all of their own in which to build their cars. A production line was laid down for chassis assembly, stores were established to serve both the assembly lines and provide customer service, and a small part of the factory was set aside for the engine tuning work to be carried out. This consisted of grinding and polishing the valve ports and cylinder head to increase power output and careful finishing and lining up of bearings to improve refinement and reliability. A special running-in bay was installed where completed chassis had their engines connected to a supply of coal gas to provide fuel, and to a water supply for cooling, before being run for the equivalent of 750 miles (1200km). The chassis was then taken back to the main assembly area where the head was removed and de-carbonized and the valves reground. The wings and valances, bulkhead, fuel tank, etc. were then attached to make the car roadworthy for a test drive. Brake and shock absorber settings were adjusted and the car returned to the works for running on a "Comparator" designed by Hubert (H.N.) Charles, which was the equivalent of a modern rolling road. A temporary seat was then installed for its journey by road to the coach-builders where the body was fitted. Upon its return the final small fittings were added and the car readied for sale.

Much was made by the company, in a series of advertisements, of the facilities at this new factory. Cecil Kimber was justifiably proud of the achievements of this off-shoot of The Morris Garages which was fast becoming larger than its parent! To acknowledge this The M.G. Car Company (Proprietors: The Morris Garages Ltd.) was registered as a separate entity in March 1928. M.G. was slowly evolving into a builder of cars in its own right, rather than just a modifier of Morris products, and 1928 was to see another advance when the 18/80 was announced.

Above: Final chassis assembly of the 18/80 Mark I in a section of the Edmund Road factory. The massive side-members of the specially-designed M.G. chassis on this model can be seen. Smoking on the job was obviously then permitted!

Left: 18/80 chassis leave the factory on test. This would have been a pleasant job on a warm summer day, but not so popular in winter.

Below: A variety of models in the Service Department at Edmund Road. In the background are a number of bodies destined for installation on new M-type Midget chassis.

Top and above: An 18/80 Mark I Fabric Saloon with body by Carbodies. This car was driven 346,000 miles (556,800km) by its first owner, who ran it for 38 years. It is now in the hands of the noted expert on early M.G.s, Phil Jennings.

Right: A beautiful 18/80 Mark I two-door saloon owned by Fred Body. These handsome cars were described in the 1930 advertisements as "The mile-a-minute cruiser" and they still provide fast and comfortable transport today.

In an effort to take the Morris cars up-market, it was decided that an entirely new six-cylinder engine be designed. Initially this was installed in an unsuitable chassis with the result that the car was something of a failure. However, Cecil Kimber still wanted the engine for an M.G., but not the chassis, so he set about having a new frame drawn up and produced which incorporated all the features he wanted. The result was a strong chassis with suspension and steering able to cope with the power output of the 2468cc six-cylinder engine. The standard of construction was very high and the cast aluminium bulkhead, incorporating the M.G. octagon in the side brackets, was a work of art. The braking system was thoroughly in keeping with that of a sports car and, for the first time on an M.G., had the "fly-off" handbrake lever that was set by pressing the button at the end and released by merely pulling it upwards and letting it go. This system was to become familiar to owners of many of the later models. The most imposing feature of the M.G. Six, as it was called, was the new radiator. No longer did the car have to

suffer a re-badged Morris item, for the 18/80 was given a specially designed radiator with a handsome polished surround and with the M.G. octagon sitting on a crest-shaped nose-piece. This was to be the "face" that would adorn all subsequent production M.G.s until the TF was announced in 1953.

Show Time

In 1928, for the first time, The M.G. Car Company had taken their own stand at the London Motor Show which was held at Olympia each Autumn. Such was the reception for the new M.G. when it was launched at this show, and when it was road-tested by the motoring press, that Kimber was certain he was going to sell large numbers of them. Unfortunately, the car was much more expensive than the previous model with the chassis-only price up from £280 for the 14/40 to £420 for the 18/80 – a rise of 50 per cent – while the cost of a completed two-seater climbed from £335 to £480. Although the car was to sell well initially, the poor economic climate then (1929 was the year of the stock

market crash in the USA which precipitated the Great Depression) meant that the numbers of potential buyers for such a large and expensive car were dwindling all the while. However, the fortunes of M.G. as a marque were to survive this set-back, almost entirely due to the announcement at the same show of a completely different type of M.G. – the 8/33, or M-type, Midget two-seater.

This model was, once again, a modified and re-bodied Morris. In order to compete with his arch rival in the British motor industry, Herbert Austin – who had enjoyed great success with his Austin Seven – William Morris decided to produce a car to challenge for a share of the small car market. Luckily, Morris' recent purchase of the Wolseley Car Company gave him access to their range of engines, which were of a much more advanced design than those used in the current Morris products. The Wolseley engines had an overhead camshaft which was driven by bevel gears from the front of the crankshaft by a vertical shaft which also formed the dynamo armature. For its time this was a powerful little

engine, although at Morris' insistence it was detuned somewhat before being installed in his "baby" car – the Morris Minor.

Cecil Kimber immediately saw the virtues of this car and obtained one of the new chassis which he proceeded to modify in line with current M.G. practice. The springs were flattened slightly and Hartford shock absorbers fitted to improve roadholding. The steering column was lowered and lengthened by three and a quarter inches (83mm) to facilitate the installation of a rakish two-seater body which he had designed. Photographs of the prototype cars used in the early publicity material show that they featured a flared scuttle which was not incorporated on the final production versions.

Critical Acclaim

The car was enthusiastically received at the 1928 London Motor Show. Many orders were placed, in spite of the fact that it was really not yet ready to go into production. This was not at all unusual at that period when manufacturers would deliberately gauge public reaction to new cars at such shows and then base production plans on the numbers of orders received. The largely hand-built nature of the average car made this way of building and selling them a lot easier than it would be now, when each new model takes many years, and vast fortunes, to develop. Things were changing even then, however, and the introduction of all-steel bodies for volume cars built in the United States led eventually to the demise of this kind of low-volume coachbuilt car production.

The first cars for customers, which were priced at just £175, were delivered in the April of

Above: The interior of a later fabric-bodied M-type Midget. The doors of the early cars were rear-hinged, and a different dashboard instrument panel had light-faced instruments.

Left: The engine compartment of a fabric-bodied car. Early engines produced only 20bhp, although most have been subsequently modified. Note scuttle-mounted fuel tank.

Below: This pretty fabric-bodied M-type is owned by Martin Bissex, who carried out the restoration.

1929. A team of four of the new Midgets appeared in the 1929 Land's End Trial, with both C.F. Dobson and J.A. Watson-Bourne earning gold medals. Contemporary reports talk of how the small M.G.s impressed with their hill-climbing ability and roadholding. There was no doubt that these cars were going to move the marque into a new sector of the sports car market, and that they would enable the younger and less affluent enthusiasts to own a car well suited to this type of competition, as well as to everyday road use.

Although the owners of the later, faster and more desirable OHC (overhead camshaft) cars tend to dismiss the M-type as something really not worth having, they were thoroughly good cars for their time and well deserving of their place in M.G. history. Without them the M.G. marque might well have gone the way of other vintage cars and died out through lack of orders for the larger vehicles. It was also the enthusiasm of the band of young men attracted to the M-type that started The M.G. Car Club in 1930, and led to John Thornley joining The M.G. Car Company – a fact which was to be of enormous benefit to the marque in later years.

The press were very enthusiastic about the Midget and "The Motor" described their test car as "a fascinating small car with exceptionally good performance". They obtained a maximum

Above: This M-type, owned by Keith Portsmore, started life fitted with a fabric-covered body but now has metal panelling similar to that used on the last few hundred cars produced. Early Oxford-built cars had hybrid cable/rod braking and can be identified by the levers and rods for the front brakes protruding through the louvred side valances.

Right: The single carburettor engine in later cars produces 27bhp. Efficiency of the M-type engine was impaired by having the inlet and exhaust ports on the same side of the cylinder head. This was remedied when the J-type was introduced.

speed of 65mph (105kph) and were at pains to point out how much space there was in the small body, although any one of a reasonable size trying to sit in the car these days would be unlikely to agree with them. Part of any road test of the time involved finding out how slowly the car would run in top gear and "The Motor" was very pleased to find that the M-type could be run at 5mph (8kph), although I doubt that many owners ever made use of this facility. The car was taken to Brooklands during the test and it was found that "the M.G. Midget is an absolute

revelation on hills and the Brooklands Test Hill with its maximum gradient of 1 in 4 was taken as though it did not exist". They concluded their test saying they thought the M.G. Midget filled a real niche in the sports car world and was capable of holding its own with any other cars of a similar type. "The Motor" decided it was one of the most fascinating little vehicles they had ever driven. A real boost to sales!

The Midget was to be assembled at the new Edmund Road factory where a separate production line was installed. Here the chassis modifications were carried out and bodies, made by Carbodies of Coventry, were fitted to the chassis. This represented a change for the company as previously all their cars had been sent away for the body to be fitted. The new arrangements obviously were much less costly as they did not involve ferrying the cars to and from Coventry, which was both a time-consuming business and an unpopular one with drivers on cold winter days. The bodies were delivered by lorries, packed three to a crate, and each body cost M.G.s just £6.10s.

In spite of having a brand new factory the company was already running out of space, and this was partly overcome by Kimber acquiring the use of a redundant bus garage in Leopold Street where some of the service work for Morris Garages could be carried out alongside the final assembly of the Midgets. Just how many of these were built at this site, instead of at the Edmund Road factory, is not clear, but a picture taken in October 1929 shows a line of cars at Leopold Street receiving finishing touches before passing on to the sales department.

Promoting The Marque

Selling the new cars was obviously a priority and one of the earliest sales brochures produced for the M-type Midget called the new model "The M.G. Midget Sports Mark 1". This was illustrated with an attractive drawing of the car and the text stressed that because the engine was small the tax was only £8 per annum, the petrol consumption was 40 to 50 miles per gallon, and other running costs were proportionally low. It listed the fabric colours available for the body as red or light blue. The bonnet, valances and wheels were cellulosed to match the fabric and the wings were black.

In addition a lavish booklet bearing the slogan "It Passes – and Surpasses – The M.G. Sports" was produced for the model range and this proudly announced inside the front cover that "The M.G. Car Company . . . is an entirely independent manufacturing concern specialising in the sole production of the M.G. Sports Cars. Whilst the vast resources of the associated companies (controlled by Sir William Morris) are behind its production, it cannot be too clearly emphasised that all M.G. Sports models are designed and built from the start to meet an ever increasing demand for a car with high sporting performance at a reasonable figure. They bear no resemblance or relation whatsoever to the other cars produced under the ægis of Sir William." Cecil Kimber was all the time trying to establish M.G. as a separate marque although to say that the cars illustrated in this booklet "bear no resemblance" to other cars when they included the 14/40 and M-type was perhaps stretching truth a little! Modern manufacturers would find it hard to get away with statements like that under the watchful gaze of consumer groups.

Cecil Kimber was keen to produce visually attractive sales literature as he felt strongly that good brochures and advertisements helped to sell his cars. To provide the illustrations he used a number of artists over the years, but the major-

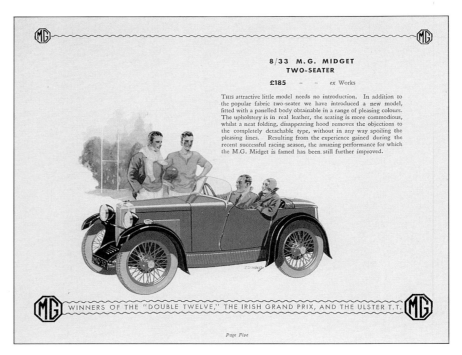

Left: The catalogue for the later M-type was one of a large number illustrated by Harold Connolly in the 1930s. He pictured the cars with appropriately dressed people.

Right: This diminutive coupé appealed to buyers looking for a car with the charm of the small open sports cars but with more comfort and weather protection. The 8/33 M.G. Midget Sportsman's Coupé, as it was called, cost £245 – £60 more than the open car.

Far right: Like the open cars, the coupé bodies were fabric-covered, except for the last few constructed. The sliding sun roof had four little windows set into it to give more light in the cabin. Few of these cars survive.

ity of the brochures issued in the 1930s featured the work of the talented Harold Connolly. Kimber felt that Connolly was able to portray his cars well and also that he imbued the drawings with atmosphere by incorporating stylishly dressed people pictured against appropriate backdrops. Many of these beautifully drawn sketches featured "hunting, shooting and fishing" scenes that he felt were appropriate for the sort of customers he was trying to attract.

The immediate success of the Midget had placed considerable strain on factory space in a building that had been designed initially to produce relatively small numbers of M.G. 14/40s

and 18/80s, and which could not cope with assembling as many as required of the new small sports cars. The only solution lay in yet another move of premises. The search led Kimber to look outside the immediate Oxford area in the nearby market town of Abingdon where there existed suitable vacant buildings.

The leather industry had been established in Abingdon since the early years of the 19th century. The industry flourished and expanded, reaching a peak in the 1914-1918 War when the Pavlova Leather Company increased production to cope with the huge demand for military coats, boots, belts, harnesses and a host of other items for the Allied war effort. The company enlarged its premises and built a new administration block in Cemetery Road to cope with all this work. The declaration of peace in 1918 led to an inevitable fall in orders, a decline in the business, and a surfeit of factory space. By 1929 the area of the factory alongside the Marcham Road was largely unused and it was this area, and the administration block, that was leased by Morris Garages for M.G. car production.

The deal was announced in July 1929 but considerable work was needed before the new factory could be brought fully into use. It was September before all the car assembly work could be transferred from Oxford to Abingdon. The key personnel also moved to Abingdon, including Kimber's friend, Hubert Charles in the post of chief designer, George Propert as General Manager and George Tuck who was in charge of publicity. Most of the original work force, who had spent countless hours working under diffi-

cult conditions to develop and produce the first M.G.s, also moved to the new factory and of these Sydney Enever and Cecil Cousins were later to prove vital ingredients in the M.G. story.

Abingdon In Full Production

By January 1930 the factory was sufficiently established for an inaugural luncheon to be held where the guest list included Sir William Morris, many dignitaries from the motoring and motor sport world, and members of the press. There was a deal of speechmaking and mutual self-congratulation but the main objective, as far as Kimber was concerned, was to establish firmly in the minds of those present that M.G. had arrived as a separate entity and that M.G. cars were no longer just mildly-modified Morris products sold at higher prices. The full separation of the M.G. marque from the parent Morris Garages was to occur a few months later when a separate limited company was formed with Sir William Morris as Chairman and Cecil Kimber as Managing Director. At that time Kimber resigned from the post of General Manager of The Morris Garages, enabling him to devote all his time to his work at Abingdon.

"The Light Car and Cyclecar" writer, H.S. Linfield, visited the Abingdon factory in

Left: Once production of the Midget was underway, space at Edmund Road was limited and some work was carried out at Morris Garages' premises in Leopold Street. This picture was taken in 1929 when work was progressing on a batch of early M-types. The board on the wall indicates that chassis carrying numbers around 350 were being completed.

Right: As well as the catalogued M-types, some cars carried specialist bodywork. This early Jarvis bodied car is fabric-covered but later they were metal-skinned. The Jarvis M-type had a better windscreen and hood than standard cars.

February 1930 and wrote of his experiences in the magazine. He was given a tour of the facilities and noted that production of the cars was now well under way. He wrote that he was astonished to see the extraordinary activity on the assembly line and that some 60 Midgets a week were being delivered. He said that everywhere there were rows of axles, springs, steering sets, engines and gear-boxes. Chassis frames were piled in huge stacks and bodies descended in a continuous flow from the floor above. Of course, Abingdon was really only an assembly plant, as no components were made there, all the items coming from other parts of the Morris empire or outside suppliers. However, at Abingdon at least the cars were built up from separate components and not assembled from rolling chassis that had been towed from the Morris plant as had mostly been the case in Oxford days.

Midget Modifications

By the time production moved to Abingdon a number of changes had been made to the Midget design to eliminate some weak points in the original Morris Minor chassis. The main change was to the braking mechanism where the Morris-designed rod and cable system, with a separate transmission brake, were done away with and the standard M.G. arrangement of Bowden cables, operating from a cross-shaft in conjunction with the hand-brake, was adopted. This gave four-wheel braking on the hand brake and it remained in use on all the M.G. models up to the introduction of hydraulic brakes on the T-series cars in 1936. The body was changed only slightly with the most important alteration being to the doors, which were now hinged on the forward edge instead of the rear. It was said to make entry more convenient – something the designers seem to have forgotten when subsequent models were drawn up.

In addition to the open two-seater, Kimber decided to produce a closed coupé to cater for customers requiring a little more in the way of creature comforts. A very attractive little two-plus-two was introduced, at first with fabric covered bodywork, but later these were metal

Above: Miss Victoria Worsley and the M-type alongside her pit counter at the Junior Car Club Double Twelve-Hour race at Brooklands.

Right: 1930 Twelve-Hour Race. Car 76 was driven by Randall and Montgomery and 80 by Stisted and Black. M.G.s won the Team Prize. Note the cut-down doors.

Below: The Mark II version of the 18/80 was heavier and more costly than the Mark I which continued in production. The Mark II had a four-speed gearbox.

panelled. Although described as an occasional four, it really was no more than a two-seater with a very tiny bench seat in the back suitable for young children, or perhaps an adult sitting sideways across the car. There was a large sunshine roof, with four little roof-lights let into it to make the interior seem light and airy, and a luggage compartment at the back with a top-hinged lid that also carried the externally mounted spare wheel. The tool kit was in a

locker beneath the floor of the luggage compartment. The Midget coupé was really very well equipped and one can see the appeal of these cars for use in all weathers. They were, of course, at £245 rather more expensive than the open two-seater, but for this price one was getting a car that was faster and more exclusive than other small saloons on the market. Unfortunately few of these survive.

Although adequate for most owners, the modest engine power of the early M-types was certainly insufficient for them to indulge in serious motor racing. John Thornley, in his book *Maintaining The Breed*, tells how M.G. chief designer, H.N. Charles, was horrified to discover that the valve timing on the engine was such that there was a period when both inlet and exhaust valves remained shut rather than having the usual overlap. A new camshaft was made, which gave an immediate increase in power, and the modified engines were first fitted to cars being prepared for the 1930 Double Twelve-Hour race at Brooklands. This race was to herald the first really serious foray into motor racing for the fledgling company and the success they earned was to pave the way for greater achievements in the years that followed.

Kimber had been approached by two enthusiasts of the M-type Midget who were keen to enter three of the cars for this event in an attempt to capture the team prize. They felt that they stood a good chance of success, provided the cars could be modified to make them more suit-

Right: A page from the University Motors catalogue for the 1931 model year illustrates the M-type and both the Mark I and Mark II versions of the 18/80. The Speed Model had the lighter 18/100 body on the Mark I chassis and is now one of the most popular 18/80s. A small number of Mark II Speed Models were built. It is interesting to see that the picture of the M-type shows the earlier type of brake gear and rear-hinged doors – both of these had long since disappeared from the production cars.

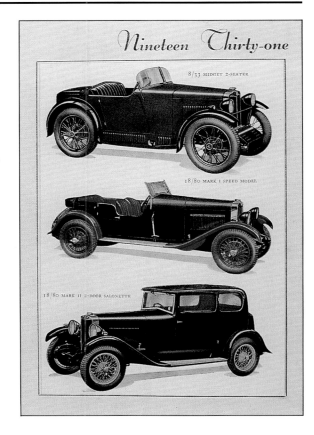

Below: A splendid two-seater 18/80 Mark II. Records show that only seventeen such cars were built, the majority of production being four-seater saloons and tourers.

able, especially as five M-types had acquitted themselves well at a Junior Car Club Member's Day at Brooklands the previous June. Engines fitted with the new camshaft, raised compression ratios and polished cylinder heads were installed in cars that had modified bodywork incorporating cut-down doors, an undershield to reduce drag and staggered bucket seats. The headlamps were re-positioned, exhaust systems

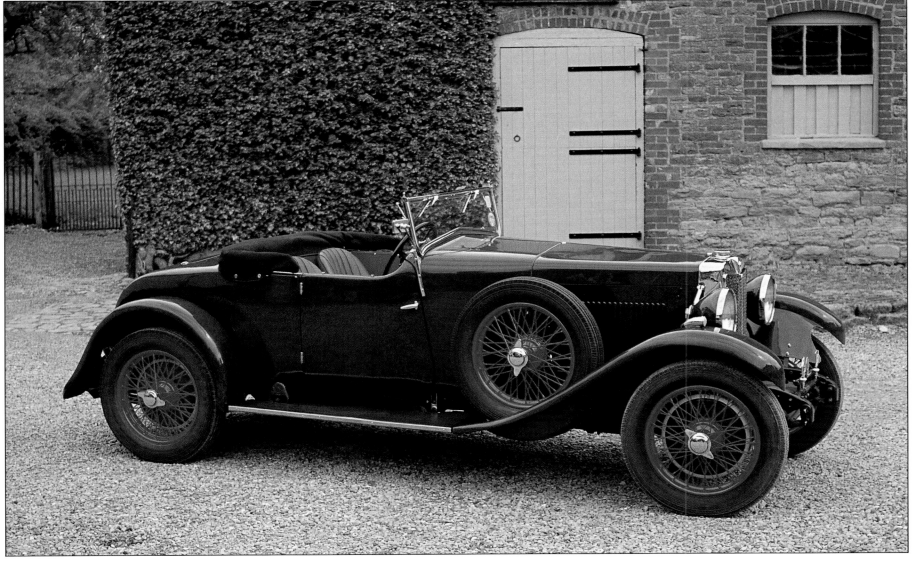

1930 18/80 MARK II TOURER

The introduction of the 18/80 in 1928 heralded the emergence of M.G. as a proper car manufacturer, rather than just as a modifier of Morris products. Called the "M.G. Sporting Six", it was designed from the outset as an M.G. Although using many components from the parent company most were modified for their new application and were mounted in a specially designed chassis. The Mk II version appeared in 1930 and changes included a stronger chassis, four-speed gearbox and better brakes.

Left: The 2468cc six-cylinder engine is an impressive sight and its high torque output provides good performance. Drive to the gearbox is via a double plate, cork-faced clutch running in oil.

Below: Club badges like this one issued in the 1930s by The Brooklands Automobile Racing Club were popular accessories at the time.

Below: The space within the streamlined airfoil section of the running boards provides useful stowage for the comprehensive tool kit.

Above: Such a large car but with only room for two! The body provides considerable comfort for the driver and passenger and the well

stocked dashboard is a feature of all the 18/80 models. When parked, the gear lever can be secured in neutral by a Yale lock.

Right: In 1986 this car was taken to the United States and entered in the Challenge America Race where, driven by Ron Gammons and Philip Mann, it was second overall and first in the pre-war class!

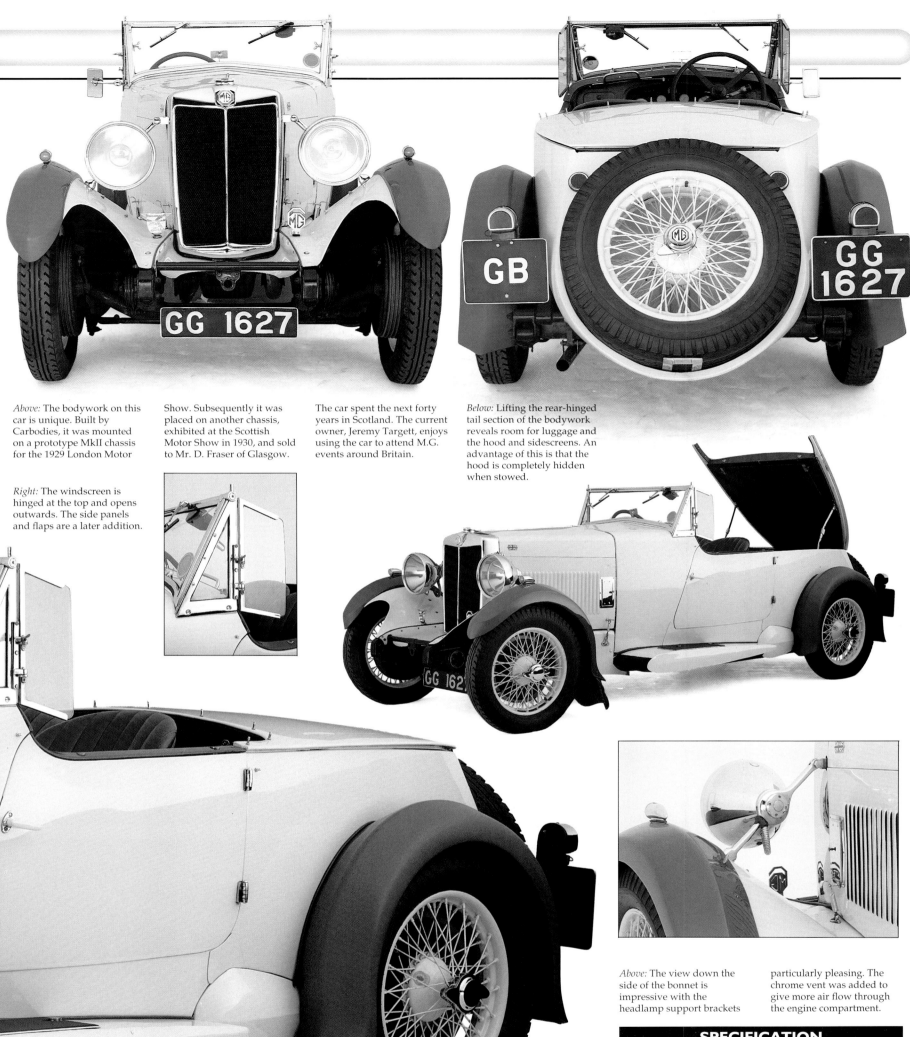

Above: The bodywork on this car is unique. Built by Carbodies, it was mounted on a prototype MkII chassis for the 1929 London Motor Show. Subsequently it was placed on another chassis, exhibited at the Scottish Motor Show in 1930, and sold to Mr. D. Fraser of Glasgow. The car spent the next forty years in Scotland. The current owner, Jeremy Targett, enjoys using the car to attend M.G. events around Britain.

Right: The windscreen is hinged at the top and opens outwards. The side panels and flaps are a later addition.

Below: Lifting the rear-hinged tail section of the bodywork reveals room for luggage and the hood and sidescreens. An advantage of this is that the hood is completely hidden when stowed.

Above: The view down the side of the bonnet is impressive with the headlamp support brackets particularly pleasing. The chrome vent was added to give more air flow through the engine compartment.

SPECIFICATION

Model: 18/80 Mk II two-seater

Engine: Six-cylinder in line, overhead camshaft, water cooled. 69 x 110mm, 2468cc

Gearbox: Four-speed non-synchromesh

Final drive: 4.27:1

Suspension: Solid axles mounted on half-elliptic leaf springs

Dimensions: Wheelbase 9ft 6in (2896mm). Track 4ft 4in (1321mm). Overall length 13ft 4in (4064mm)

Unladen weight: 24cwt (1219kg)

Cost when new: £550 in chassis form and approx. £650 with this body

Performance: (From contemporary reports): Top speed 85mph (137kph)

Owner: Jeremy Targett

changed, fold-down gauze racing windscreens fitted and all the cars had larger fuel tanks and a smart paint scheme in the M.G. colours of cream and brown.

In all, six Midgets were entered in the race with the "team" cars driven by Randall and Montgomery, Townend and Jackson and Roberts and Pollard taking the Team Prize. In addition to participating in the British version of the twenty-four hour Le Mans race, two M-types were specially prepared to enter the French event in June 1930, one to be driven by Sir Francis Samuelson and Freddie Kindell and the other by Murton-Neale and Hicks. These cars were fitted with bodies that featured a flared scuttle and extra-large fuel tanks. They did not fare all that well with one car suffering big-end failure and the other a broken crankshaft, but their participation did signify a start for the marque in international racing.

In a way that was later to become company practice, replicas of the "Double-Twelve" cars were catalogued for sale to the general public. Called "The 8/45 hp M.G. Midget Sports Double-Twelve Model" these replicas were priced at £245 and in all 21 cars were built. The majority were used from the outset for competitions but at least one was bought purely as a road car – the owner obviously feeling that the price premium was worth paying in order to have a car that was out of the ordinary.

The Racing Tigress

The M-types were not the only M.G.s entered in the 1930 Double-Twelve race. With an eye on the chance of an outright win against other large sporting cars, like the Bentley Speed Six, The M.G. Car Company had embarked on an ambitious project to build a racing version of the 18/80, called the 18/100 or Tigress. It was to be offered for sale to the public at £895. In October 1929 the company had announced a Mark II version of the 18/80, although deliveries to customers really only got under way in April 1930, and it was the Mark II that was modified to produce the Tigress.

The original 18/80 Six – now to be called the Mark I – was to remain in production alongside the new Mark II, with the latter cars costing around £100 more than the earlier model. For the extra money the buyer had better ride and road-holding but less performance as the power output of the engine was unchanged, but the weight of the car had increased appreciably. The two versions of the 18/80 differed considerably in detail. The chassis of the Mark II was stiffer and the rear springs were both wider and set outside, rather than under, the frame. The M.G.-designed front and rear axles gave a four-inch (102mm) wider track to aid stability, and braking was improved by the adoption of 14-inch (356mm) brake drums in place of the 12-inch (304mm) drums used on the Mark I. To eliminate the need for frequent attention to a large number of chassis lubrication points with a grease gun, the new model had an ingenious system of automatic lubrication which was pressure-fed when the car was in motion. A larger, 12-gallon (55lit)

Above: This is one of the five 18/100 Tigress models built. Owned in 1930 by Victor Rothschild, it was subsequently bought by Christopher Barker of Winchester in 1943 who kept it until his death in 1997.

Right: The Tigress was designed from the outset as a racing car to compete against the likes of Bentley and Lagonda. Unfortunately, in its first and only race – the 1930 Double-Twelve – it failed to impress and its development ceased.

Below: One of the few Mark II Speed Models. These are fast cars, even by modern standards, and able to cruise at over 70mph (113kph).

Above: The start of Midget production. M-type chassis are piled up awaiting fitting of springs and axles, and subsequent addition of first the wheels, and then engines, before going down the line.

Right and below right: The end of the line at Abingdon. Brakes are set and tested. Once cars were returned from the coachbuilder, they were thoroughly cleaned and prepared for sale.

fuel tank was fitted and the two-gallon (9lit) reserve tank in the bulkhead from the Mark I was retained, as was the reserve oil tank.

The Mark II was the first M.G. for which the vast majority of its components were specially designed and built. The new chassis and axles were only used on this model, as was the braking system, and this must have added considerably to the building costs. Unfortunately the higher price, and a lack of sufficient wealthy customers, meant sales were comparatively slow and it was not until well into 1933 that the last of the 236 cars built was finally sold.

Competition Engines

The development of the special racing version of the Mark II involved making more special parts, and even building a batch of modified engines. The intention was to assemble at least 25 cars and Kimber obviously thought that there was a market for these amongst the wealthier members of the racing fraternity. The engine was extensively re-worked with fully-machined and balanced crankshaft and connecting rods, a different cylinder head of "cross-flow" design with the exhaust gases feeding into three siamesed manifolds on the opposite side of the engine to the twin, down-draught carburettors. The "dry-sump" lubrication was fed from a large oil tank which was mounted between the front dumb irons. Power output now exceeded 80bhp – a 35 per cent increase over the standard engine. With the competition driver in mind, brakes could be adjusted from the cockpit, any nuts and bolts that could work loose were wired or split-pinned and the lightweight body complied with International Racing regulations.

In spite of all this preparation, the single 18/100 entered in the 1930 Double-Twelve race driven by Callingham and Parker failed to finish when the engine expired. The success of the Midgets, and a distinct lack of orders for the larger car, forced abandonment of the project after just five cars had been built. The remaining bodies from the batch of 25 ordered from Carbodies of Coventry were used to create a new version of the Mark I 18/80 – the "Speed Model". Thought by many to be the best of the 18/80s, the combination of the light bodywork on the earlier chassis meant that the Speed Model, which cost £525 when it was introduced for the 1931 model year, was the fastest of the 18/80s, with a guaranteed top speed of 85mph (137kph). The narrow body inherited from the 18/100 meant that the brake lever remained outside the bodywork on the earlier cars, although a later batch of bodies had room for the lever to be moved inside the cockpit. Towards the end of production just a handful of Speed Models were built on the heavier Mark II chassis.

Looking back now at the early years in the history of the world's favourite sports cars, one can only wonder at the rate of growth of the business at a time when many other car companies were struggling to stay out of bankruptcy and, indeed, a great many were disappearing from the motoring scene. There is no doubt that the fortunate arrival of the Midget, just in time to take advantage of the move to smaller and more economical cars, played a large part in this growth. It is interesting to speculate just how long the shrewd William Morris would have allowed Kimber to build ever more expensive cars against the current trends before calling a halt to the enterprise and thereby consigning the M.G. marque to history.

That The M.G. Car Company was firmly established, and building ever increasing numbers of sports cars in its own factory at Abingdon, just seven years after the first special-bodied Morris Cowleys had been constructed as a sideline by The Morris Garages, must rate as a landmark in the annals of the British motor industry. That this growth had been achieved at a time when many other specialist car manufacturers were struggling just to survive was a tribute both to Cecil Kimber and his team, and to the cars they were building.

Any company setting out to establish the reputation of a new make of car with the buying public can either rely on the traditional route of taking advertisements in the press, attending motor shows and encouraging dealers to promote their products, or they can take the more rewarding, but riskier, route of involving the cars in record-breaking or participation in motor sport. We see many modern car manufacturers today spending millions of pounds to enter teams in rallies, or in touring car championships, in the hope that the public will associate the highly modified cars entered with the standard vehicles they can buy from their local dealer. For some reason people still see a sporting pedigree as being important for cars likely to spend the majority of their lives in traffic jams or supermarket car parks!

Left: Record-breaking with EX120 at Brooklands on a cold March day in 1931. George Eyston sits in the car while Reg Jackson changes the plugs. Towering over everyone else, Cecil Cousins looks a little worried! They went on to take the flying kilometre and mile records.

Below left: The first production model to benefit from the chassis developed for EX120 was the D-type. Whilst the performance failed to measure up to the looks, these four-seater Midgets did provide stylish transport for a small family.

Record-Breakers

Initially, the reputation of the M.G. versions of the Morris Cowley was as much founded on the sound construction of the basic cars as on the changes made by Cecil Kimber. Any sporting achievements were limited to production car trials and occasional club speed events at Brooklands and other venues. However, by 1930 the company was seriously considering a more ambitious sporting programme and the arrival of the Midgets had given them a car that could be made competitive in its class. It has to be said that Kimber's approach to competition entries seems to have initially been as much led by his customers as by a wish to gain publicity for

M.G.s. After all, it was the approach by Cecil Randall that had led to the entry in the 1930 Double-Twelve race and the building of the limited run of special M-types, and it was customers who encouraged the company into the record-breaking field – an activity in which they were to excel in later years.

Within M.G. there were a number of key personalities who shaped the way the marque developed and without whose efforts The M.G. Car Company would have ceased to exist many years ago. In addition to these men, there were also a few people who, whilst not directly employed by M.G., had a vital role to play in

establishing the reputation of the cars and bringing them to the attention of the general population. The most important among these was George Eyston whose legendary record-breaking and racing efforts did much to build the reputation of the marque and whose warmth of personality and good nature benefited generations of enthusiasts through his association with The M.G. Car Club.

George Eyston was born at Bampton, in Oxfordshire in 1897 into a wealthy land-owning family. Friends of his parents used to visit their house in the early 1900s driving cars like Daimlers and White Steamers which fascinated

Above: There are seats for four adults but the car is better suited to carrying two adults and two children. A hood and sidescreens give good weather protection.

Right: The instrument panel has a centrally-mounted speedometer but no tachometer. The "butterfly" gauge on the right shows red when oil pressure is low.

Below: The single-carburettor engine was basically the same as that fitted to the M-type and was mated to a three-speed gearbox with a neat remote-control for the gear lever. Power was a modest 27bhp.

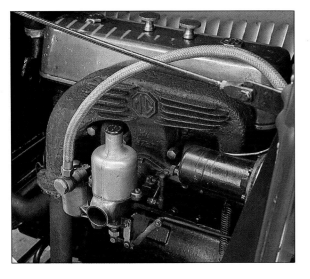

young George, who was also lucky enough to see an early hill-climb event where a cousin of his competed in a new Humber car straight from the Coventry factory. This interest in things mechanical led to a schooling at Seafield Engineering College and an apprenticeship with a firm of marine engineers where he was also involved with experimental aircraft work. He started riding motorcycles and used a succession of machines to compete in hill-climbs, reliability trials and for racing at Brooklands, where he used an assumed name to hide his activities from his family.

An active army career in the First World War left George Eyston with the rank of Captain but no permanent employment when hostilities ceased and, after a return to Cambridge University to finish his education, he was signed on by another firm of marine engineers. By this time he had moved from two wheels to four and had owned a succession of interesting cars, as well as having learned to fly at his own expense during a period of army leave. Purchase of a 1.5 litre Aston Martin led to racing successes at Brooklands and elsewhere. His career in motor sport at the highest level had started.

Developing EX120

George Eyston's long association with M.G. began when he was introduced to Cecil Kimber by a university friend, Jimmy Palmes. Jimmy was preparing a car for an attempt on the 750cc 24-hour world speed record, which was at the time held by an Austin at 64mph (103kph), and he wanted George to drive it. A car based on the M-type Midget was to be used for the attempt and, to bring it within the 750cc class, the engine capacity had to be reduced from its standard 847cc. However, Kimber felt that the standard M-type chassis was unsuitable and offered a new chassis that was under development at that time.

In spite of it having gained some success on the track, Kimber had realized that another chassis was really required if the Midget was to be developed into a better car for both road and racing. The M-type suffered from having too short a wheelbase and a high centre of gravity. To address both of these faults a new frame was designed, most probably based on examination of the chassis used for the French Rally sports car, an example of which spent some time in the M.G. experimental shop. The new chassis, designated EX120, was to form the basis of all M.G. sports car chassis design until the TD was announced in 1949. It was a simple ladder frame with the two main chassis members set parallel to each other and passing under the rear axle.

100mph From 750cc

The side frames were separated by tubular cross members, brazed into cast and turned mounting brackets, which were riveted to the chassis frames. These cross members also formed mounting points for the springs. Each spring was pivoted at the front but held at the rear by bronze trunnions, rather than by conventional shackles. This system was said to stiffen the chassis and to stop the springs moving laterally. The radiator was mounted on an extension of the front engine mounting and the entire engine, gearbox and radiator were carried on two tubular supports, the front support also providing the mounting for the steering box and the rear passing beneath the clutch bell-housing. The effect of what was a "three-point" mounting was to isolate the power unit and radiator from chassis flexing.

The new chassis was fitted with an engine reduced to a capacity of 743cc and special bodywork and, after much development work including installing a Powerplus supercharger, EX120, as the record-breaker was to become known, became the first 750cc car to exceed 100mph (161kph). The high-speed runs were made at the banked Montlhéry track near Paris and attracted huge publicity. On the back of this success Kimber announced that a new 750cc racing car was to be made available to the public – this was to be the M.G. Midget Mk ll, Montlhéry Model – the C-type. The M-type continued in production but a new Midget, originally called the 8/33 long chassis but better known as the D-type, utilized an EX120-based chassis fitted with four-seater open or closed coachwork.

The D-type had the M-type engine, in its later, modified form, mated to either a three-speed gearbox with remote control or later, when the J-type box became available, a four-speed gearbox. This new model was introduced as an addition to the M-type which continued in its two-seater form. The first 100 D-types produced had four-seater open bodies, almost identical to the body fitted to the six-cylinder F-type which was introduced the same year. After 100 chassis had been produced, from chassis number D0350, the wheelbase was increased from 7ft to 7ft 2in (2134 to 2184mm) and the chassis rail section strengthened to reduce damage to the body caused by the frame flexing. The new chassis had exactly the same dimensions as used later for the J1/J2. Some of the modified chassis were built with the closed salonette-style body similar to that fitted to the six-cylinder F-types. A number of chassis were sent to outside coachbuilders and it is on record that two of these

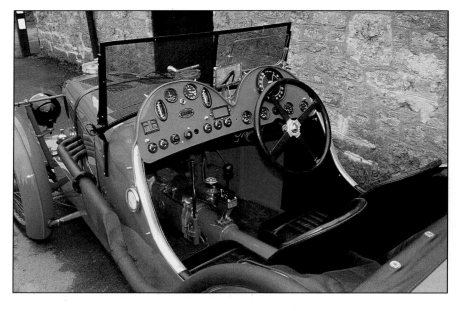

Right: The cockpit of the C-type Montlhéry Midget was designed for racing. Owned by University Motors, this car was entered in the 1931 Brooklands Double Twelve-Hour race and driven by "Hammy" Hamilton into third place, despite some problems.

Below: The attractive lines conceal considerable potential. Fitted with a supercharger and later 12-inch brakes, C0261 is now a fast roadgoing racing car. Surprisingly, the mesh screen does give some protection to driver and passenger.

were bodied by Jarvis and three by Stiles. The Stiles bodywork was particularly attractive and exactly the same as that fitted to a number of six-cylinder F-type chassis.

Although M.G.s had originally fitted their coachwork to chassis built elsewhere, they were now in a position to be able to supply other coachbuilders with chassis. This process started with the 18/80s that were sold as chassis to coachbuilders and and continued with the few M-types that were fitted with Jarvis bodies.

The D-type, having only the M-type engine with a power output of 27bhp, was not a fast car. Indeed, with the heavier Coupé bodywork progress must have been fairly pedestrian. The car designed to cater for the motor sport enthu-

siast was the C-type Montlhéry Midget. The first outing for the initial batch of these cars was to be the 1931 Double Twelve-Hour race at Brooklands and the Abingdon factory worked at full stretch to ready the cars for this event. The body was entirely new, although at this stage it was still of ash-framed construction, and incorporated a pointed tail that concealed the spare wheel – a similar arrangement to that used on the M-type. Ahead of the driver and passenger, the twin humps in the scuttle were to become a feature that was to be carried over in M.G. sports car design until the end of production of the TF in 1955. A shaped cowl enclosed the radiator. Overall the C-type looked both pretty and businesslike – every inch a true racing car.

The Montlhéry Midget

The engine was a version of the M-type unit which had been modified by H.N. Charles to retain the existing 57mm bore of the 847cc engine but with the stroke reduced to 73mm to bring the capacity down to 746cc. The special engine used in EX120 had retained a longer stroke crankshaft but for the C-type Charles decided to increase the diameter of the crank

Above: This C-type had an interesting racing career. By 1932 it was in the hands of Norman Black, and was run, unsupercharged, in the 1000 Mile race at Brooklands. The same year he had a lightweight body fitted and entered the car in the Tourist Trophy race where he retired with engine failure.

Right: The pretty tail houses the spare wheel and the fuel tank. Many cars were later fitted with slab tanks.

Below right: The 750cc engine is capable of high-speed running. The fuel/air mixture is fed under pressure from the front-mounted supercharger.

pins and reduce the stroke to help reliability at sustained high speed. An advantage of this was the retention of the standard block and head, as fitted to the production cars. The engine was mated to a four-speed gearbox which was operated by a remote-control gear lever. There was a scuttle-mounted oil tank that fed a replacement supply of oil directly into the sump as the level fell during a race. This was particularly important on blown cars where the supercharger used engine oil for lubrication.

Fourteen C-types were entered for the race and all were immaculately turned out after much last-minute work at the factory. The result was a triumph for the Abingdon cars and, as almost all the work force had travelled to Surrey to cheer on their team, this was shared by the people who had toiled to finish them in time for the race. The car driven by The Earl of March and C.S. Staniland was placed first overall and the M.G.s took the team prize and the first five places in the race – triumph indeed. The high speeds and bumpy track took their toll of the entries and the M.G. teams didn't escape problems. Valve spring failure, blamed on a faulty batch of springs, claimed a number of victims but some teething troubles were only to be expected. Overall the factory had good reason to be proud of themselves.

In the Double Twelve the cars ran unsupercharged but the factory offered the option of a supercharged version which was fitted with a number 7 Powerplus blower. Although initially announced as being on sale to the public at £295 for the un-blown version and £345 with the supercharger, prices soon rose and unsupercharged cars cost £490 with the blown version being priced at £85 more. Presumably the earlier prices were announced before anyone had properly worked out just how much it cost the factory to make these hand-built cars.

"C" For Competition

The C-types were very successful competition cars over a number of years and some of them received considerable modifications to keep them competitive. The C-type also made a potent road car with the short-stroke 746cc engine capable of running effortlessly at high revolutions for long periods, and in supercharged form they were more than a match for most sports cars of the period. In June 1932 a Mark lll version was announced featuring a different gearbox and a cross-flow cylinder head that gave increased power. Many of the earlier cars were updated to this specification by their owners. The new cylinder head was incorporated into the production Midgets when the J-series cars were introduced two months later.

Just what varied lives the average C-types led can be judged from the account in a 1933 motoring magazine of the career, up to then, of just one of these cars. Built for the 1931 Double-Twelve race, where it took second place in the hands of

Gibson and Fell, it was later supercharged and entered for the 1931 German Grand Prix where it crashed into a ravine. On return to Abingdon it was rebuilt and used as a demonstrator before being fitted with a single-seater body and raced in the 500 Mile Race at Brooklands. Following some record attempts it was again rebuilt as a standard, unsupercharged C-type and passed to the development department. Here it was again supercharged, used in gasket development work, taken to the Tourist Trophy as an official car and raced at the Shelsley Walsh Hill Climb. Entered for the 1932 German Grand Prix it crashed again, was rebuilt and raced at the Craigantlet Hill Climb with some success. Following entry in the 1932 Tourist Trophy as a team car it was yet again rebuilt as a standard car, without a supercharger, and used as a demonstrator before being sold to a customer.

The six-cylinder F-type was introduced in October 1931, at the same time as the four-cylinder D-type. There was a considerable vogue in the 1930s for small six-cylinder engines which were thought to be far more refined than four-cylinder engines of similar capacity and also to produce their power over a wider range allowing for fewer gear changes. Much was made in contemporary road tests of top gear flexibility at a time when "crash" gear boxes made changing gear a skilled process – there were even such feats as "travelling from London to Edinburgh in top gear" to consider.

Along with the engine used in the Morris Minor and the M-type, the acquisition of the Wolseley concern also allowed Kimber access to some six-cylinder units. He was conscious that he needed a car to fill the huge gap between the Midget and the 18/80 and looked to a six-cylinder version of the Wolseley engine already employed in the M-type. This shared the overhead camshaft with vertical dynamo layout of the four-cylinder unit but also had the same conservative valve timing that stifled power output. Nevertheless, this engine was fitted to an EX120-derived D-type chassis which had been lengthened by 10 inches (254mm) to give the company a "small six" to sell alongside the M-type Midget two-seaters and the four-seater D-type.

Extending The Range

To disguise its Wolseley Hornet origins, the engine had sheet-metal side covers which had the unfortunate effect of making it run rather hot – a tendency later partly cured when water flow was modified with the introduction of the F3 model. The engine was mated to a superb ENV gearbox that was a delight to use and very strong – if a little heavy. Even with a fairly modest power output of around 37bhp, the F-type performed well and gained many admirers. It is probably fortuitous that the available power was not greater as the heavier car was initially fitted with eight-inch (203mm) brakes from the lighter Midget and only had more powerful 12-inch (304mm) drums when the two-seater F2 and upgraded four-seater F3 models arrived.

The company issued attractive brochures for both the D-type and F-type illustrating by way of Connolly coloured drawings the four-seater

Above: The 1931 Double Twelve-Hour race at Brooklands was the first outing for the C-type. The cars were very successful and number 60, driven by The Earl of March and C.S. Staniland, won the event. Some cars were troubled by a faulty batch of valve springs. The slower cars were most affected, suggesting that a vibration period in the engine at lower speeds accelerated failure.

Left: The C-types at first had a radiator cowl similar to that used on EX120. However, these caused overheating and were replaced by conventional radiator surrounds, as seen on H.D. Parker's car in the Irish Grand Prix at Phoenix Park.

Right: The team of C-types entered for the 1931 Irish Grand Prix at Phoenix Park, Dublin line-up at the docks. Number 33 was driven by R. Watney and number 31 by H.D. Parker, but number 32 in the experienced hands of Norman Black won the event. By a lucky chance, the gearbox on this car seized just half a mile after being driven out of Liverpool docks on its way to Abingdon – it could have happened in the race!

open and closed coachwork available. The F-type, in particular, was a handsome car. Christened "The 12/70 M.G. Magna" the longer bonnet and sloping radiator gave it the well proportioned lines that the dumpier four-cylinder cars lacked. Although far more of a touring than true sports car, the Magna appealed to many who had previously found their needs satisfied by much larger machines. In addition to the standard factory products, there was on offer a plethora of special bodied versions of the F-type. M.G. were now well into the business of supplying cars in chassis form and a considerable number of F-types found their way into the hands of specialist coachbuilders. Customers had the choice of two-, three- or four-seater cars – some closed and some open – from coachbuilders such as Stiles, Jarvis and Windover.

Abbey Coachworks Limited of North Acton offered a roomy four-seater body on either the Magna or the similarly powered Wolseley Hornet Chassis. Unlike the standard factory version, the Abbey Coupé featured a sloping windscreen and had side windows for the rear passengers who, according to the makers, were also provided with a rear seat "of ample propor-

tions". Shortly after this model was announced, Abbey came up with a much more radical design for a two-seater coupé. Described as having "low and rakish lines" this car featured elegant swept wings that formed a continuous, flowing line from their pointed tips at the front to the tail of the swept-back rear wings. To accentuate the "long and low" design, the bodywork was barely large enough to accommodate the driver and passenger and the luggage capacity was limited to the small area behind the seats. The same wing design was also available on Abbey open four-seaters in preference to the standard factory separate wings.

Bespoke Coachbuilding

There was an established tradition at that time for customers to have their cars built to order and a certain class of purchaser would no more have thought of buying a standard production car than they would of wearing an "off-the-peg" suit. Many of the coachbuilding companies advertising their services started business in the era of horse-drawn carriages and a lot of the woodworking, upholstering and painting skills they employed were learned in that earlier age.

These skills then came under threat as fewer and fewer people could afford to buy specially built large cars and so the availability of a reasonably priced chassis, with the added appeal of the six-cylinder engine, must have been seen as providing an alternative source of work.

An example of this was the two-seater coupé built on the Magna chassis by Windovers Limited of Oxford Street to a design by Lord Portarlington. Windover were better known as builders of high-class bodies on Rolls-Royce and Daimler chassis and they had built a number of luxuriously-appointed cars previously for Lord Portarlington, a wealthy pioneer motorist who had started driving in 1900. Called "The Windoverette", this special-bodied Magna was strictly a two-seater with the aluminium covered, ash-framed body affording a high degree of comfort for both driver and passenger. The single seat back and twin seat bases were internally sprung, rather than having the more usual pneumatic cushions, and were generously proportioned to give a greater degree of comfort than was usual on this type of car. Buyers had a free choice of exterior and interior colours and finishes for a total price of £360 – compared to

Above: Like many of the F-types running today, here the sheet-metal side plates fitted to the Wolseley Hornet engine when it was installed in the M.G. have been removed. These served no purpose, save that of a disguise, and hindered engine cooling. Unlike later six-cylinder cars, the F-type engine had the inlet and exhaust placed on the same side of the cylinder head.

Left: The smooth power delivery and torque of the F-type engine makes the cars it powers pleasant vehicles to drive.

Left: The four-speed ENV gearbox has a reputation of being strong but many of the early owners complained of excessive noise and other problems. Note the reversed gate, with 1st and 3rd gears towards the driver.

Below: The family similarity to the D-type pictured earlier is evident, but the longer bonnet on the six-cylinder car, as well as the handsome, sloping Magna radiator shell, give it better balanced lines. This F1 would have left the factory with 8-inch (203mm) brakes, but a subsequent owner has fitted 12-inch (305mm) drums on the front axle. As it is now used daily on a school run this was a wise precaution.

the factory coupé which cost £289, in which one had the benefit of a minuscule rear seat.

As previously mentioned, the Magna was really more of a touring car than an out-and-out sports machine but this did not stop a large number of them being used in production car trials and even in continental rallies. One F-type in particular was destined to earn a place in M.G.

history when it was bought by the author, John Heygate. John ordered the car through his local dealer, Knott Brothers of Bournemouth, but collected it from Abingdon. He recounts in his book *Motor Tramp* how he went to the factory to collect the black-painted four-seater, with its red wings and red upholstery, from a line of similar cars and how proud he was of his new possession.

Once it was run-in, he decided to take the car on an extended continental tour through Germany, France, Austria and Italy; this lasted a year and he covered a considerable mileage. He visited the factory at Abingdon to have his car repaired and serviced on his return and later returned to Europe with the Magna to make yet another trip; his stories of his encounters with the evidence of the increasing power of Fascism make interesting reading. For the M.G. enthusiast, however, it is the loyalty and affection he felt towards the car, and just how well it coped with the difficult road conditions, that speaks most eloquently.

In spite of all the company's efforts to develop their road cars, record-breaking had not been forgotten. George Eyston, having already taken the 750cc class record at over 100mph (161kph) in EX120, was keen to improve on this to keep ahead of his rivals in the Austin camp. There was obviously little point in proceeding with the EX120 design as this was just not good enough for the task in hand – an entirely new car was needed. A C-type chassis, brakes, front axle and springs were used to build up the car – called EX127 – which had an off-set drive to allow the

driver to sit alongside the transmission rather than above it. This was achieved by using a special rear axle, with the banjo set off-centre alongside the left-hand rear wheel, and the engine and transmission mounted diagonally in the chassis. The advantage of this set-up was a reduction in total frontal area and thus a lower wind resistance – a vital ingredient for any successful record-breaker.

With a streamlined body and aircraft-style surface radiator fitted, the car was driven at Montlhéry by Ernest Eldridge, who was the project engineering consultant. George Eyston was still recovering from burns sustained when EX120 had caught fire during a previous record attempt and Eldridge was only able to raise the five kilometre record by a small amount before the special radiator burst. The car was returned to Abingdon for modification to the supercharger drive to allow room for a conventional radiator to be used. Late in 1931 the team returned to France and this time EX127 was driven by George Eyston and four records were taken at over 114mph (183.5kph).

Early in 1932 the car was taken to the sand flats at Pendine, on the South Wales coast, to try to raise the speed to 120mph (193kph). Although these sands had been used by a succession of record-breakers they were far from ideal for the purpose. Depending on the prevailing wind

direction and the weather at the time, each high tide left the sands in a different state when it receded and it was often quite unsuitable for high speed record attempts. Many days were wasted whilst the frustrated members of the team waited (usually in the bar of the local hotel!) for an improvement, and often this frustration led to runs being made when conditions were far from ideal. Attempts were not without peril and a few years previously Parry Thomas had lost his life at this spot whilst trying for the world speed record. His car, Babs, was buried in the sands by his friends and remained there until dug up and carefully restored to running condition in the 1970s.

"The Magic Midget"

The M.G. team with EX127 – now called "The Magic Midget" – had mixed fortunes experiencing trouble with the timing apparatus and with the weather conspiring to keep the officially recorded speed to 118mph (190kph) – just below their goal of 120mph. Unofficially the car had easily passed its target speed but the team returned to Abingdon unable to claim that they were the first "baby" car to attain a speed of two miles per minute. This goal was eventually reached later in the year when further runs at Montlhéry in December, with the car driven by George Eyston, raised the mile, kilometre and

five kilometre records to speeds of over 120mph (193kph). Yet another motoring landmark for M.G.!

1931 saw M.G.s boasting a model range that spread from the original two-seater M-type Midget, through the four-seater D-type and six-cylinder F-type to those large and expensive 18/80s which were to remain in limited production whilst there was still any chance that customers could be found for them. A measure of just how long some cars took to sell can be gauged from surviving factory records that reveal some unsold cars that had been built in 1930 or 1931 being returned from dealers as late as 1933 for renovation at the factory before subsequent sale as "brand new" cars. The classified advertisements in motoring magazines like "The Autocar" occasionally offered for sale unregistered 18/80s as late as 1935!

The M-type was by now beginning to look a bit dated and the more advanced chassis of the C, D and F-type models must have made some enthusiasts wonder just how much longer the

Right: The F Salonette is a pretty little car which provides comfortable 1930s' style transport for those less wedded to open air motoring. The sliding sun roof has small windows set in it to increase the amount of light in the cabin.

Below top: The side-mounted spare wheel replaced the rear fitting seen in pictures of the early prototypes. Moving the spare gave room for a luggage compartment lid.

Below bottom: The nicely-mellowed interior of this beautiful car exhibits the charm of these little saloons. Unfortunately very few survive fitted with this type of body, and some cars that were originally salonettes have been subsequently fitted with open two- or four-seater coachwork.

Below right: The petrol tank is in the luggage compartment. The lid of this can be left open to increase its capacity. It is supported by two struts, only one of which has been lowered here.

earlier Midget design would survive. To help sales, the car was now available with metal-covered bodywork and those fitted with the last of the fabric bodies were offered at a reduced price. Additionally, the supercharging experience gained with the C-types led to the factory offering supercharged M-type Midgets at £250. A contemporary road test of such a car praised the improved performance, not so much for the maximum speed of nearly 80mph (129kph) as for the extra power available at lower speeds. Apart from the installation of the supercharger, which was driven directly from the front of the crankshaft, and a boost gauge on the dashboard, these cars were just standard 1932 model Midgets fitted with the usual three-speed gearboxes. The metal-panelled bodywork was praised for having a little more interior room than the earlier cars and the only drawback noted for the supercharged car was the need to add oil to the fuel to lubricate the supercharger. However, small improvements and the introduction of a performance model could not keep the M-type soldiering on much longer and the

When the J2 arrived on the market in 1932 to replace the M-type Midget, it was regarded as the ultimate expression of small sports car design. The 80mph (129kph) top speed recorded by road test cars was sufficiently fast to beat rival models with twice the engine capacity. The car sold well not only because it was fast, but also because it was one of the prettiest cars on the road. Whether by accident or design, M.G.s had produced a car that set a style that was to be fashionable for sports cars for many years to come.

SPECIFICATION

Model: J2 two-seater

Engine: Four-cylinder in line, overhead camshaft, water cooled. 57 x 83mm, 847cc, 36bhp

Gearbox: Four-speed non-synchromesh

Final drive: 5.375:1. Top gear 14.7mph/1000rpm (24kph/1000rpm)

Suspension: Solid axles mounted on half-elliptic leaf springs. Each spring is fixed at leading end and in sliding trunnions at rear

Dimensions: Wheelbase 7ft 2in (2184mm). Track 3ft 6in (1067mm). Overall length 10ft 4in (3150mm)

Unladen weight: 11.5cwt (584kg)

Cost when new: £199.10s.0d.

Performance: (From contemporary reports): Top speed 80mph (129kph)

Owner: Peter Dunn.

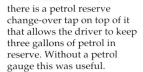

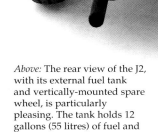

Above: A four-speed gearbox was standard equipment on the J2 and the ratios were chosen to take full advantage of engine power. Like all the OHC units, J-type engines thrive on hard work and frequent gear-changing is necessary to extract the best performance from the cars.

Above: The rear view of the J2, with its external fuel tank and vertically-mounted spare wheel, is particularly pleasing. The tank holds 12 gallons (55 litres) of fuel and

there is a petrol reserve change-over tap on top of it that allows the driver to keep three gallons of petrol in reserve. Without a petrol gauge this was useful.

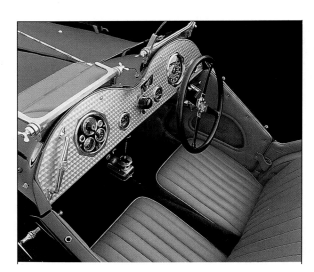

Above: The basic J2, which cost £199.10s.0d., was supplied with an engine-turned aluminium dashboard that had a combined tachometer and speedometer mounted in front of the driver, and an oil pressure gauge, ammeter and ignition/light switch set in front of the passenger. Additional instruments, like those fitted to this J2, were available as extras to be fitted when the car was built.

Below: When this car was built at Abingdon in July 1933 it was a standard J2. Following a total restoration by M.G. expert Roger Thomas, owner Peter Dunn decided to have it converted to J3 specification which included fitting this crankshaft-driven supercharger that runs on 5lb (0.3bar) boost. The car is certainly a lot quicker than it was when it first left the factory in the 1930s.

Above: The car looks just as smart as it must have done when the first owner, Sydney Pearlman of North London, took delivery in September 1933. Although J2s were supplied with full-width windscreens, many of these were replaced with aero-screens of the type seen here.

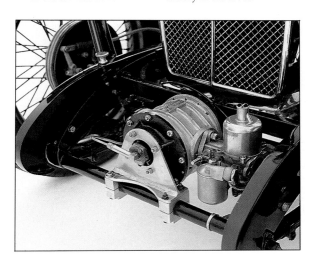

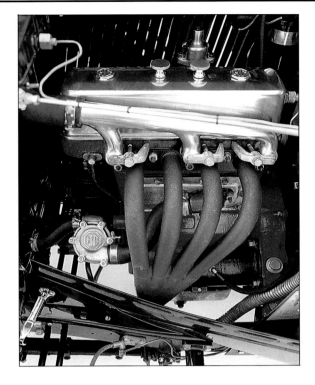

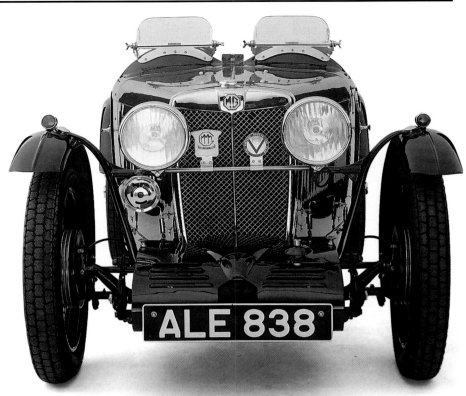

Above and left: This J2 retains the standard engine capacity of 847cc, although it has been otherwise converted to J3 specification. Factory-built J3s had a short-throw crankshaft reducing the capacity to 746cc, allowing the engine to run at sustained high speed and bringing the car into the 750cc class for competitions. Originally just 22 J3s were built and few of them survive.

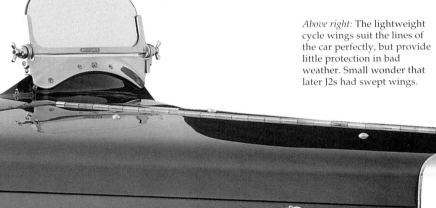

Above right: The lightweight cycle wings suit the lines of the car perfectly, but provide little protection in bad weather. Small wonder that later J2s had swept wings.

The badges on the chromed bar between the headlamps are for the Triple-M Register of the M.G. Car Club and The Vintage Sports-Car Club. The horn is below one headlight.

Right: Easily-adjustable Hartford friction shock absorbers are fitted to front and rear axles. These suit the limited suspension travel allowed by stiff springs.

announcement in August, 1932 of its replacement – the J-type Midget – came as no surprise.

Like the preceding four- and six-cylinder D and F models, the new J-type was much more a recognizable M.G. design than the M-type had been. In spite of modifications, and notwithstanding that the cars were completely assembled at Abingdon, there was no disguising the fact that the chassis and running gear used for the M-type was still basically Morris. For the J-type the chassis was similar to the later D-type which was two inches (51mm) longer than those used for the earlier cars. The familiar 847cc engine was was fitted with the cross-flow head developed for the C-type and was mated to a four-speed gearbox.

The Versatile J-type

From the outset the J-type was designed to replace not just the two-seater M-type but also the underpowered D-type in both its open and closed forms, and the racing four-cylinder C-type that was sold in small numbers to those intending to take part in competitions. The J was, therefore, listed as being available in four different guises. The J1 four-seater open tourer and closed salonette were similar in appearance to the D-type, with the exception that the open car now had cut-away doors although early publicity pictures of the new cars still showed them having D-type bodywork. A J2 two-seater was offered to replace the M-type with the J3 listed to provide a supercharged version of the J2. The J4 was an out-and-out racing car for use in competition at the highest level in the 750cc class. This was also supercharged but additionally had lightweight bodywork, better brakes and steer-

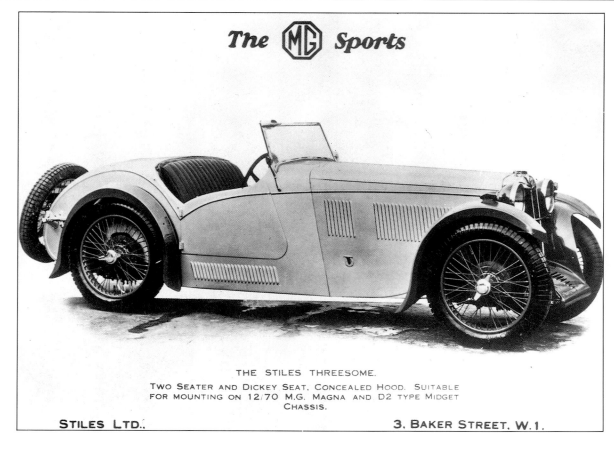

THE STILES THREESOME.
TWO SEATER AND DICKEY SEAT. CONCEALED HOOD. SUITABLE FOR MOUNTING ON 12/70 M.G. MAGNA AND D2 TYPE MIDGET CHASSIS.
STILES LTD.   3. BAKER STREET. W.1.

ing and much more comprehensive dashboard instrumentation. Initial announcements spoke of a J5, which was essentially an unsupercharged J4, but this model was not widely publicized and none was ever sold.

If it was the M-type that set the company on the road to volume car production, it was the J2 that established an M.G. sports car style that was to last for over twenty years. I am not sure just how much the appearance of the J2 was designed in the accepted sense, and how much it

just evolved both from what had gone before and from the style being adopted by M.G. for their racing cars. Nevertheless, the car that emerged was exceptionally good to look at as well as being at the pinnacle of small sports car design at that time. The combination of an elegant body and the low build allowed by the EX120-derived chassis produced a timeless classic. The simple cycle wings were a little impractical from the point of view of weather protection but they looked just right and the rear

Above: The Stiles Threesome body was available on the D-type and F-type. It has a dickey seat in the rear compartment but anyone sitting here has to be warmly dressed as they are outside the soft-top when this is raised.

Left: EX127 with George Eyston and Sir William Morris. Wheel discs to aid streamlining are fitted but these were often removed when the car was raced. George Eyston and Bert Denly ran the car at Brooklands in the B.R.D.C. 500-mile race just after the Pendine record attempt.

Right centre: The four-seater J1 Midget with the hood and sidescreens up. The sidescreen on the driver's side has a signalling flap whilst the glazing is carried down to the top of the door on the passenger's side.

Right lower: The most noticeable difference between the J1 tourer and the D-type is the cut-away tops to the doors which were *de rigueur* for 1930s' sporting cars. The J1, however, also has much improved performance.

esting to see from the catalogue that the J1 and J2 could be bought in chassis form for £175 with a set of four wings costing £2.5s.0d. The same price was charged for a bonnet.

Press reports for the J2 were enthusiastic and sportsmen were soon queuing up to buy the car, which was said to be capable of exceeding 80mph (129kph). Some were initially disappointed when their cars failed to match up to expectations and a trip to the factory for some work on valve timing and carburettor adjustment was often required. Hard driven J2s were prone to crankshaft breakage, and this failing has gone down in M.G. lore as having afflicted most J2s at some time, but the writer has seen a number that have survived on their original crankshafts for most of their long lives. The poor service record must have been the spur that prompted the development of the stronger engine used in subsequent models.

In its production life the J2 experienced one major external change when 1934 model year cars were given swept mudguards. Other minor modifications over the production run included an extra outrigger ball bearing at the front end of the crankshaft to try to reduce crankshaft breakage, fully-floating gudgeon pins for the pistons and stiffened windscreen frame to reduce the tendency for the glass to crack. The J1 was discontinued in mid-1933 and no more J3 or J4 models were constructed. The last J2 left Abingdon on 10th January 1934 being replaced by the heavier, and slower, P-type. Abingdon's baby – the Midget – was growing up.

K-type Magnette

The 1932 Motor Show must have been an exciting one for the staff manning the M.G. stand at Olympia. In addition to the re-designed Midget that was bound to attract attention, the company launched an entirely new model – the K-type Magnette. Having had four-cylinder Midgets and six-cylinder Magnas, I suppose it was only to be expected that this car, with its slightly smaller capacity six-cylinder engine, would be called a Magnette. The existence of these three names for the ranges of overhead-camshaft cars built between 1929 and 1935 later led the members of The M.G. Car Club forming a register to cater for them, calling it the "Triple-M Register" – a title that still causes considerable confusion amongst the uninitiated!

The Magnette was announced at the show as offering a range of models to cover the needs of both the family man and the motor-racing enthusiast. The K1 chassis was available with either an open four-seater body of generous proportions or as a four-seater, four-door saloon of "pillarless" construction. This ingenious body style had no pillar between the front and rear doors which allowed easy access to front or rear seats when both the front-hinged front door and the rear-hinged rear door were opened at the same time. Unfortunately, this style of bodywork deteriorated rapidly resulting in many complaints about poorly fitting doors and few examples of the model have survived. The K2 chassis carried two-seater bodywork and the K3

Above: George Eyston took EX127, accompanied by the M-type service van, to Pendine Sands for a record attempt. Runs were restricted by weather and tides, but the mean speed for runs in both directions over the measured mile was 118.39mph (190.52kph).

slab fuel tank and rear-mounted spare wheel set a fashion copied by other manufacturers.

The company produced a whole range of publicity material to promote the new model and in the brochure "The New M.G. Midget – The Car With The Racing Pedigree" they listed the features as including an "entirely new head design, two carburettors, ten miles an hour faster, more commodious coachwork, twelve volt lighting and starting, brakes better than ever, racing type wheels on all models". They said that its modest price of £199.10s.0d for the J2 was out of all proportion to the lavish equipment but the catalogue listed the stop, tail and reverse lamp as an extra costing £1.19s.0d. All the models now had leather upholstery and were available in quite a range of colours. It is inter-

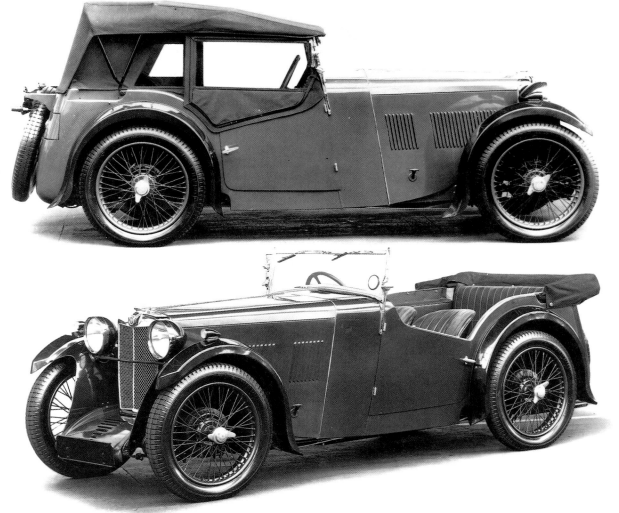

The K engine was really an entirely new design essentially based on the features of the six-cylinder F-type engine. Although still built by Wolseley, unlike the unit fitted to the F-type, the new 1100cc engine was built only for use in M.G. cars. The basic design of the block was retained but the crankshaft, oil pump and lubrication arrangements were changed, the connecting rods were strengthened and the cylinder head totally re-designed. As with the recently-introduced J-type, cross-flow porting placed the inlet and exhaust on opposite sides of the engine to improve efficiency and the valve gear and camshaft were strengthened to reduce wear. The result of these changes was to produce a strong and efficient engine that produced greater power, more reliably, from 1086cc than the F-type engine had from 1271cc. More importantly, from the point of view of future M.G. racing programmes, here was an engine that fell conveniently into the international 1100cc racing category and was capable of being supercharged to produce more than three times the power of the standard engine.

This engine was fitted to the K1 in two forms.

was a purpose-built racing car that was destined to become the most famous and most coveted of all M.G.s.

The K chassis was altogether a more substantial affair than the Magna although of basically similar design. The track was increased by six inches (152mm) to four feet (1.22m) giving the cars a much heavier look, and two lengths of chassis were available, the longer wheelbase being used for the K1 saloon and open tourer and the shorter for the K2 and K3 models. A feature adopted for the K-series cars was a divided track rod. Designed to overcome the transfer of "kick back" from the front wheels to the steering wheel, this system used an idler arm on the front axle to transfer steering movement from the steering box drag link to twin track rods.

Above: Edward and Ian Gillett make their debut at Brooklands in a J3 under the watchful eye of their father, an experienced racing driver.

Below: The ultimate J-type. The supercharged, 750cc J4 is an exciting car today – in 1933 it was sensational.

Below left: The same car, the same place, but more than sixty years later. The ex-Gillett J3 returns to an event at The Brooklands Museum.

Below: The redoubtable Evans' family team of J2s on the Barnstaple Trial tackling a water splash near the foot of Tarr Steps in 1933.

Above: Doreen Evans' J2 smartly painted in the family colours of Cambridge Blue with a cream stripe. In early events she was too young to hold a driving licence and Nevil Lloyd would drive the car on the road, as he was when the picture below was taken. The J2 is now owned by Keith Hall.

In the heavy saloon it was mated to an ENV "Wilson" preselector gearbox where the engine camshaft timing was modified to suit the characteristics of this gearbox. The more sporting K1 tourer and K2 two-seater had a conventional Wolseley four-speed gearbox with remote control. Both versions of the engine had triple SU carburettors which are even more difficult to set up than the more usual twin carburettor arrangement.

The K3 racing cars used the shorter K chassis with additional bracing and with the brakes featuring elektron brake drums. The specially prepared engines had front-mounted superchargers and were mated to preselector gearboxes. These gearboxes were popular then for racing cars as they offered a quick and reliable gear change at the press of a clutch pedal. The driver's task was limited to selecting the next gear he required in advance – the box would change to this ratio when the clutch pedal was depressed.

A Family M.G.

The Magnette saloon weighed in at well over a ton and with less than 40bhp available was never destined to be a fast car. However, the preselector gearbox allowed frequent gear changes to keep engine speed up, handling and road-holding was good, and average journey times were reasonable for a 1930s' saloon car. The factory were aware of the cars' shortcomings and

before it had been on general sale for twelve months a larger-capacity version of the engine was offered. This engine, known as the KD and usually installed with a preselector gearbox, had a longer stroke crankshaft returning the capacity to 1271cc and increasing the power by 8bhp.

In September 1932 the Magna had gained 12-inch (304mm) brakes and various engine modifications were made to the F1 four-seater salonettes and tourers to produce the F3 Magna, and also a new two-seater version called the F2. The F2 had the neat J2-style body and wings enhanced by the longer six-cylinder bonnet and sloping Magna radiator shell. Only forty F2 Magnas sold, however, as the extra £50.10s.0d. asked for the six-cylinder car over the visually similar and almost as quick J2 Midget proved a deterrent to most buyers and, anyway, the F-type Magna was coming to the end of its time.

To those more used to the modern motor industry where the life of any particular model is measured in years rather than months, the story of The M.G. Car Company in the 1930s must appear bewildering. Remembering how comparatively recently the company had started building cars in their own right, the seemingly never-ending announcements of new models every few months during this period is a constant source of confusion and amazement. The original M-type was in production for quite a long period, April 1929 to August 1932, when compared with some of its successors. The D-

1933 K3 MAGNETTE

Of all the beautiful cars in this book this must be the most coveted. K3011 was purchased as a rolling chassis by Whitney Straight through Jarvis and Sons in June 1933. Thomson and Taylor built the body and the car was raced extensively by Straight, and then by Richard Seaman, before being sold to Reggie Tongue who drove it in a number of events. In 1935 it was bought by Sam Collier who took it to America in 1936, where it remained in original condition until it was purchased by Peter Green in 1979.

Right: A large tachometer sits ahead of the driver behind a close-set steering wheel. There is no speedometer. The knob below the rear-view mirror is the handle for a pump pressurizing the fuel tank to force the fuel through the pipe to the carburettor. In a race the driver or riding mechanic pumped to maintain 3psi on the gauge to the left of the handle.

Above and below left: The secret of the high power output of the K3 engine lies in the supercharger. This is driven directly from the front of the crankshaft and fed by an SU carburettor. The performance of K3011 has been amply demonstrated at a number of record attempts in recent years and the car currently holds ten British speed records ranging from 200miles at 105.14mph (169.2kph) to 79.81mph (128.4kph) for 24 hours – not bad for a 1933 car!

SPECIFICATION

Model: K3 two-seater

Engine: Six-cylinder in line, overhead camshaft, water cooled. 57 x 71mm, 1086cc, supercharged, 120bhp

Gearbox: Four-speed Wilson preselector

Final drive: 4.89:1. Top gear 17.85mph/1000rpm (29kph/1000rpm)

Suspension: Solid axles mounted on half-elliptic leaf springs. Each spring is fixed at leading end and in sliding trunnions at rear

Dimensions: Wheelbase 7ft 10.1875in (2392mm). Track 4ft (1219mm). Overall length 12ft 1in (3683mm)

Unladen weight: Approx. 17cwt (867kg)

Cost when new: £795 (with standard two-seater body)

Performance: Top speed approx 110mph (177kph)

Owner: Peter Green

Below: An aero screen provides the only weather protection, even though this car is regularly driven on the road all year round.

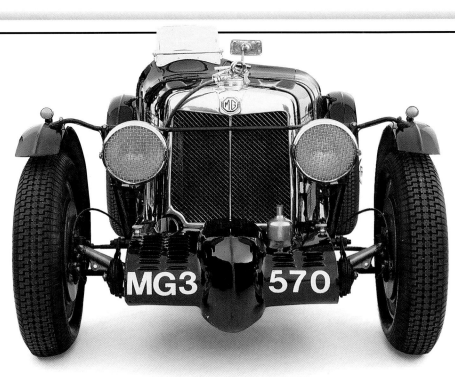

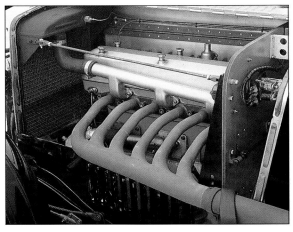

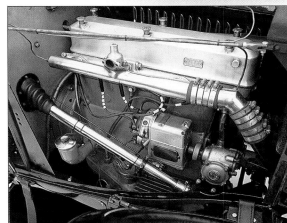

Above: The radiator and headlights are protected by mesh grilles. The small mudguards are a legal requirement for road use, but are removed for racing or record-breaking.

Right: The six-cylinder OHC M.G. engine at its best. In spite of its immaculate appearance, this K3 is no museum piece and appears regularly in historic races in Britain and abroad.

Above: The tail houses a large fuel tank fitted with tightly-sealing twin filler caps. When refuelling during a race, both of these are opened – one to take a funnel for the fuel and the other to let the displaced air escape.

Left: The fuel/air mixture, under pressure from the supercharger, is fed to the cylinders via a slightly tapering inlet manifold which incorporates a blow-off valve to stop a backfire damaging the supercharger.

Below: The elegant body on K3011 differs from that used for standard 1933 factory-bodied K3s, which were all fitted with the heavier, slab-tanked Mille Miglia style coachwork.

type, for example, lasted just nine months and the F1 ten months – with the F3 carrying on for a further seven months before this too was replaced. The advertising agencies must have enjoyed the business this brought whilst the accountants, and the men responsible for maintaining stocks of spares, must have been sent prematurely grey!

The Legendary K3

The announcement in late 1932 of the racing version of the K-series Magnette, the K3, brought with it a period of feverish activity for those working in the racing shop at Abingdon. In search of international racing honours it was decided that a team of K3s be sent to take part in the 1000 mile Italian road race, the Mille Miglia, under the control of the enthusiastic Earl Howe. By January 1933 – the race itself was scheduled for early April – one of the two prototypes was ready for testing and this was taken to Italy to see how it performed. Poor weather precluded a trial run over the full route but much was learned from the trip and some modifications were incorporated into the team cars being hurriedly assembled.

The prototype car returned to the factory towards the end of February – just six weeks before the race and with only three weeks available to ready the cars for shipment to Italy. Much midnight oil was burned preparing the team cars and rebuilding the prototype for use as a practice car. The trial had exposed shortcomings in the gearbox and the road wheels, and a substantial redesign of these components was needed in the short time available. In spite of this the cars were finally completed just in time for shipment to Italy on a cargo boat leaving from Fowey in Cornwall. The team's troubles were not at an end, however, as practice runs in the now hot climate revealed weaknesses in the brake drums and erratic steering. A batch of brake drums had to be hurriedly modified at Abingdon and shipped to Italy and the steering fault was traced to wrongly-positioned torque reaction cables on the front axle. One problem that was not resolved before the race was that of oiling sparking plugs. The combination of steep hills and tight corners, allied to the need for an adequate oil feed to the superchargers, made selecting the correct grade of plug a difficult task, and frequent stops to clean or change plugs proved necessary.

In the race one car was to be driven by Sir Henry Birkin and Bernard Rubin and to this pairing fell the task of driving as fast as possible right from the start in an attempt, successful as it turned out, to break their Maserati-mounted rivals in the 1100cc class. The other team members in their two K3s, George Eyston and Count Lurani and Earl Howe and "Hammy" Hamilton, were to follow at a more moderate pace to try to preserve their cars during this gruelling event.

The Birkin car broke the class record to the first control, which was 220 miles (354km) after the start, but then had to retire with a burned exhaust valve. His average speed on ordinary roads for the first 130 miles (209km) was 88mph

(142kph) – quite remarkable in 1933 for an 1100cc car. The whole event was a tremendous feat of endurance for both cars and drivers; to put it into perspective remember that a modern Grand Prix race only lasts a maximum of two hours and covers around 200 miles (320km). The

Above: When the swept-wing version of the J2 arrived the company issued a completely new coloured brochure. M.G.'s competition achievements were always fully exploited in their sales campaigns.

Below: The swept-wing J2 is heavier than the cycle-wing model but much more practical. This very original car is owned by Brian Wigg, who drives many thousands of miles a year in the J2 to attend M.G. events.

K3 was a fast car and, with a top speed of well over 100mph (161kph) without any streamlining to assist it, it compares well with many a modern sports car. Where current cars score is in the areas of ride and roadholding, rather than outright speed, and the driver of a 1933 K3 had to work a lot harder to maintain high average speeds over rough, winding roads.

With the Birkin/Rubin car out of the running, it was left to the two remaining K3s to uphold the honour of Abingdon and, indeed, Great Britain as the Italian fans and press had welcomed the arrival of these foreign competitors with enthusiasm. The main opposition in their class to the M.G. team, the supercharged Maseratis, had been unable to match the pace set by Birkin and were effectively out of the running so to take class honours it was merely a matter of beating the four Fiats and, of course, finishing. By Rome, Eyston and Lurani had taken 25 minutes off the existing class record with Howe and Hamilton following on 20 minutes later.

With just over 600 miles (965km) of the route completed Ancona was reached and the average speed, including stops for fuel and changes of spark plugs, was a remarkable 55.7mph (89.6kph). Although both M.G.s were doing well, the Fiats were far from out of the running and the one driven by Torriani was not far behind. Because the cars started at one minute intervals, their position on the road did not always reflect the final results and the situation was further complicated because the slower cars

Above: The K1 tourer used the longer version of the K chassis which enabled the factory to fit a body that provided ample room for four adults. Carrying a price tag of £399, only 97 K1 tourers were built.

Below: The two-seater K2 built on the shorter chassis cost just £9 less than the four-seater tourer and only 20 were built. A 1271cc-engined K2 must be rated as the most desirable roadgoing pre-war M.G.

started before the faster, which inevitably resulted in a lot of overtaking.

Both of the remaining cars finished the 1000 mile race ahead of their rivals to the applause of the enthusiastic crowd at Brescia. The blow inflicted on Italian national pride by beating the local cars in the 1100cc class on their own ground was offset by the overall victory notched up by their hero, Tazio Nuvolari, who was driving one of the magnificent straight-eight 2.3 litre Alfa-Romeos. The M.G. team took the first and second places in their class and won the team prize – the first time this had been awarded to a foreign team in the Mille Miglia.

International Honours
Following this success, 1933 was to prove a mixed year for M.G.'s racing efforts. At Brooklands Ron Horton set a new class record in his K3 at 115.55mph (185.95kph); whilst at the Mannin Beg race held on the Isle of Man in July all the K3s failed to finish after a succession of problems, the most serious of which was a number of rear axle failures. Even the gruelling Mille Miglia had not highlighted this weakness which only a strengthening of the differential components cured. In August Whitney Straight recorded another K3 victory on foreign soil when he won outright the Coppa Acerbo at Pescara in Italy.

However, it was a victory closer to home, in the Ulster Tourist Trophy, that did most to establish the reputation of the cars. Run over closed roads in Northern Ireland where speed events

Above: The 1933 Tourist Trophy Race was held on the circuit outside Belfast, Northern Ireland. With Alec

Hounslow as mechanic, Tazio Nuvolari gained the lead just before the fall of the flag, winning by 40 seconds.

on the public highway were permitted – unlike in mainland Britain where they had been banned for many years – the Tourist Trophy was a handicap event. Under this system the K3 suffered from being given a target average speed of 77.93mph (125.4kph) which was actually faster than the then current class lap record. Consequently the team regarded outright victory as unlikely with the four-cylinder Midgets being far better placed to take this honour. However, neither the team nor the handicappers had made sufficient allowance for the extraordinary qualities of the driver chosen to lead the K3 challenge.

Above: The Mille Miglia in April 1934 with Lord Howe in K3017. After an appeal to Sir William Morris, a team of three cars was entered at Lord Howe's expense. Unfortunately, his car was eliminated by a crash but K3105, driven by Count Laurani and C. Penn-Hughes, was second in the 1100cc class.

Imported Talent

Tazio Nuvolari, the winner of the Mille Miglia a few months earlier, was probably the best racing driver of his era. Indeed, there are many who would accord him the position of being the best driver of all time. In any case, to give him a seat in the K3 was the equivalent, in modern terms, of employing a Senna or Schumacher to drive in a sports car or touring car event – quite simply, he outclassed almost all the other drivers.

From the start of the race Nuvolari drove like a man possessed, breaking the lap record at speeds over four miles an hour (6.4kph) faster than similarly-sized cars had done the previous year. He beat his handicap by 0.72mph (1.16kph) and won the race, although it has to be said that an overlong pit stop by his main rival for honours, Hamilton in one of the more favourably handicapped Midgets, allowed him to take the chequered flag. Nevertheless, the brilliant drive, which was shared by his riding mechanic Alec Hounslow from the factory at Abingdon, must rank as one of the greatest M.G. victories.

The publicity given to the K3 successes in the Mille Miglia and the Tourist Trophy did the marque a lot of good as the motoring magazines devoted many pages to these events. Never one to shun publicity, Cecil Kimber made the most of

Right: The second race meeting at the Donington Road Race Circuit took place in May 1933. On the start line Robin Mere in a K3 (race number 33) watches the frenzied activity around a fellow competitor's car. Car number 6 is a Lea-Francis. Robin Mere made a good start but had to stop during the race owing to problems with the supercharger. Donington was the first true road-racing circuit on mainland Britain where racing on public roads was banned.

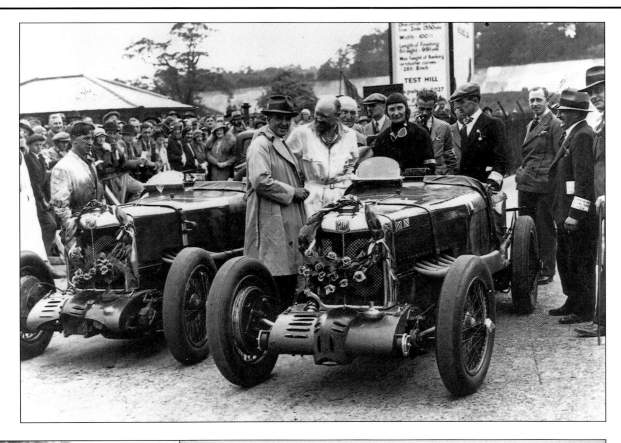

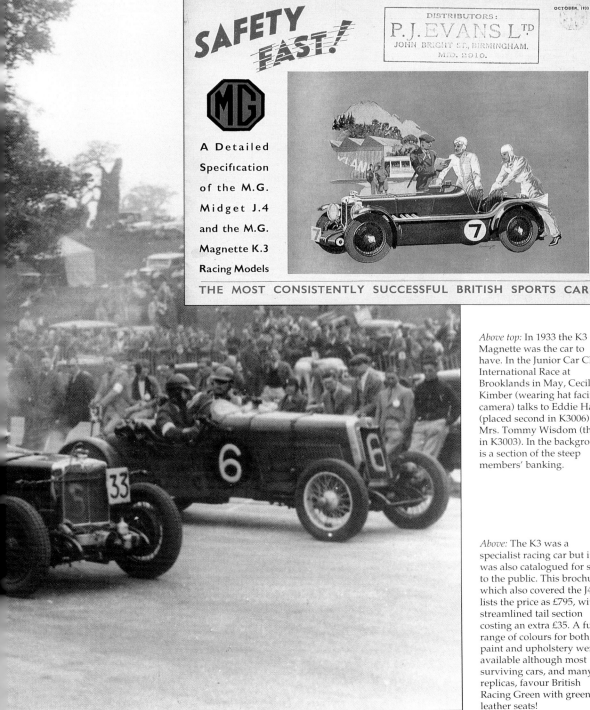

Above top: In 1933 the K3 Magnette was the car to have. In the Junior Car Club International Race at Brooklands in May, Cecil Kimber (wearing hat facing camera) talks to Eddie Hall (placed second in K3006) and Mrs. Tommy Wisdom (third in K3003). In the background is a section of the steep members' banking.

Above: The K3 was a specialist racing car but it was also catalogued for sale to the public. This brochure, which also covered the J4, lists the price as £795, with a streamlined tail section costing an extra £35. A full range of colours for both paint and upholstery were available although most surviving cars, and many replicas, favour British Racing Green with green leather seats!

the limelight by placing advertisements and issuing a lavish, 48-page booklet to celebrate the Mille Miglia success. This attractive publication, now much prized by collectors, was designed not just to advertise the victory but also to help sell the rest of the 31 production K3s that were being built. These were sold at £795 as production racing cars fitted with Tourist Trophy regulation coachwork and preselector gearboxes. The 1933 cars mainly left the works fitted with this body although a lightweight "skimpy" body of similar pattern could be specified. For racing a detachable streamlined tail could be ordered at an additional cost of £35 and in 1935 most of the cars were supplied fitted with lightweight bodies and pointed tails. On these cars the usual pattern slab fuel tank, which held around 23 gallons (105lit), was replaced with a larger tank mounted directly behind the seats and shaped to match the rounded contours of the pointed tail. Placing the fuel load slightly further forward on the chassis helped the handling when the tank was full.

Flying The Flag

The growth of the M.G. marque as a force in international motor racing and the publicity this gained was something of an antidote to all the bad news that was appearing in the press. Following the Wall Street crash of October 1929, unemployment in the industrial countries in the early 1930s had risen as high as 25 per cent. Heavily hit was the United States where President Franklin Roosevelt introduced vigorous state intervention to provide work on road building and other projects in his "New Deal" in 1933. In Europe the economic devastation that followed the First World War, and dissatisfaction in Germany over the terms of the Versailles Peace Settlement of 1919, was leading to the rise of Fascism. In Italy Benito Mussolini founded the original Fascist movement in 1921 and had acquired dictatorial powers by 1922. In Germany the National Socialist Party had used intimidation, violence and racial hatred to gain popular support that led to their taking power in 1933. After abolishing the constitution, their leader, Adolf Hitler, assumed dictatorial powers the same year.

One result of the growth of nationalism in these countries was the interest taken in motor sport by their leaders. Seen as a way of demonstrating the power and technical superiority of their nation, the Germans spent vast sums supporting the Mercedes-Benz and Auto-Union teams resulting in the most exciting and technically-superior racing cars ever produced. Lacking such state support, the British cars were left to compete for honours in the smaller-capacity classes – luckily an area where M.G.s excelled in both motor racing and in record-breaking.

In March 1933, before all the racing activity with the K3s, a replacement for the F-type Magna was announced. The chassis dimensions were similar to the earlier car, it retained the narrower (3ft 6in, 1066mm) track of the F-type and the Midgets and also kept the 12-inch (304mm) brakes fitted to the later Magnas. The engine,

1933 L1 MAGNA TOURER

The four-seater tourer M.G.s provided sporting motoring for the 1930s' family man and the introduction with the L-type of full-length swept wings to keep road dirt away from the sides of the body made the cars a lot more practical. Although the tourer versions of the four-cylinder cars tended to be a little underpowered and tail heavy, the six-cylinder L1 tourer was much better. Aesthetically, the longer bonnet gave a better balanced design making the L-type one of the prettiest of the pre-war M.G.s.

Right: Comfortable bucket seats are provided for driver and passenger. Unlike some of the other six-cylinder M.G.s, the L-type retained a manual four-speed gearbox with a remote control and octagonal (of course!) gear lever knob. Controls for the choke and idling speed are mounted low down in front of the gear lever.

Below right: All the seat facings are leather and the rear seats are shaped to sit passengers as low as possible over the rear axle. Also there are recessed foot wells to give extra room.

Above: When erected, the hood and sidescreens provide good weather protection and reasonable visibility. However, as with most open cars, the L1 is much nicer when used with the hood stowed away!

Below: The fuel tank with its attractive, chromed filler cap is mounted low at the back of the chassis, behind the spare wheel. The stowed hood frame and folded fabric rest on brackets and are held in place with leather straps.

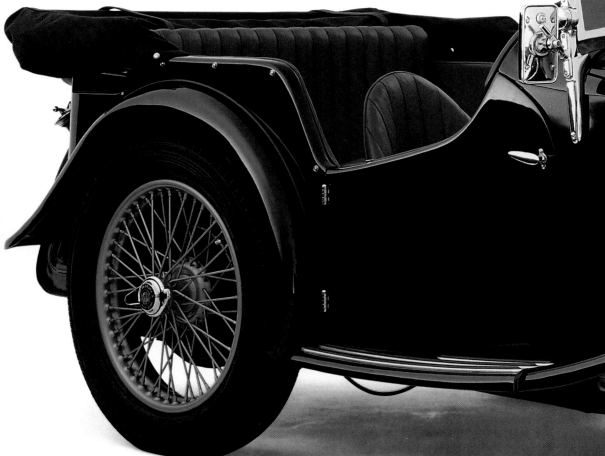

SPECIFICATION

Model: L1 four-seater

Engine: Six-cylinder in line, overhead camshaft, water cooled. 57 x 71mm, 1086cc, 41bhp

Gearbox: Four-speed non-synchromesh

Final drive: 5.375:1. Top gear 15.2mph/1000rpm (24kph/1000rpm)

Suspension: Solid axles mounted on half-elliptic leaf springs. Each spring is fixed at leading end and in sliding trunnions at rear.

Dimensions: Wheelbase 7ft 10.1875in (2392mm). Track 3ft 6in (1067mm). Overall length 12ft (3658mm)

Unladen weight: 16.5cwt (838kg)

Cost when new: £299

Performance: (From contemporary reports): Top speed 75mph (121kph)

Owner: Chris Cook

Above: The epitome of a 1930s touring car – cut-away doors, folding windscreen, and double-humped scuttle. All one needs to enjoy Chris Cook's beautiful car now is sunshine, and roads as free of traffic as they would have been in that golden age of the M.G. sports car!

Above: The engine-turned aluminium dashboard has a combined speedometer and tachometer placed in front of the driver and a control and instrument panel on the passenger's side, both with octagonal bezels. A clock and water temperature gauge flank the centrally-mounted combined horn push and dip switch which is placed so as to be easily reached without moving a hand from the steering-wheel rim.

Above: All Magnas had sloping radiator shells, making them easy to distinguish from other models. The wing stays were attached to the engine-mounted radiator.

Right: The engine, which was fitted with twin carburettors, derived from that fitted to the K-type Magnette and they shared all the major components.

however, was the K-type unit, with some minor differences, and was mated to a four-speed gearbox with a remote control similar to that used on the J-type. The engine was a vast improvement over the F-type and although it was of smaller capacity, 1086cc, the power output given in twin-carburettor form was greater than the earlier unit. The car retained the sloping Magna radiator grill inherited from the F-type but adopted elegant swept wings that totally transformed the appearance. Initially the new Magna was available as the L1 in four-seater open and closed form, and as a two-seater sports model, the L2. A number of improvements had been made to the design of the four-seaters to give greater room and comfort to passengers, with new seat frames for the front seats on both models and larger rear seats. There were now separate windows for the rear-seat passengers on the closed car, and the bodies for these were built by Abbey Coachworks.

L-type Magna

The L-type Magna made a superb road car as well as being used in competitions. The strong and powerful engine, good brakes and safe handling made it an ideal mount for club racing and long-distance trials. In the Light Car Club's third annual relay race, run at Brooklands in blazing heat, a team of three L-types, entered by The M.G. Car Club and driven by Martin, Wright and Hess, won the event at an average speed of 88.62mph (142.62kph). In August 1933 the Alpine Trial was also the scene of a win for the new Magnas. Cars driven by Watkinson, Welch and Wisdom won the Team Prize in this demanding event that included climbs of many of the notorious Alpine passes. In recent years the heyday of the Alpine Trials and Rallies held before and after the Second World War have been re-created in a number of successful Historic Marathons where M.G.s have once again featured amongst the winners.

With unemployment still rife and many men forced to rely on state benefits and charity to feed their families, M.G. workers were fortunate to have a job. In spite of the popularity of the cars, life was not always easy for the assembly line workers. Granted, average pay rates in the motor industry then were well above those of agricultural workers and there is no doubt that jobs at M.G.s would have been desirable, but employment was not all that secure. Then, as now, demand for cars was seasonal and there were times when workers could be laid off because of a shortage of orders. Often employees would have work for just two or three days a week and have to sign on "the dole" for the rest of the time. When busy, full employment and even some overtime was the order of the day and then workers would be considerably better off than many of their neighbours. At Abingdon,

Left: To publicize the L2 two-seaters, in August 1933 The M.G. Car Company lent ten brand new cars for a celebrity race of former Brooklands drivers. The race was won by Sidney Cummings. I wonder if the cars then went back into stock?

Right: The dashboard of the L2 owed much to that fitted to the J2 although the six-cylinder car did have the clock and oil thermometer as standard equipment.

Far right: The L2 was a particularly good-looking car and is now high on most enthusiasts' "wish list". Ninety L-types left the factory as two-seaters but, in recent years, a number of four-seaters have acquired L2 bodies.

Right: This magnificent car is owned by Dave Jarvis, who totally rebuilt it himself. As a jeweller he is used to painstakingly detailed work, and this talent was evidently put to good use on his beautiful L2. The door cappings are a period extra, as are the headlight guards and the Junior Car Club member's badge.

when work was available, preference was given to workers previously laid off over new recruits. Those working in development or on the racing cars were less likely to be short of work, and the more usual complaint in their case was of excessively long hours.

In September 1933 it was time to announce the changes for the 1934 model year. In August the first of the J2s with swept wings, like those now appearing on the larger Magnas and Magnettes, left the production line. The revised J2 was destined to appear at the Autumn Motor Show alongside the Magna and the K-type Magnettes, with the advertising brochures produced for all these models making much of the large number of competition achievements gained by the marque in previous years.

Continental Style

An interesting addition to the Magna range was the Continental Coupé. Later criticised as one of Kimber's less successful designs, this closed car provided comfort, even luxury, for two, with the tiny rear seat best used as luggage accommodation. From the outside the car appeared to have a large luggage trunk at the back but this was merely a cover for the fuel tank and spare wheel. The main selling point was the appearance and interior appointments. The brochure lists a number of striking two-tone colour schemes designed to enhance the lines of the coachwork. Two-tone colour schemes were popular in the 1930s, with many of the exotic makes like Bugattis and Delahayes producing striking examples, and Kimber was once again trying to sell M.G.s to a different market by "gilding the lily".

For the occupants much was done to make the cars attractive, with door panels featuring the M.G. octagon at the centre of a "sunburst" design, a sliding roof with inset glazed windows and comfortable seats. The cars failed to appeal to buyers in the numbers the company expected, however, and remained in the price lists long after the rest of the L-types had been sold. An advertisement was placed by one London dealer as late as March 1935 offering brand new Continental Coupés at £250 – which was £100

THE M.G. MAGNA, CONTINENTAL COUPÉ

The M.G. MAGNA "L" Type
Continental Coupé . . . £350
Ex Works

under the previous list price. Perversely, it is now regarded as one of the more desirable of the prewar cars.

As already mentioned, the Magnette had by now gained a larger-capacity engine for the production models where the advantages of remaining in the 1100cc class for competitions were likely to be of lesser interest to owners than the benefits of more power. Both the K-type Magnette and the L-type Magna were sold in chassis form to coachbuilders who produced a number of differing designs. University Motors continued to offer their customers non-standard products and the University Foursome Folding Head Coupé was available on the J-type at £295, the L-type at £395 and on the K2 chassis at £490. In exchange for the performance loss resulting from the weight penalty of the University Motors body, customers had the advantage of enjoying the "three position" folding top that was so suited to the British climate.

More Records Fall

Record-breaking had not been forgotten and the "Magic Midget", EX127, was out again at Brooklands in the hands of George Eyston in 1933 to recapture some of the longer-distance records – 50 and 100 kilometres and 50 miles – which had been wrestled from his grasp by the Austin team. He raised these records to speeds of between 105.65mph (170kph) and 106.72mph (171.74kph). Bodywork modifications made to reduce wind resistance restricted the room for the driver so much that it was difficult for George Eyston to fit in the car. For further record attempts, held at Montlhéry in October 1933, the much shorter Bert Denly took the wheel. The results were amazing for a 750cc car. The speeds for the mile and kilometre records were raised to 128.62mph (207kph) and the 10-mile record to 125.43mph (201.85kph). Bearing in mind how recently a 750cc car had exceeded 100mph gives some measure to this achievement. EX127 was then sold to Bobby Kohlrausch, a German racing driver of note, who first entered it in road races and then went on to use it for record-breaking with much success.

Above: The sales brochure for the oddly-styled Magna Continental Coupé – this was the least commercially successful of the various versions of the L-type Magna on the market.

Above: The interior of the Continental Coupé was extremely well appointed. The "sunburst" pattern door trim, the ashtray, zipped map pocket and sliding windows are neatly done.

The Abingdon factory had been continually updated to keep pace with changes of models and increases in production since the company moved there in 1929. A journalist visiting in late 1933 remarked on these alterations and visited the new paint shop and a new machine shop where he saw the very latest lathes and pressing tools. A special workshop was set aside for the preparation of racing engines which were tested on a dynamometer and he also saw a standard K2 being tested on a system of rollers which recorded performance and allowed faults to be rectified before the body was fitted. When ready for sale, all the cars were taken out of the factory for a road test. The company were obviously keen to show both journalists and ordinary members of the public round their factory, a tradition that continued after the war and an experience I was pleased to enjoy on a number of occasions.

The J-type Midgets were very successful and popular little sports cars but hard use, and competition work, had shown up the weakness of the crankshaft, which flexed at higher revolutions. In March 1934 a replacement for the J-type was announced to the public with the new model, called the P-type, addressing some of the criticisms that had been levelled at the earlier cars. Design work on the six-cylinder engine carried out for the introduction of the L-type Magna and K-type Magnette models had shown the way ahead and a completely revised four-cylinder engine for the new Midget was drawn up. The crankshaft was larger and now ran in three main bearings which were lubricated by filtered oil fed from a gear-driven pump. The diameter of the camshaft was also increased and the valve gear strengthened. The capacity of the engine remained the same at 847cc, as did the power output. The improvement in cylinder head design was counteracted by the greater

Right: London M.G. distributors, University Motors, offered their own versions of various models. This brochure shows their rather heavy-looking Folding Head Coupé.

Left: At the end of the chassis production line the brakes were adjusted and tested on these powered rollers. All M.G.s also underwent a full road test, a tradition that was to endure into the 1970s.

Below: For any modern restorers of the pre-war M.G.s, detailed factory photographs like this provide inspiration. Here L-type chassis are assembled and engines installed.

weight of the crankshaft and increased friction from the larger bearing surface area.

A new chassis was designed which was based on the J-type, but lengthened at the rear to provide a more rigid mounting for the spare wheel. The axles now carried 12-inch (304mm) brakes which improved the stopping power considerably over the lighter eight-inch (203mm) brakes. Two- and four-seater bodywork was available, as well as an Airline Coupé, and, although the general layout was similar to the swept wing J-types, the whole effect of the slightly larger size and the tidying up of details produced a very pleasing car.

The other improvements included a new instrument layout with the centre panel containing a mileometer but no speedometer. As had been the case on the J2, the speeds in each gear were shown on the tachometer in front of the driver. The wood-veneered finish of the dashboard, with its chromed edging, and the pair of brown dash lamps was very smart and rather less utilitarian in appearance than the dashboards of the earlier Midgets.

In spite of the extra weight of the chassis and coachwork, the smooth delivery of power from the modified engine gave the new model similar performance to the J-types, but a fully laden four-seater was still not a fast car. The new engine was a strong unit well able to stand considerable tuning and many owners resorted to fitting one of the superchargers being offered by performance specialists. A Zoller blower installation that was approved by the M.G. Car Company for the P-type cost just £27, complete with all the parts needed to install it – including a set of spark plugs with a different heat range to cater for the more exacting requirements of the supercharged engine.

The Airline Coupé

The P-type Midget was a stronger, better equipped and more comfortable car than the previous models and a far cry from the first Midget, the M-type. However, it continued to appeal to the same sort of owner and many were used in competitions. Unlike the D-type and the

Bought originally by a Mr. McGregor-Fry, who owned the Cambrian Ashfelt Company and was apparently a member of the Fry's Chocolate family, this car covered no less than 18,000 miles (29,000km) in the first year of his ownership – a high mileage in the 1930s when there were no motorways. A few months later the car was damaged in an accident and was returned to the factory for repair. The owner asked if the factory would update it to the more powerful PB specification, but they refused and suggested he purchase a new PB!

SPECIFICATION

Model: PA two-seater

Engine: Four-cylinder in line, overhead camshaft, water cooled. 57 x 83mm, 847cc, 36bhp

Gearbox: Four-speed non-synchromesh

Final drive: 5.375:1. Top gear 14.73mph/1000rpm (24kph/1000rpm)

Suspension: Solid axles mounted on half-elliptic leaf springs. Each spring is fixed at leading end and in sliding trunnions at rear

Dimensions: Wheelbase 7ft 3in (2210mm). Track 3ft 6in (1067mm). Overall length 10ft 11in (3327mm)

Unladen weight: 13.5cwt (686kg)

Cost when new: £222

Performance: (From contemporary reports): Top speed 72mph (116kph)

Owner: Terry Andrews

Left: The M.G. octagonal trademark was employed wherever possible, hence the shape of the side lights!

Right: The flowing wing lines and attractive bodywork make the P-type one of the prettiest of the prewar M.G.s. The car was heavier than the J2 it replaced, and for competition these wings were often discarded, but in normal road use they provided the occupants much more protection than cycle wings.

Right: This petrol cap is of the type installed as original equipment on the PBs, but it was often fitted by owners of the earlier PA cars to update them.

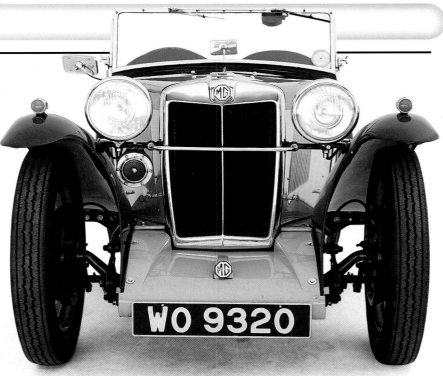

Above: The dashboard is veneered with sequoia wood which, after 1935, was a protected species. Burr walnut was therefore used for the PB. This car has the deluxe instrument layout with a water temperature gauge and clock.

Above right: Although the PA now looks as good as it did when new, at the time that it was purchased by Terry Andrews in 1978 the car was in a very sorry state. It had moved to the Isle of Man at some time, and had been involved in yet another accident. Repairs then had involved fitting a T-type petrol tank and rear axle.

Above:"Trafficators" were a popular fitment in the 1930s. Switches on the dashboard operated the semaphore arms which were lit when extended. Unfortunately, often they either failed to close after use, or to emerge when required, to the confusion of following traffic!

Above: The small capacity, high-revving engine fitted to the PA was a gem. In standard form it was capable of giving the car good performance but could also be tuned, or supercharged, to give even more power. The "crossflow" design of the cylinder head – with the carburettors feeding one side and the exhaust gases leaving from the other – was efficient. The polished pipe above the exhaust manifold is to take the cooling water from the cylinder head to the radiator. The canister to the left of the exhaust pipe is the oil filter. The water pump (with the M.G. logo attractively cast into the cover) is to the left of this.

Above: The attractive shape of the M.G. radiator complements the superb body styling. The PA had a honeycomb pattern radiator grille, which was replaced on the PB by slats. Mechanical misfortune had taken this car off the road in 1953 and it languished for 25 years before being rescued.

Right: The friction-type shock absorbers fitted to the front of the PA were an efficient way of controlling the heavy beam axle. Hard wooden discs are sandwiched between metal plates and damping is increased by progressively tightening the central nut. The pointer indicates the setting.

J-type, the P-type was not offered as a four-seater saloon but a closed two-seater with extremely striking bodywork, called the Airline Coupé, was produced. Once again Kimber was influenced by current styling trends and the 1930s saw quite a vogue for the streamlined look. Buildings, furniture and even tableware were designed to look modern and streamlined and there had been some attempts by the more advanced car designers, particularly in Europe, to make their products look more up-to-date.

The elegant sloping rear bodywork of the Airline Coupé complemented the flowing lines of front and rear wings and contrasted with the upright radiator shell and angular bonnet. Overall the result was pleasing and quite a number were sold to customers wishing to limit their exposure to the weather to that afforded by opening the sliding sunshine roof. A number of these cars have survived with some fetching at auction three times as much as restored open two-seaters. Closed coupés have always been popular with people looking for something out of the ordinary, without having to endure the disadvantages of an open sports car.

Another new model announced in early 1934 was the N Magnette. The enlarged-capacity, 1271cc KD engine fitted to later K-type road cars was further improved by fitting a modified cylinder head and having the crankshaft running in main bearings of similar design to those used in the new P-type engine. This twin-carbu-

rettor, six-cylinder engine produced 56bhp, which was a useful amount more than the 48bhp available from the earlier engine. The chassis for the new model generally followed established M.G. practice but was both stiffer than previous designs, and had side frames that were not parallel to each other but placed so that the chassis was wider at the rear than at the front. To insulate the body from the chassis, sub-frames were rubber mounted on each side of the chassis frame and parallel to it and these provided mounting points for the ash frame of the bodywork. The front and rear body mountings were likewise isolated from the chassis by the use of rubber with the result that the N-type bodies suffer less from being twisted on rough roads than did the earlier cars and they also gave their occupants a more comfortable ride.

Space And Comfort

On announcement only two- and four-seaters were available but the press releases mentioned that an Airline Coupé and an open two/four-seater were also to be available very shortly. The Airline was similar to that available on the P-type chassis but the open car was of a design unique to this model. Known as either the Airline convertible or the Allingham N-type, this car could be used either as a pure two-seater, with the rear seat concealed by closing the rear decking, or as a full four-seater when the rear panel is open. Unlike other "dickie" seat designs, rear-seat passengers sat within the cockpit and benefited from the weather protection offered by the soft top when it rained. This body had the advantages and looks of a two-seater, with the bonus of having those additional rear seats when required.

Both the Airline Coupé and the two/four-seater were built at the instigation of M.G. dealer, W.H. Allingham of Stratford Place, London W1, but, unlike some other special bodied cars, these models were offered as stock M.G. products alongside their other catalogued cars.

Left: The slightly heavier appearance of the closed cabin on this PA does not spoil the appeal of these cars. The curving shape of the wings nicely frame the radiator grille and large headlights.

Right: The dashboard of the Airline differs from those fitted to the open cars, although instrumentation is identical. The windscreen opens outwards and there is a sunshine roof with inset windows to provide light.

The standard two- and four-seat open cars were, perhaps, rather less attractive than some of the earlier models but they were fast and comfortable, and probably the best of the overhead-camshaft pre-war cars for normal, everyday use. The engine was both powerful and robust and the bodywork offered the occupants rather more space and comfort than they had previously enjoyed.

Variations On A Theme

In addition to the standard two-seater, the company also built a number of N-types fitted with unsold K2 bodies and it called these cars the ND. The result was a car of somewhat unusual design that found favour with competition enthusiasts and a few examples still exist. The K pillarless saloon was updated by fitting the more powerful N-type engine and in this guise it was called the KN, this variant was also available with the four-seater K1 body as "The University Motors Speed Model" and was advertised and sold by these well-known London M.G. dealers.

Changes in the regulations meant that the factory could no longer rely on the K3 Magnettes when entering the 1934 Tourist Trophy race. Having won the 1933 race so convincingly, Cecil

Kimber was anxious to repeat this in 1934. Perhaps because of the K3's success, a ban on superchargers was announced in early 1934 for that year's race. As an unsupercharged K3 was considered unsuitable, the factory turned to the then current model, the N type, and decided to develop that. Lightweight aluminium, narrower-than-standard two-seater bodies were fitted to the N chassis to comply with the regulations, and the 1271cc engines tuned to increase the power output to 74bhp. The extra power was

transmitted by a two-plate clutch through a standard gearbox with different ratios. These racing cars were given the factory designation NE (see pages 78-79).

To try out the new cars, a team of three were entered for the LCC Relay Race at Brooklands on the 21st July. The cars were driven by Miss

Below: The striking shape of the Airline Coupé must have seemed as modern in 1934 as the most outrageous of "concept" cars does today. The same body was used for the N-type and suits the larger car even better.

The new M.G. MAGNETTE Type 'N'

and The M.G. MAGNETTE K.N. Type Saloon

Left: To bring the completely new N-type Magnette to the attention of the public, the company issued a lavish brochure. As can be seen, this also gave details of their attempt to boost flagging sales of the K-type saloon by upgrading the mechanical specification.

Below: One of the nicest of the N-types is this pretty Allingham-bodied two/four-seater owned by Keith Portsmore. In these cars the back seat is concealed under the rear deck, which opens up to form the seat back when needed. Unlike other dickey seat designs, rear seat passengers share the covered accommodation with those in the front when the soft-top is erected.

the sides. Two of the other cars were painted dark green and the third, JB 4607 driven by W.G. Everitt, was painted Italian Racing Red as this was originally intended to be for the great Tazio Nuvolari to drive. In the race one of the Eyston team cars, driven by Charlie Dodson, won – just beating Eddie Hall's Bentley by 17 seconds after over six hours of racing. M.G. had repeated their 1933 success.

Four-Cylinder Racer

Shortly after the P-type Midget had been introduced the factory announced a new four-cylinder racing car. The engine was based on that used for the road car but with the capacity reduced to 746cc and the power boosted to well over 100bhp by fitting a Zoller supercharger. The chassis was longer than that used for the P-type and was actually the same length as the K3 but not as wide. The axles fitted gave it a track of 3ft 9in (1143mm) which was wider than a P-type but narrower than the 4ft (1219mm) axles on the K3. The bodywork was visually similar to that fitted to the 1934 K3s with the shaped fuel tank ahead of the rear axle and with the twin batteries stowed under the lifting, pointed tail.

Although exceptionally fast, the Q-type Midget, as the new car was called, attracted few buyers at its list price of £550. The availability of the charismatic K3 was probably one reason and the other was the difficulties experienced by

I. Schwedler, Miss Margaret Allen and Miss Doreen Evans and the team was placed third overall. As a relay race the cars and drivers had to visit the pits periodically to hand over the sash to the next team member, with the incoming driver leaving the car and climbing onto the pit counter and handing the sash to the next driver who could then leap down from the counter and climb into the car – it must have been fun for spectators to watch.

After this successful debut for the new machines, the factory entered six cars for the TT. Three were entered under the Eyston banner – one for George Eyston to drive himself and the others for Wal Handley and Charlie Dodson, who were both ex-motorcycle racers. The other three cars were driven by Norman Black, A.P. Hamilton and W.G. Everitt. The three Eyston team cars were painted in cream with brown wings and sported a pair of brown stripes down

Left: A two-seater NA Magnette. Although this model lacked some of the delicate beauty of the earlier cars, the taller and roomier body, and the rubber-mounted sub-frame that isolated this from chassis flexing, made travelling in the car a more comfortable experience.

Right: Leather-covered seats and attractively-patterned trim panels make the interior of the four-seater NA look particularly inviting. The stowed soft-top packs neatly out of the way.

many drivers coping with such a high power output given the limitations of the solid axle chassis. In the end just eight of these potent racing cars were built. The Development Department were already looking at a more radical solution to the handling problems.

With all the new models introduced during 1934 it is hardly surprising that the London Motor Show season brought no further changes for the 1935 model year. The range was now

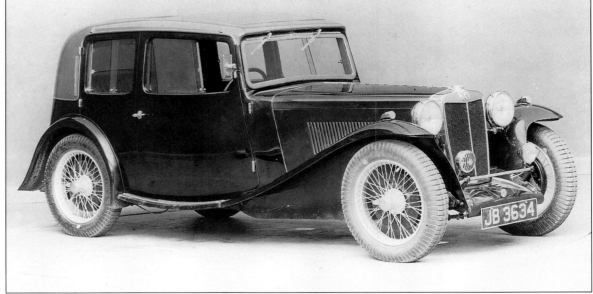

listed as the P-type Midget, in two- and four-seater form together with the Airline Coupé, the remaining stocks of the hard-to-sell L-type Continental Coupé, N-type Magnettes in all four versions, the KN saloon and the racing K3 and Q-type models. With prices ranging from £222 for the two-seater PA to £795 for the K3, there was surely something to suit all tastes. M.G. were establishing their reputation and widening their market year on year, which was remarkable given the current economic climate. The world recession was still having a severe effect on the numbers in employment and on wage levels. In Britain car ownership was still enjoyed by a minority of citizens. Rearmament brought on by the likelihood of another war was soon to improve employment prospects; however, the salesmen on the M.G. stand at the 1934 Motor Show knew that many of the visitors had little chance of affording one of their cars.

Considerable effort by those working in the Research and Development Department at Abingdon over the 1934/35 winter resulted in a revolutionary new racing car being announced in April 1935. Called the R-type, the 750cc class racing engine from the Q-type found a new home in a car with a chassis design better able to cope with its power output. This car, engine

Above: The KN Pillarless saloon is an interesting design, but one that has drawbacks. To give the appearance of a two-door coupé with convenient entry to the rear, there is no central pillar between the front and rear doors. However, only the front doors have exterior handles and a lack of body rigidity caused many owners problems before the cars were very old.

apart, bore little resemblance to any previous M.G. and was such a radical departure from earlier designs that the development team of Cecil Cousins, Syd Enever and Bill Renwick, working under the direction of the designer H.N. Charles, were stepping into uncharted territory with its development.

New Chassis

The chassis devised for the R-type by Charles consisted of a central backbone that ran from just behind the rear differential mounting point, underneath the driver's seat to the back of the gearbox where it divided with separate arms running to the front each side of the power unit. Electrically welded from 16 gauge steel, the box-section chassis was was light enough to be easily carried by one man but immensely strong. It resembled an enormous tuning fork with the "prongs" joined at the front by a box section and with the differential mounting attached to the end of the "handle".

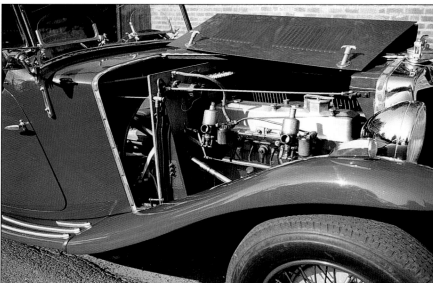

Above: One of the few surviving Abbey-bodied N-types. This car is owned by Rod Martin who has extensively researched the history of the cars produced by this coachbuilder. His car was supplied new fitted with Michelin 16-inch low-pressure tyres and wheels, rather than the standard 18-inch wheels.

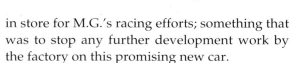

Left: The 1271cc N-type engine was the final development of the pre-war OHC six-cylinder design. With twin carburettors it produces a healthy 56bhp at 5500rpm and, if even mildly supercharged, considerably more than that.

In place of beam axles and leaf springs, all four wheels were carried on double wishbones independently suspended by torsion bars. These bars were mounted parallel to the frame, and were adjustable, and damping was provided by a set of hydraulic shock absorbers. Power from the engine was transmitted to the rear by a short prop-shaft via a preselector gearbox and a clutch that was not controlled by the driver but was merely inserted into the drive line to act as a sort of safety valve to prevent excessive torque from damaging the final drive. When operated by the driver the clutch pedal changed to the gear ratio that he had previously selected on the "gear lever" that was mounted on the steering column. The differential was fixed to the chassis and power was transferred to the rear wheels by two short drive shafts that incorporated sliding splines and universal joints, and looked like short prop-shafts.

The driver sat over the top of the transmission tunnel with the "clutch" pedal to the left of the gearbox and the brake and throttle pedal on the right. The fuel tank was set behind the single seat and was shaped to match the external panelwork. The instrument panel was carried by a steel framework. The brakes were still cable-operated and the external handbrake worked on all four wheels in line with usual M.G. practice. The easily-removed aluminium body panels gave the car an attractive appearance which was complemented by the sloping version of the M.G. grille that covered the air intake.

End Of An Era
The Q-type engine had been slightly modified to improve reliability and the front-mounted Zoller blower gave induction pressures of around 28lb (12.7kg) and an output of over 110bhp. With a chassis that was now able to cope with the tremendous power output of the 750cc engine, great things were expected of these cars. Immediately following their public announcement, a team of four were entered for an event at Brooklands. Driven by Norman Black, W.G. Everitt/Sir Malcolm Campbell, Wal Handley and Doreen Evans, the cars ran well over the bumpy track but exhibited an alarming amount of roll on the corners. However, two of the cars completed the gruelling race and finished in first and second places in their class. Additionally they proved as quick as the larger-capacity K3s with only one of these able to finish ahead of them. The next outing was not so successful as problems with the rear driveshaft forced three of them to retire. However, a much worse fate was

in store for M.G.'s racing efforts; something that was to stop any further development work by the factory on this promising new car.

Morris Garages, and later The M.G. Car Company Limited, were owned personally by William Morris (who became a Baron in 1934 taking the title of Lord Nuffield) and were quite separate from Morris Motors Limited. As part of a reorganization of the financial structure of all of the Morris empire, The M.G. Car Company was sold by Lord Nuffield to Morris Motors Limited on 1st July, 1935. To enable the parent company to better control the activities of The M.G. Car Company, the dictatorial Leonard Lord was appointed Managing Director with Cecil Kimber relegated to the position of just being a director and General Manager. Lord Nuffield had never been all that enthusiastic about The M.G. Car Company's participation in motor sport and it is not surprising that the opportunity was now taken to close down that part of their activities.

The announcement that M.G. was to cease its involvement in racing forthwith came as a shock to the motorsport world. In the company-sponsored magazine, "The Sports Car", the statement by Cecil Kimber carried in the August, 1935 issue makes clear that the orders to cease build-

ing racing cars came from the very top: "Lord Nuffield has said there are to be no more M.G. racing cars. This announcement came as a shock to all and sundry connected with or interested in the sport, for since 1931 one or other of the highly successful M.G. racing types has either won outright, or most certainly been well in the picture, in almost every British and Continental event, for which the cars have been eligible." He went on to say that "First of all the directors have decided that at all events for the present time racing for the purpose of development has, in our case, served its useful purpose. Another reason, rather more obscure, purely concerns racing itself . . . that we are handicapped out of British racing, through no fault of the handicapper."

No doubt, Cecil Kimber was upset by both the racing ban and by the change in the structure of the company he had created. The excuse about handicapping has some merit as it is true that, by its very nature, such a system penalizes success – every time a car wins its handicap is reassessed, making future victories more difficult to achieve. Had there been more racing circuits in Britain, and had the cars run in more races where they could take outright or class wins based purely on performance rather than by beating handicap times, things may have been different. However, no matter what reasons lay behind them, the results of the changes were to have far-reaching consequences for M.G., and for the cars they built. 1st July, 1935 was the day that shut the door on the most exciting period in the history of the M.G. sports car, and henceforth the future course of the development of both the company and the cars was to owe more to the whims of accountants than success on the race track.

Above: Californian owner Pete Thelander took this picture of the extremely nice NE Magnette he has owned for over twenty years. The racing body it carries was carefully rebuilt by Pete a few years ago, but almost none of the original metal was replaced. In 1934 it was painted Italian Racing Red as the intended mount for the 1933 TT winner, Tazio Nuvolari, in the 1934 event. He did not compete and the car was driven by Bill Everitt, who retired when a wheel collapsed.

Below: The revolutionary R-type had a backbone chassis and independent suspension all-round. Lack of development limited its potential but it could have been a world-beater.

The takeover of M.G. by Morris Motors not only brought with it the racing ban but also, in due course, a complete revision of the models in production. Immediately after the announcement the staff of the Design Department were either dismissed or transferred elsewhere within the Nuffield Group. Luckily, a few key personnel remained at Abingdon to liaise with the Morris Motors' designers, but H.N. Charles was moved to work in the main Nuffield Group design office at Cowley.

Prior to the takeover and the transfer of Hubert Charles and some of his staff, Cecil Kimber had made a decision to build a big car again. Whilst the Midgets, Magnas and Magnettes had been the mainstay of the Company's production, and had put The M.G. Car Company firmly on the map, they needed to be keenly priced and produced but small profits. Kimber longed to return to making larger and more luxurious cars, rather in the style of the old 18/80 Mk II, whilst retaining sports car performance and handling.

He envisaged building a stylish, four-door saloon car that was as technically advanced as possible and fitted with the all-round independent suspension that was already being adopted by some Continental manufacturers. As we have seen, Abingdon had already produced the startling R-type single-seater racing car with its backbone chassis and independent all-round wishbone suspension and Kimber was determined to build on this significant work and gave

Left: The PB has a burr walnut dashboard, instead of sequoia, and a separate speedometer replaces the PA central panel which has trip and mileage recorders. The auxiliary instruments flanking the central speedometer were optional extras on new PBs.

Below and opposite: Externally there is little to distinguish the PB from the less-powerful PA and, indeed, a number of unsold PAs were converted by the factory to PB specification. The main distinguishing feature is the radiator grille which has slats. This beautiful car was restored by the owner, Tom Metcalf of Ashland, Ohio, and the pictures were taken by Jon Mazu. The black paintwork and green interior was a popular colour option when the cars were new. The standard wheel colour was aluminium, although occasionally other colours were chosen – at a price.

his chief engineer, H.N. Charles, instructions to produce a new large saloon with similarly advanced specification.

Given the designation "S-type" and the Experimental Department code EX150, this new car was designed around a chassis of 10ft 3in (3124mm) wheelbase. Extra draughtsmen were recruited to produce the hundreds of detailed

drawings necessary and a prototype chassis was soon completed. Mulliners Ltd. of Birmingham designed an elegant body for the S-type that looked similar to that fitted to the more conventional SA saloon when it eventually appeared. EX150 was listed in the EX Register as a "3.5 litre all independent car" but it is not clear which power unit would have been chosen for it. Had

the axe not fallen on the Abingdon Drawing Office with the reorganization, then a world-beating machine may have resulted from these efforts, although it would have probably been expensive to build and perhaps not as profitable for the company as the car that did finally emerge. However, the project was cancelled and it fell to the Cowley design office, including the personnel transferred from Abingdon, to produce the large M.G. saloon which now had to utilize components available from within the Nuffield Group, rather than ones specially made for The M.G. Car Company.

More Power For The Midget

Whilst all these behind the scenes changes were taking place, the day to day business of selling production cars continued. August 1935 saw the announcement of revisions to the model range for the 1936 model year. The P-type Midget had been well received and was popular but it was obvious that more power was needed to help it keep up with increased competition from other marques. The answer was to increase the size of the engine by modifying the block casting to allow it to be bored out to 60mm – enlarging the capacity by 92cc and increasing the power by 7bhp. In addition there were modifications to the gear ratios, steering box and prop-shaft, and the driver was now provided with a separate speedometer and rev. counter.

The new model was called the PB and to boost flagging sales the price of the PA-type two-seaters, with the smaller engine, was reduced to £199.10s 0d. from the £222 still asked for the PB model. However, this ploy was not altogether successful and the company resorted to modifying a few unsold P-types to full PB specification. The PB was the last Midget designed by the team at Abingdon as the next model was to be the Cowley-designed T-series which utilised the Morris 10hp push-rod engine.

The N-type was also revised and benefited from price reductions. To improve their rather heavy appearance, the bodywork on both two-seater and four-seater had been changed to lower the scuttle line. The doors were now front-hinged using distinctive curved, chromed hinges with the top one aligned with the division between the colours on two-tone painted cars. Like the PB, the dashboard carried a separate speedometer and tachometer, rather than the combined dial seen on the NA, and there were improvements made to the seats. Externally, the radiator stone guards on both the N-types and the PB now sported the slats first seen on the later 18/80s. These were to remain a feature of M.G. design until the late 1960s.

The S-type development was continuing at Cowley, but in a much modified form. The car now had a conventional chassis and suspension but the body style chosen for EX150 was retained virtually unchanged, as were the track and wheelbase dimensions. Renamed the M.G. Two Litre (Cowley had specified a 2062cc Morris engine for the prototype which was increased to 2288cc prior to the cars going on sale to the public) the "S" designation did not appear again until the car was well into production. Announcement of the new car appeared in the motoring press in October 1935 but it has to be said that this early proclamation of an important

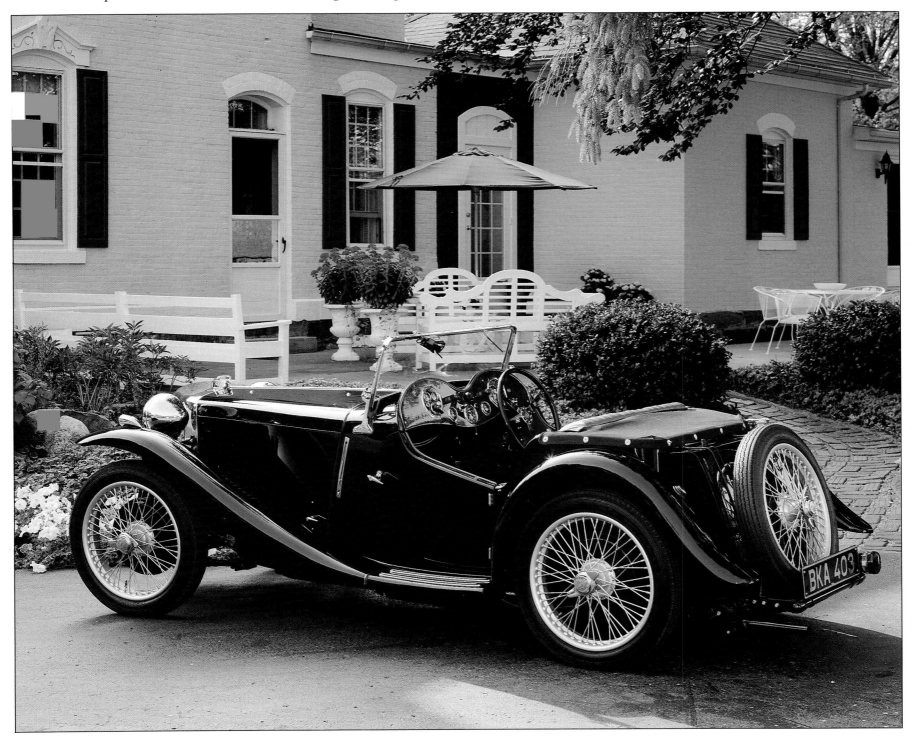

Above: Hinging the doors from the front edge, rather than at the back, means that long hinges are needed to keep them parallel to the ground when they open. These hinges immediately identify NBs from NAs.

Left: This two-seater NB has been restored by its owner, C. Roeleveld from Holland, and his care, and attention to detail, is evident in this picture of the 1271cc engine.

Below: The NB cockpit provides ample room and comfort for two and these cars are amongst the best of the pre-war OHC M.G.s to use for longer journeys.

new model for the company was ill-judged. No longer could M.G.s be designed and brought into production in the short time spans that were such a feature of the early 1930s. With the much larger and more bureaucratic regime at Cowley, delays were inevitable and design changes during the development period took longer to be incorporated into the production cars. The result was that a large number of customers who had ordered the new car after its announcement, and at the Motor Shows, were very upset when they had to wait over six months for their cars to be delivered to them.

The Lap Of Luxury

The M.G. Two Litre, or SA model as it was later to be called, was certainly radically different from the KN saloon it replaced. Not only did it have an OHV engine of almost twice the capacity of the OHC engine in the K-type, but it was well over 16 feet (4876mm) long and weighed over one-and-a-half tons (1525kg)! Luxury was the keynote of the design. Generous space was provided for the four occupants with deeply-upholstered seats, arm rests and all manner of creature comforts to distract their attention from the relative lack of the pace and agility they may have expected from an M.G. That is not to say that the SA was a slow car. They were, and are, capable of cruising for long periods at 65 to 70mph (105-113kph) and were much more comfortable on long journeys than the previous models. Indeed, they could be called more a touring car than a sports car.

The vastly changed product that the new M.G. saloon was led to much speculation about what form the replacement for the Midget and Magnette sports cars would take. Therefore, the announcement of a new Midget was awaited with some trepidation by enthusiasts who must have studied with particular attention the articles in the June 1936 issues of motoring magazines that featured the new model. The revised Midget, which was to be called the T-series, in many ways followed the design of previous M.G. Midgets. The chassis first used for EX120 and then for the C-type, D-type and subsequent models was retained for the T-series Midget but strengthened with the front part of the side members reinforced by including a boxed-in section.

Hydraulic brakes were beginning to become universally adopted for family saloons of the period, and had been fitted for the first time to an M.G. in the Two Litre, so it was logical that this system was also used for the new sports car. Drivers must have welcomed the change although, aesthetically, the smaller drums fitted to the new car did not look as impressive as the large, 12-inch, drums used for the P-type Midgets. The handbrake was similar to that fitted to the earlier cars but now only worked on the rear wheels.

M.G. had developed the OHC engines to the point where they were capable of giving higher power outputs per litre than almost any other production engines. However, these were not fitted to any other Nuffield products and even

camshaft and manifold changes, and twin SU carburettors, to increase the power to 50bhp. The final version of the four-cylinder OHC engine, used for the PB, produced 43bhp at 5500rpm from its 939cc, whereas with the larger, 1292cc, TA engine, maximum power was produced at only 4200rpm. This, then, was the essential difference between the two engines. One was a high-revving and very sporting unit capable of producing a good power output for its capacity, whereas the other was rather less free-revving but was capable of good performance and a high torque output at lower engine speeds. The TA engine was, however, larger and much heavier than the earlier OHC unit.

Greater Refinement

In an effort to improve refinement, the new engine was provided with rubber mountings to mate it to the chassis, and the previous three-point cross tube mounting used for the OHC engines was discontinued. The radiator was fitted directly to the chassis, rather than to the engine mounting as was previous practice. The four-speed gearbox gained synchromesh on the two upper ratios and was driven from the engine via a cork-faced clutch running in oil. This system was very popular at the time as it was thought to give a smooth feel to the clutch and, as a bonus, also eliminated any problems that arose from oil leaking onto the clutch face from rear crankshaft oil seals.

the Wolseley engines, originally the basis for the OHC range, were now quite different. This situation could not continue, so for the T-series the design team turned to the new OHV engine destined for the Wolseley 10/40 and Morris Ten. This unit, designated the MPJG, was given

Above: A four-seater NB. Like the PB, the radiator has a slatted grille and the dashboard a separate speedometer. The car is the original two-tone red, but the wheels would have been aluminium colour.

Below: Although now owned by Suzette Arnell, the car was in the hands of the first owner for over 40 years. To date it has covered just 27,000 miles (43,450km) from new and the body has never been off the chassis.

The body followed the style first set when the J2 was designed in 1932. However, the two-seater, ash-framed bodies had more generous room for both driver and passenger than the earlier cars. In particular there was now a lot more room behind the bench-style seats to carry a reasonable amount of luggage for touring holidays. The sports car was becoming a much more serious form of everyday transport.

Broad Appeal

With an engine capacity larger than even the N-type Magnette, and as it was really now the only proper sporting car available from Abingdon, the T-series Midget had to be good enough to appeal to both the owners of previous M.G. Midgets and to those who would have earlier bought the larger and more powerful two-seater Magnettes. Judged by contemporary press reports, the average buyer welcomed the new car and was happy with the performance. Those using the cars competitively were, perhaps, rather less sure that they were an improvement but, as we will see later, this was to change.

The first road tests to appear stressed that, although there had been a great many changes made for the new model, the essential character

of the car had remained unaltered. They said that it had exceptionally good performance for that engine capacity and that its handling was vastly better than that offered by the average touring cars of the period. They remarked upon the appearance of greater solidity given by the longer wheelbase, wider track, bigger body and longer bonnet. On the road the car felt different when compared to the earlier models and it was altogether softer, quieter and the engine was far more flexible at low engine speeds. Altogether it was easier to drive, although many still han-

Above: An early two-litre SA saloon. These are large cars and very different from the high-revving out-and-out sports models that had

dominated M.G. production for the previous six years. In spirit, it owed more to the earlier M.G.s, like the 18/80, although more up-to-date.

kered after the pleasures of driving a more demanding machine.

The performance figures recorded by road testers, 23.1 seconds to 60mph (97kph) and maximum of 77mph (124kph), compared well with those for the previous model, the PB, which were 27 seconds to 60mph and a maximum of 71mph

Below: The earlier SAs (like that in the picture above) have a series of little doors down the bonnet sides that can be opened to let hot air out. Owners of the later cars have to make do with sets of louvres in the panels.

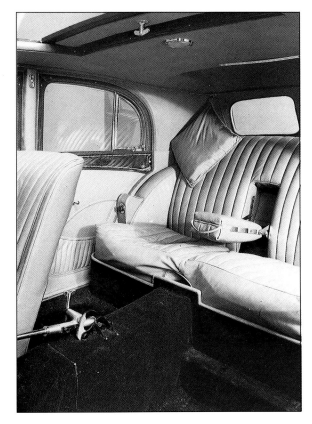

THE M.G. TWO-LITRE TOURER
Four seater open model by Charlesworth
£375 *(ex works)*

(114kph) – albeit these figures had been recorded under adverse conditions. Tests in some magazines gave even better figures for the new car, a top speed as high as 80mph (129kph) – very good for a small car in 1936. One headlined their report with the statement that the new model "outshines its predecessors in speed, acceleration, comfort, braking and ease of maintenance" which was quite a vote of confidence and an opinion which should have helped sales no end.

Although the Midget had grown up, it still seemed to appeal to the same sort of customers and many part-exchanged their older models for the new car. The price was £222, the same as that charged for the PB, so this was in its favour and those deserting the ranks of six-cylinder M.G. owners to buy the Midget were actually purchasing a cheaper car, but one of similar size and possessing comparable performance and roadholding to their old one.

The Sumptuous Tickford Coupé

In 1938, to widen the appeal of the car further (which, remember, had to replace a number of models that had been available in a variety of body styles) a more luxurious model on the same chassis, and with the same mechanical specification, was announced. This new car was the Series T Tickford Drop-head Coupé. Salmons and Sons Limited of Newport Pagnell, later to become part of Aston Martin, built special bodywork for a number of different makes of car incorporating the versatile three-position folding drop-head soft top. This hood could be used either fully closed, with the front section opened, or fully open. Allied to proper winding windows and higher-sided doors this coachwork was, perhaps, better suited to the British climate than the standard open cars. Of course, it was a bit heavier, and this affected performance, but, nevertheless, the new model was a practical alternative to the open two-seaters, and even to saloons from other manufacturers.

Above left: The space and comfort enjoyed by rear-seat passengers in the SA saloon can be judged from this picture of the interior of an early car.

Above right: This picture of one of the separate sheets included with the 1936 SA brochure illustrates an early Charlesworth tourer. The drawing by Harold Connolly exhibits the spirit of the age.

Right: As a comparison with the previous picture, this one of a page from the 1937 catalogue shows cut-away tops to the two front doors. These appeared on the later cars. Few examples of either model survive.

The MG Two-Litre Tourer
FOUR SEATER OPEN MODEL BY
CHARLESWORTH

Unlike the normal two-seater, the Tickford coupé was built as a rolling chassis at Abingdon and then driven to Newport Pagnell for the special coachwork to be fitted. For the journey the chassis were fitted with rudimentary bodywork that provided the delivery drivers with little protection and one can imagine this was not a pleasant task in mid-winter! The Tickford coupés were available in a wider choice of colours than the standard cars and, in addition to the better weather protection, they were also fitted with separate bucket seats, fully carpeted interior, semaphore style direction indicators, an ash tray and an interior light just above the glass rear window. The windscreen wiper motor was no longer fitted on the top of the windscreen frame, but was installed beneath the bonnet, and the dashboard was modified to fit the differently shaped bodywork.

The greater bulk of the lowered hood restricted rearward visibility a little, when compared to the ordinary TA, but the higher doors reduced wind buffeting for the occupants and

when the soft top was raised the extra layers of material and wadding in the Tickford hood made the car much quieter to travel in. The TA Tickford was an extremely attractive small car and it is just a pity that so few, just 252, were built. The Airline Coupé designed by H.W. Allingham and built by Carbodies that was previously available on the P-type and N-type chassis was also offered as an alternative on the T-type chassis but only one or two were built.

At Abingdon the change of emphasis towards greater productivity brought some benefits. Although cars were still moved along the production line by hand, a higher degree of organization had been introduced to speed up production. Some of the space previously used for the racing and development activities was given over to assembly lines, increasing the number of lines from two to four, and a mechanical conveyor system now moved the wheels from one part of the factory to another. A spray plant capable of dealing with up to 200 cars a day was installed.

1939 VA TICKFORD

Although meant to replace the OHC N-type as the medium-sized car in the range, the VA saloons, tourers and Tickford drop-head coupés appealed to a different, and wider, market than had their predecessors. While less overtly traditional sports cars, they still possessed reasonable performance for their size, and the extra comfort and space was appreciated by owners. The Tickford bodywork was particularly attractive, as well as being more practical for the English climate than the standard open tourer.

Left: Style was everything when trying to sell cars that were more expensive than rival products, and the VA has a beautifully appointed interior. The dashboard has a full range of instruments, as befits a sporting image.

SPECIFICATION

Model: VA Tickford DHC

Engine: Four-cylinder in line, overhead valve, water cooled. 69.5 x 102mm, 1548cc, 55bhp

Gearbox: Four-speed with synchromesh on second, third and top gears

Final drive: 5.22:1. Top gear 16.35mph/1000rpm (26kph/1000rpm)

Suspension: Solid axles mounted on half-elliptic leaf springs.

Dimensions: Wheelbase 9ft (2743mm). Track 4ft 2in (1270mm). Overall length 14ft 8in (4470mm)

Unladen weight: 25cwt (1270kg)

Cost when new: £351

Performance: (From contemporary reports) Top speed 68mph (109kph)

Owner: Peter Pimm

Below: Work started on VA 2214 at Abingdon on 13th January, 1939. In early February the rolling chassis was driven to Salmons and Sons at Newport Pagnall to have the body fitted. The car was ready by 15th February.

Above: The advantage of the Tickford "three-position" soft-top is its ability to suit every type of weather: either fully open for sunny days, or in "coupé-de-ville" form or fully closed when more protection is needed.

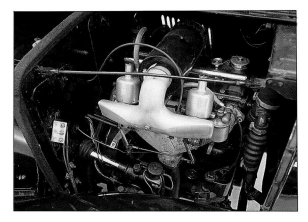

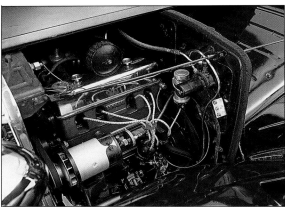

Left and below left: The 1549cc VA engine is a sturdy, if unexciting, unit and the change from a cork-faced clutch running oil, used for the early cars, to the Borg and Beck dry clutch fitted to this car was an improvement. This was one of a number of detail specification changes made to the VA during the three-year life of this model. The two groups of three nipples, one set on each side of the firewall, are lubrication points for the chassis. Heavy oil, not grease, was used. The first owners of this car may have been the Royal Navy. Certainly the car had been painted Battleship Grey over its original Maroon cellulose by the time it was registered for civilian use in 1950.

Right: The heavy chromed bumpers are typical of the period. The round weights at each end, as well as looking good, were thought to be an aid to damping unwanted vibrations. The small rear window does make parking tricky and so, perhaps, strong bumpers were an asset.

Below: Unlike the standard tourers, Tickford Coupés have winding side windows and full-height, rear-hung doors, which are much heavier and need substantial hinges. The "trafficators" were standard equipment.

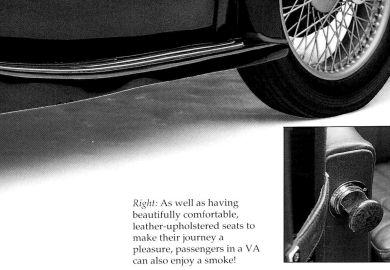

Below: Lowering the hood requires care. The front rail is secured to the windscreen frame by wing nuts, and the cant rails above the doors fold across the car in front of the rear section before this is pushed down.

Above: The comprehensive tool kit is stowed within the luggage compartment lid. Having the original sales brochures with the car is typical of the care that is lavished upon it by owner Peter Pimm.

Right: As well as having beautifully comfortable, leather-upholstered seats to make their journey a pleasure, passengers in a VA can also enjoy a smoke!

These improvements were mainly introduced to cope with assembling sufficient of the Two Litre saloons to meet orders. Being larger and more complicated than the cars they replaced, they occupied more space on the assembly lines and took longer to build. The two-litre SA was available as a four-seater open tourer and was also fitted with Tickford Coupé bodywork similar to that later available on the TA.

The open tourers were fitted with Charlesworth-designed bodies and a number of changes were made during the time these cars were in production. The shape of the rear of the body was modified after a few cars had been built, and later the top of the front doors was changed to provide a "cut away" for driver's and passenger's elbows, as was fashionable on sporting cars of the period. The windscreen was also modified to provide a greater area of glass. Never as popular with buyers as the Tickford, only around 90 tourer SAs were built and few survive today. A few Two Litre chassis were supplied to outside body builders, particularly on the Continent, and some elegant cars were built in this way.

Style And Performance

In October 1936 the last of the new Nuffield M.G. models was announced. The 1.5 litre VA fell conveniently in size and price between the SA and the T-series Midget and was offered as a saloon, tourer and with Tickford bodywork. The design of the chassis frame owed more to the Two Litre than to the Midget and other previous M.G.s. It had a strong frame that was swept over the rear axle with the road springs being suspended by shackles rather than by the sliding trunnions that were used on the Midget chassis. Like the SA, the brakes were hydraulic and much attention was paid to comfort with soft springing and roomy bodywork.

The OHV pushrod engine was less highly stressed than the OHC unit in the Magnettes that the VA was replacing. With a capacity of 1548cc it produced just 55bhp, against the 56bhp available from the 1271cc engine in the N-type, but the larger capacity did give the engine greater torque which was certainly needed to propel what was a fairly heavy car. Performance was adequate for the period, and few full four-seater

Above: The prototype TA, which differed slightly from production models. About the first 1000 TAs built had narrow, rounded rear wings and wider fuel tanks. Later cars had wider rear wings, with a raised line down the centres, and narrower fuel tanks, as did the TB and TC.

Left: Once again a folding windscreen was standard equipment, as was the FT27 spot lamp on the badge bar. This lamp was also used on the TB and early TCs. The cars cost £222 new.

Below: TAs are comfortable cars for winter travel. The hood erects easily and the four sidescreens have a good area of glazing. The twin rear windows in the hood are rather small, and this feature was carried over to early TC production.

1.5 litre saloon cars then gave their owners the combination of good looks, comfort, handling and performance offered by the VA. Both the VA and the SA had a large number of detail changes to their mechanical specification during the time they were in production. The SA engine was increased in capacity to 2322cc and the gearbox gained synchromesh on third and top gears whilst later VAs had the cork faced, oil-immersed clutch replaced by a conventional Borg and Beck single plate dry clutch.

With the M.G. model range now catering for most tastes, the factory settled down to building sufficient cars to satisfy demand. Although there were many detail changes, the Midget, VA and SA models were to remain basically unchanged right up to the outbreak of war in 1939, in contrast to the frequent model changes seen in the early 1930s. Although many enthusiasts mourned the loss of the overtly sporting M.G. OHC cars, the models produced during the late 1930s gained many converts to the marque and there is little doubt that, in many ways, they provided more suitable transport for long journeys than did their predecessors.

The racing ban introduced in 1935 did not curtail The M.G. Car Company's sporting activities altogether. The growth of interest in trials, and the increasing numbers of events being staged during the early 1930s, led manufacturers to take

a greater interest in the sport. Some companies ran their own trials teams whilst others merely supported the endeavours of private owners. In the case of M.G. this support was considerable, and much was made in advertisements of successes gained by M.G. cars. However, on occasions some of the drivers in the teams were also Abingdon employees and this possibly could have been regarded as being paid to drive.

The best-remembered of the M.G. trials cars were those used by the Cream Crackers and

Above: The TA, and TB, Tickford coupés are practical little cars. The hood makes the interior cosy when up and, in addition, the car can be used with the rear section raised but with the part above the occupants folded back – like a large sun-roof. The Tickford bodies were fitted at Newport Pagnell, the chassis being driven there from the Abingdon factory.

Right: At £269.10s. 0d. the TA Tickford cost rather more than the sports two-seaters but buyers enjoyed greater luxury and a wider choice of colour finishes for the extra money. Today Tickfords are highly prized.

Musketeers teams. With factory support, these cars were successful in many of the events they entered, gaining much publicity for the marque. The story of the Cream Crackers teams starts with the 1935 Land's End Trial which was the debut for the P-type Midgets wearing the M.G. cream and brown colour scheme, but support for cars by the factory had been evident before this. Two of the members of the team, J. Maurice Toulmin and R.A. "Mac" Macdermid, had acquired their PAs early in 1934 and the third

1934 NE MAGNETTE "MUSKETEER"

This car is one of seven NE Magnettes built to compete in the 1934 Tourist Trophy Race. In 1933 a K3 had won the event but, as supercharged cars were banned from the 1934 race, new cars were constructed using N-type chassis fitted with tuned 1271cc engines and lightweight bodies. Driven by Charlie Dodson, this car won the six-hour race for M.G. at an average speed of 74.65mph (120kph). In 1935 the car was driven in a trial with its racing body and then fitted with a two-seater body for use by the "Musketeer" team.

SPECIFICATION

Model: NE two-seater

Engine: Six-cylinder in line, overhead camshaft, water cooled. 57 x 83mm, 1271cc, 68bhp

Gearbox: Four-speed non-synchromesh.

Final drive: 4.875:1. Top gear 16mph/1000rpm (26kph/1000rpm)

Suspension: Solid axles mounted on half-elliptic leaf springs. Each spring is fixed in bushes at leading end and in sliding trunnions at rear

Dimensions: Wheelbase 8ft (2438mm). Track 3ft 9in (1143mm). Overall length 12ft 7in (3835mm)

Unladen weight: 16.3cwt (828kg)

Cost when new: Not catalogued

Performance: Top speed approx. 90mph (145kph)

Owner: Peter Green

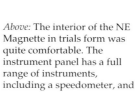

Above: The large fuel tank on this NE has a "quick-action" filler. These were also popular extras for those wanting to make their cars look more sporting.

Above: The interior of the NE Magnette in trials form was quite comfortable. The instrument panel has a full range of instruments, including a speedometer, and

this car has a full-width windscreen. Unlike the 1933 K3s, in 1934 the NEs used conventional four-speed gearboxes, rather than Wilson preselector units.

Left: "Quick-action" radiator filler caps were essential for competition work where the water may need to be replenished rapidly. Also, with these there is no risk of losing a separate cap.

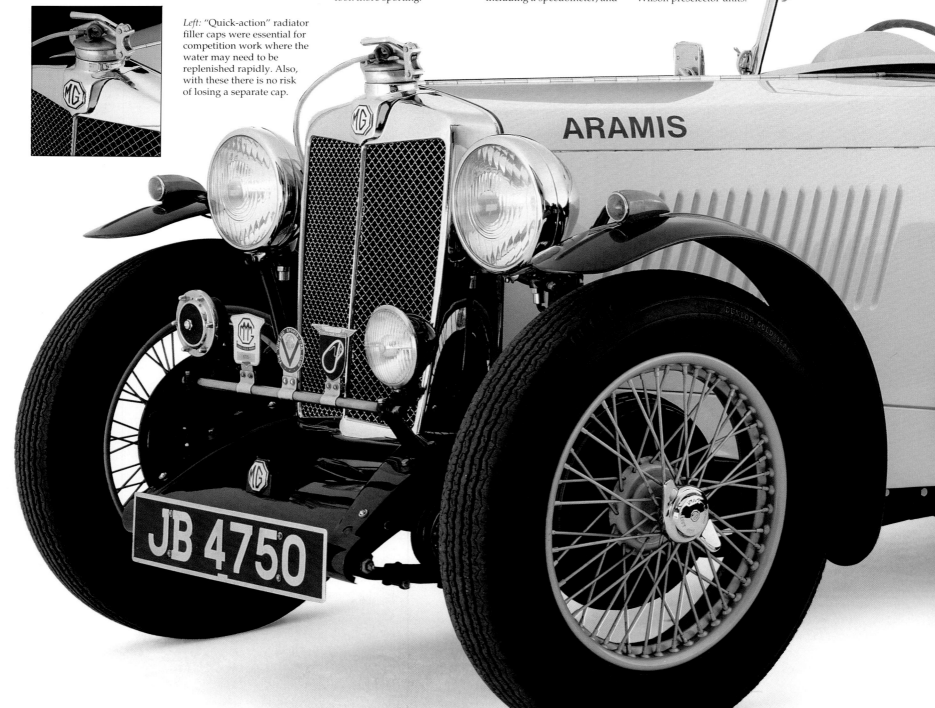

ARAMIS

JB 4750

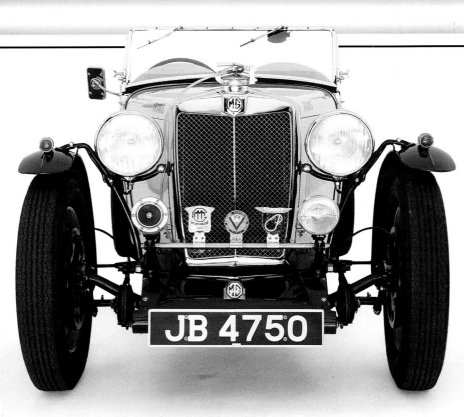

Above left & right: With a production run of just seven cars, the NE is one of the rarest of all the M.G. models. JB 4750, apart from being the Tourist Trophy winning car, has an interesting competition history. Miss Margaret Allen drove it in the Wye Cup Trial in 1935 and it, and two other NEs, were later entered as the "Musketeers" team in a series of events. They won First Class Awards in The Land's End and Edinburgh Trials and in The Welsh Rally this car, driven by Sam Nash, won the event outright. During this period the TT bodies had been replaced by ones adapted from P-type frames. The racing bodies were then refitted and the cars sold to Bellevue Garage to enter in the 1935 TT, in which event this car was driven by Kenneth Evans. The car was raced by various owners up to the early 1950s, including Betty Haig. When she raced the car it had a lightweight body, which it carried until 1994. JB 4750 was bought in the mid-1950s by Pat Green, the uncle of the present owner, and used by him to attend club events. Peter Green subsequently acquired the car in 1994.

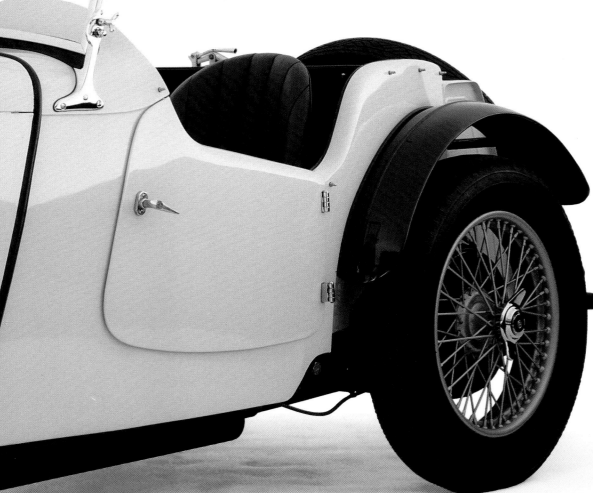

Above: The P-type style body worn by "Aramis" is similar to the one fitted when the car joined two other NE Magnettes – JB 4606 "Athos" and JB 4608 "Porthos" – to form the "Musketeers" trials team, which collected a number of awards.

Above: The standard N-type engine was modified to increase the power output for use in the NE. While not capable of matching a supercharged K3, the NE was quite fast enough to ensure some competition successes.

Below: The high standard of preparation achieved by Peter Green for his cars is all the more remarkable bearing in mind that they are constantly in use on the road and track, where they are enjoyed by many.

member, Jack A. Bastock, his in September that year. At first the cars remained in their original colours although later they had brown and cream stripes along the sides of the bonnets. As they were still fitted with the heavy swept wings, and were thus overweight, they were not as successful as expected and the cars were all returned to the factory for comprehensive modification before competing in the Exeter Trial at the end of 1934.

"The Cream Crackers"

The swept wings were replaced by cycle wings and they were fitted with lightweight aluminium bonnets, lighter eight-inch (203mm) brake gear from the earlier J2 model, locked differentials, while much of the equipment, such as hoods, windscreens and sidescreens, was discarded. Thus modified, the cars were more successful and took two First Class Awards and one Second Class Award on the Exeter Trial. When they were returned to Abingdon to be prepared for the 1935 Land's End Trial it was decided to call the team "Cream Crackers" and to repaint the cars.

By the end of 1935, the factory had replaced the PAs with a team of three PBs, JB 7521, driven by Toulmin, JB 7524 for Ken Crawford and JB 7525 for J.E.S. Jones. The lessons had been well learned and the new cars, although similar in appearance to the earlier PAs, were more powerful, lighter and altogether more effective. In this form the cars enjoyed considerable success but replacement by the company of the PB with the

Above: The 1.5 litre VA Tourer had cut-down doors, in sporting style, and it remains popular with enthusiasts looking for an open four-seater M.G. for family use. A total of 2407 VAs were built between 1936 and 1939.

Right: The VA Tourer has four comfortable leather-covered seats of generous proportions and some luggage space behind the rear seat. The spare wheel is mounted on the tail.

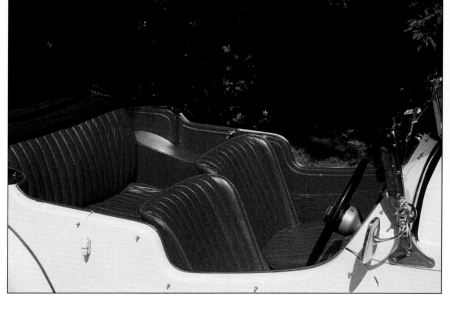

T-series Midget meant that the trials teams had to follow suit if publicity they gained for the cars was to have any meaning to potential customers. A new Cream Crackers team of three TAs was formed for 1937 with the registration numbers ABL 960, ABL 962 and ABL 964 for Toulmin, Crawford and Jones respectively. Initially these were not as popular as the P-types with the drivers but eventually they were developed into very effective trials cars. For 1938, VA (1548cc) engines were fitted to the replacement cars, BBL 78, BBL 79, BBL 80 and BBL 81, and later the capacity was increased to 1708cc by over-boring and fitting WA pistons. Godfrey "Gof" Imhof joined as driver of the last car.

Alongside the Cream Crackers team, the company also supported the Musketeers cars. Initially this team ran the specially built NE Magnettes that had successfully competed in the 1934 Tourist Trophy. Three NEs, fitted with road-going two-seater bodies in place of the special racing bodies, were driven in trials by Lewis Welch, Freddie Kindell and Sam Nash with a great deal of success. For example they won First Class Awards on the Land's End and Edinburgh Trials and the Team Award, and for Sam Nash an outright win, in the Welsh Rally.

Following this success, three special cars based on an amalgam of various current components was built for the next Musketeers team

Right: A VA Saloon outside The Barley Mow at Clifton Hampdon. The inn looks little different now, in spite of a fire and some re-building, but stopping outside is less easy. The villages around Abingdon were popular for taking publicity pictures of new M.G.s. This photograph was taken after the imposition of wartime black-out restrictions and the car has a mask for the dipped headlamp. On these cars the off-side light was extinguished on dipped beam.

Below: The 1937 Cream Cracker Team TA, ABL 964, still earning a living. Ken Selby tackles "Nailsworth Ladder", the famous pre-war trials hill, during the 1995 Kimber Trial run by The M.G. Car Club.

Below right: The NE Magnette shown on pages 78-79 after its outright win, in the hands of Sam Nash, of the 1935 Welsh Rally. Although the car later reverted to wearing the racing body, it is nice to see it today in the same condition as it appears in this photograph.

of Macdermid, Bastock and Langley. These cars proved fast and competitive and the team was very successful. Like the other M.G. team, the Musketeers changed over to TAs for 1937, running ABL 961, ABL 963 and ABL 965 to the same specification as that used for the Cream Crackers cars. Likewise these were replaced for 1938 by BBL 82, BBL 83 and BBL 84 as well as by BJB 412 for the new team member, Dickie Green. However, this last series of cars differed from those of the Cream Crackers team as they were fitted with TA engines running with Laystall crankshafts and Marshall 110 superchargers.

Record-breaking was another activity that continued to bring acclaim to the M.G. name.

The efforts of Lt.-Col. A.T G. Gardner in the EX135 stood out as a beacon of British endeavour at a time when the all-conquering Mercedes and Auto-Union teams, backed by Nazi government funds, were reaping most of the glory in motor sport. EX135 started life as a K3, K3023, that was specially built up for George Eyston. It initially had two bodies made for it – a stream-lined record-breaking body, painted with cream and brown stripes which gained it the nickname of "Humbug" after a popular type of sweet, and an ugly, lightweight body for road-racing.

Driven by George Eyston, the car ran in a number of events in 1934 with some success and was taken to Montlhéry for a record breaking

session where it took a number of class G records at speeds up to 128.8mph (207.3kph). In 1935 it was sold to D.N. Letts who raced it with little success. Following a discussion between Cecil Kimber and Goldie Gardner, Lord Nuffield's blessing was obtained for an attempt on the 1100cc world records and K3023 was located and bought to use for this purpose. The chassis was rebuilt at Abingdon and Reid Railton, who had previously designed a record-breaker for John Cobb, was asked to design a special body for the car which was now called EX135. This body was built at Abingdon and the engine used previously by Gardner in his own record car was to be fitted to the rebuilt chassis.

This car was meticulously prepared for the job in hand. Special tyres that ran at very high pressures were made by Dunlop, with the object of reducing rolling resistance, and the wheels and tyres were carefully balanced to run smoothly at the high speeds envisaged. The engine, which had been highly developed by ace tuner, Robin Jackson, was carefully checked and taken to the M.G. factory for testing. Initially many problems were encountered but Syd Enever worked on these, eventually adopting a number of radical solutions including fitting a cylinder block without any water passages between it and the cylinder head to eliminate leakage from the gasket. The engine was fed from a Centric supercharger, running at 26lb (2bar) boost, and a special heavy-duty clutch was installed to transfer the power to the gearbox. On test the engine now produced 194bhp at 7000rpm from 1100cc.

Breaking Records In Germany

The car was taken to an autobahn at Frankfurt-am-Main in Germany where it took the class G flying-start records for the kilometre and mile at over 186mph (299kph). During the run Goldie Gardner had seen the engine speed exceed its prudent maximum and it was obvious that the car would have been capable of even higher speeds given a more suitable final drive gear ratio. It was decided to delay any further record attempts until the axle ratio could be changed, and the team returned to England. With the attempt taking place a mere three months after the Munich crisis there was no

temptation for the team to spend more time than absolutely necessary as guests of the Germans.

Early in 1939 the team returned to Germany for a further record attempt with EX135, this time fitted with a revised axle gearing. The German war machine was fully mobilized and there was no shortage of help from the military with the arrangements for the high-speed runs that were, this time, to take place on a new

Above: EX135 on a German autobahn near Frankfurt in 1938. This record-breaking attempt was successful and Goldie Gardner returned home having taken the flying-start kilometre and mile records at over 186mph (299kph). He returned in 1939 and raised these 1100cc class records to speeds of over 203mph (327kph).

Below: Before it was fitted with the streamlined body seen in the above picture, EX135 had carried this track-racing body, painted with cream and brown stripes – earning it the nickname of "Humbug". In that guise at Montlhéry in 1934 it took twelve International 1100cc records at speeds of up to 128.8mph (207kph).

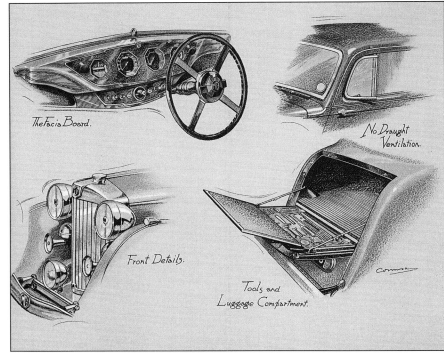

stretch of road near Dessau. The car had been carefully checked after the runs made the previous year and it performed faultlessly for these attempts. The team were delighted when the records for the flying-start kilometre, mile and five kilometre records were taken at 203.5, 203.2 and 197.5mph (327.5, 327 and 317.8kph) respectively. An M.G. had broken the 200mph barrier with only 1100cc at its disposal.

Flushed with success, they decided to attempt the records for the under 1500cc class by the expedient of boring the cylinder block, whilst it remained in the chassis, and fitting over-size pistons to take the capacity just over the 1100cc mark and so into the 1500cc class. With these changes the records for class F over the same distances as those already bagged for class G were all taken at speeds of over 200mph (322kph), and EX135 returned home now an International Record Holder in two classes. Plans were made for an attempt on the 750cc class records but world events overtook them and the car was retired. It did not emerge until after the war.

Although the company had run their existing models since introduction, some changes to the model line-up were considered necessary for the 1939 model year. The TA had already gained the Tickford body as an alternative to the standard sports two-seater and this was proving popular, as had this body style for the VA and SA. The large SA model was to be supplemented by a new model, the WA, which had an engine of 2561cc that gave a power output of 95bhp – 17bhp more than the SA.

War Overshadows The WA

The WA was the largest, heaviest and most luxurious car the company had ever built. The chassis was completely redesigned and the interior appointments improved to produce a car that looked good value at £442 for the saloon, £468 for the Tickford and £450 for the open four-seater. Unfortunately, fewer than 400 cars were built before a change-over to war work stopped production at Abingdon.

The T-series Midget benefited from the intro-

duction of a new range of engines for the Morris 10. Originally designed as an 1100cc unit, a modified version of this engine with a capacity of 1250cc and twin carburettors found its way into the Midget which was to be called the TB. This engine was the now-legendary XPAG that proved to be so strong and amenable to a considerable amount of tuning. In the TB it offered a much more suitable engine for a sports car. Gone was the oil-immersed clutch and the white metalled bearings of the TA and in its place was a

Above left and right: Pictures of a couple of pages from the most lavish of the pre-war M.G. catalogues. In keeping with the largest car in the range, the brochure is illustrated with drawings and is beautifully printed.

Below: A 2.6 litre WA saloon. These luxurious cars were available as Saloons, Tourers and as Tickford Coupés but few were built before war started. Like the VA pictured earlier, this car is fitted with headlamp masks.

thoroughly modern engine with shell bearings and an ability to thrive on hard driving. It is a pity that, like the WA, production of the TB was curtailed by world events.

The outbreak of war in 1939 brought car production at Abingdon to an end as the Government required that the factory be turned over to essential war work. All of the Nuffield Group factories were involved in this change – plans to convert factories to armament production had been formulated a few years previously. Component manufacturers, such as SU Carburettors and Morris Radiators, were easily able to switch to making similar parts for military vehicles and aircraft, and a specially constructed factory at Castle Bromwich was to build Supermarine Spitfires using motor industry production line techniques. Indeed, many of the factories were already working on military contracts before the outbreak of hostilities. The position of the M.G. factory at Abingdon was less clear and no definite plans for using it for similar work existed when war was declared in September 1939.

On A War Footing

Obviously the first job was to clear out all the machinery, fixtures and fittings of sports car production. For the hard-working and dedicated team that had built such successful and desirable cars over the last ten years this must have been a terrible wrench – some of them must have doubted that they would ever see cars built there again. There was also a large quantity of parts for the cars in current production, and for obsolete models, so a place to store all these had to be found. Luckily, Cecil Kimber was able to locate suitable premises in the form of an old clothing factory situated in West St. Helen's Street in the heart of Abingdon. The building was far from ideal, being very neglected and divided into a multitude of small offices and workshops, but after some demolition of partition walls and strengthening and re-laying of floors, M.G. had a

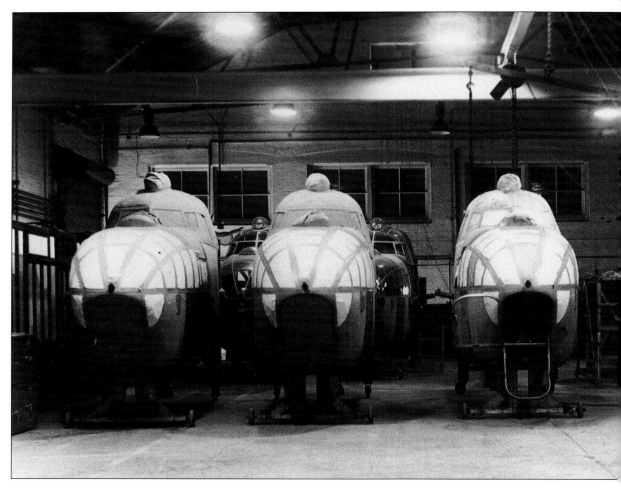

Above: The most demanding of the wartime contracts was the assembly of the main part of the fuselage for the Albemarle bomber. It is a tribute to the Abingdon workers that the job was successfully completed.

suitable site for the storage of the factory equipment and spare parts. Moving this huge mountain of material from the factory in Marcham Road to West St. Helen's Street was a formidable task and to assist this a special unit was built in the Experimental Department that consisted of a tractor and trailers constructed

Left: Much of the wartime work at Abingdon consisted of assembly and repair of light tanks and gun carriers, a task for which car workers were ideally suited. Completed vehicles were tested in the local countryside before being handed over to the army.

from redundant T-type parts! "Making do" was in the spirit of the times.

At first all this effort in clearing out the factory seemed to have been wasted. When Cecil Kimber and George Propert, the Works Manager, tried to find out exactly what contribution Abingdon was to make towards the war effort, they discovered that no plans to use the factory had been made and, to keep the remaining work force employed, they both had to spend considerable time drumming up contracts for work, any kind of work. Even when this was forthcoming there was also the problem of equipping to cope with it. M.G.s was more an assembler than builder of cars, with the vast majority of the components being manufactured elsewhere. Consequently, they had few machine tools and these were largely unsuitable for producing items to the tight tolerances necessary for the military contracts.

Initially the orders obtained were for shell racks, small bins and other similar items that could easily be made up using the existing facilities in the Press Shop. This area of the factory was to be utilized for the duration of the war producing short runs of items in urgent demand elsewhere in the works, and also for other companies. The main factory was still without suitable work and thus a contract to renovate light tanks, usually suffering from wear and tear rather than battle damage, was obtained. In typical Abingdon fashion a system to deal with these was evolved that obviated the need for the complete dismantling called for in the Ministry

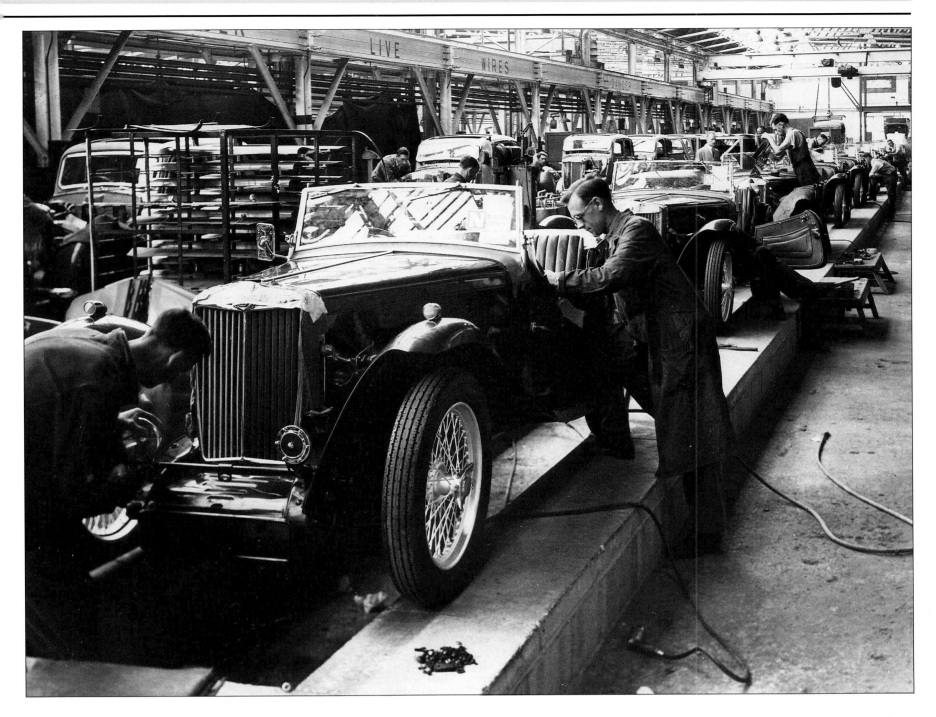

Above: A batch of export TCs. The first car is destined for a country where they drive on the right-hand side of the road – the spot lamp and horn are being fixed on opposite sides to those for home market cars.

specification, and the results obtained were sufficiently satisfactory for the factory to be awarded a contract to renovate much heavier tanks. This work required the installation of a 20-ton gantry crane to lift complete vehicles, and the introduction of a night shift, for the first time at Abingdon, to help speed up the return of the tanks to active service. These had to undergo an off-road test on part of the Berkshire Downs known as "The Ridgeway" and for security reasons these tests were often carried out at night. As a result there were occasional mishaps with tanks becoming stuck in ditches too deep for them to be recovered without the expert assistance of army teams – they were rather more demanding vehicles to test than new M.G.s.

In addition to repair work, the factory was also called upon to assemble new tanks and put into service "lend-lease" lorries shipped from the United States. The packing cases that contained these imported vehicles provided valuable materials for the maintenance staff to construct urgently-needed extensions to the Press Shop. The demand for small runs of components had made this one of the busiest parts of the factory and the control on the supply of building materials by Government departments made improvization essential.

Under Close Scrutiny

The production of aircraft parts and sub-assemblies proved to be the most demanding contracts undertaken by the team at M.G. during the war. Not only were they required to be manufactured to the highest standard, but these standards were rigorously enforced by the ministry-appointed inspectors. Having very limited manufacturing capacity, the management team looked around the engineering industry to see if they could have the necessary tools and jigs built by sub-contractors only to find that there was little spare capacity anywhere. In the end much of the equipment, including the main assembly jig which was 15 feet (4.6m) long but which was required to be accurate to a few thousandths of an inch, had to be designed and built within the factory. In spite of all such difficulties the complex fuselage assemblies of the Albemarle bomber were built and tested at Abingdon before being taken elsewhere for assembly into complete aircraft. Abingdon also assembled aircraft engines, and manufactured parts for other aircraft, contributing considerably to the country's war effort.

Members of the pre-war work force who had not been called up to join the forces had been augmented by women recruited locally and from other parts of the country. These largely unskilled people learned to work to the demanding standard necessary to assemble complex aircraft components, and the production line techniques used pre-war to assemble Midgets and Magnettes proved useful when trying to keep up with the demands of a country fighting for its very existence. The employment of a large number of women brought problems strange to management more used to dealing with a largely locally based male work force. A training school was established, at first just to train welders but later other assembly workers. There were problems, too, of accommodation. Abingdon was only a small market town that had a population of just 8000 people in pre-war years. With this figure raised by wartime demands to around 20,000, accommodation for the new recruits was difficult to find. Those living in outlying villages were served by a bus

Left: The Y-type is an attractive small saloon that was justifiably popular amongst those looking for a car that had better handling and more comfort than was offered by the average family car. Although the basic body was derived from a Morris, the longer bonnet and imposing M.G. radiator made the Y-type look completely different.

Below: The leather-faced seats, wooden dashboard and instruments with octagonal dials leave the driver in no doubt that he is driving a luxury sporting car in miniature. With new cars in short supply after the war, lucky was the owner of one of these attractive saloons.

service provided by the factory but some of the young women were housed in a hostel bought, and equipped, by the company. This hostel was provided with all the comforts of home, including a laundry and sewing room, and was appreciated by the young women, many of whom were living away from home for the first time in their lives.

With the coming of peace in Europe in 1945, the military work naturally dried up and it was imperative that the factory return as quickly as possible to making cars. Even whilst the last of the military contracts were being completed, a corner of the factory was turned over to producing Abingdon's first post-war car – the TC. When car production ceased before the war the last few two-seaters produced had been TBs. As the TB was a development of the TA, which had been in production since 1936, with over 3000 examples built, it was logical that any post-war sports car should be based on this model.

The Post-War Midget

With the benefit of the experience of seeing the TA, and later the TB, in service with customers, it was decided that minor revisions to the design could be undertaken to counter criticisms made. Some customers required more elbow room in the body so this was widened by about four inches (102mm) at the rear door pillar. This change produced one of the easiest ways to identify a TA or TB from a TC – the running boards were reduced in width and had only two tread strips on each, rather than the three fitted to the earlier cars.

Another criticism of the design concerned the chassis, or more particularly the mounting of the

road springs. The TA/TB chassis frame had the leaf springs pivoted at the front end and mounted into bronze trunnions at the rear – a system said to provide good lateral location to the springs. In spite of this advantage, when the TC was designed it was decided to change to more conventional, rubber-bushed shackles to locate them. This modification eliminated problems encountered when the sliding trunnions were insufficiently lubricated – particularly important now that it was hoped that many more cars were to be exported to countries where owners expected their vehicles to cover high mileages without much attention.

With the military work ending, the factory was stripped of all the jigs and fixtures installed to build the complicated weapons of war. The production lines were rebuilt and production of the TC started in earnest. The original pre-war work force, released for the duration when called up for military service, returned to take up their old jobs relegating the majority of the female wartime workers to their kitchens! According to factory records, in 1945 100 TCs were built and these appear to have been laid down in batches. The factory was back in business and by December 1945 they had produced a full catalogue advertising the TC.

The shortages of materials, and the difficulties of production, reduced the choice of colours for the new model to just one – Black. However, buyers had the chance to select from either Vellum Beige, Shires Green or Regency Red upholstery, although for most the choice was academic as demand far outstripped supply and the majority of M.G. owners had to put up with driving those pre-war cars that had survived the

attentions of the German Air Force and the enthusiastic ownership of young R.A.F. officers! Actually the arrival of peace didn't bring with it a freedom to enjoy motoring once again. The severe economic problems faced by the incoming Labour Government in 1945 forced them to impose severe rationing, and supplies of petrol for private motoring were to be restricted for quite some time.

When a car was subjected to a full road test by "The Motor" in 1947 the reviewer commented on the improvements that had been made and was impressed by its quality and finish. The leather interior and polished wooden dashboard with the full range of instruments, allied to the stability, comfort and performance – all for an all-inclusive price of £527.16.8d. – was excellent value and the cheapest true sports car on the

Above: Deeper wings and smaller wheels identify Peter Arnell's car as a YB. The braking system and rear axle from the TD were adopted, as was a larger-diameter clutch. To improve the handling, 15-inch wheels with wider section tyres replaced the 16-inch YA wheels, and an anti-roll bar was fitted to the front suspension.

Left: A useful-sized luggage compartment is provided and overly large cases can be accommodated by leaving the lid open. The spare wheel compartment is behind the panel that holds the rear lights and number plate. This is deeper on the YB than the YA, to give room for the wider-section tyre.

market. Looked at today, a recorded time of over 21 seconds to reach 60mph (97kph) seems very slow but compared to the average small saloon car of the period, this was real performance. Although reorganization of the factory for the transfer from wartime to peacetime production, and a shortage of materials, had limited numbers built, the TC was starting to gain new friends for M.G. all around the world.

M.G. had always marketed saloon cars alongside the open tourers and out-and-out sports cars. When production ceased in 1939, they had open and closed versions of the VA, SA and the 2.6 Litre WA models. There was a need to provide the post-war public with an M.G. saloon as soon as materials and facilities would allow. In 1938 work on a new smaller saloon car had begun at Cowley where the talented Alec Issigonis and an ex-M.G. man, Jack Daniels, had designed an independent front suspension layout for the Morris 10. In the event the new suspension was not used on that car on the grounds of cost but was incorporated into a prototype of a new M.G. saloon which was to be known as the M.G. Ten. This was based around a new chassis, with the Issigonis independent front suspension, fitted with the body from the Morris Eight and the engine from the Morris Ten – all blended to conform to established M.G. sporting traditions.

A New Saloon

As soon as production was resumed after the war, the M.G. Ten designs were brought out of retirement and dusted off to be used as a basis for the first post-war M.G. saloon – the Y-type.

The Y-type chassis was made up of welded, closed box-section side rails and tubular cross members. At the back it ran under the rear axle – a feature it shared with the TC. The rear axle was suspended on the traditional leaf springs and had a Panhard rod to give lateral location. At the front a cross member housed the coil springs and provided a mounting for the rack-and-pinion steering gear. This front suspension, utilizing coil springs, lower wishbones and with the shock absorbers providing the upper mounting for the swivel pin, was to serve the company well with the basic design continuing right through to the end of production of the MGB.

The body was closely based on the new Morris Eight but the longer bonnet, flowing wings and the Abingdon radiator gave it much improved looks. The pressed steel wheels, rather than the wires fitted to previous M.G.s, were to be a radical departure but no doubt the average motorist would have blessed the ease with which they could be cleaned. The new saloon was powered by a single carburettor variant of the XPAG engine being fitted to the TC. The power output was reduced from 54.4bhp in twin carburettor form for the TC to just 46bhp for the Y-type. The saloon weighed over a ton so performance could be expected to be adequate rather than sprightly. However, if you compare this power-to-weight ratio, about 45bhp per ton laden, to the average British saloon car of the period, it does not seem quite so under-powered.

As well as having a more up-to-date chassis design than its predecessors, the Y-type also had a more modern bodywork construction. Previous M.G. saloons were fitted with traditionally built, wooden-framed bodies that were

1949 TC MIDGET

The TC was both the first post-war car from Abingdon and also the last of the traditional pre-war, cart-sprung M.G.s. Based closely on the 1936 TA Midget, and having a powerful little engine that first saw use in the short-lived 1939 TB model, the TC started a boom in sports car sales that was to maintain the factory in full production for over 30 years. Although already dated when it first appeared, its attractive appearance and good performance guaranteed the car a lasting place in the history of the marque.

SPECIFICATION

Model: TC two-seater

Engine: Four-cylinder in line, overhead valve, water cooled. 66.5 x 90mm, 1250cc. 54bhp

Gearbox: Four-speed with synchromesh on the three higher ratios

Final drive: 5.125:1. Top gear 15.6mph/1000rpm (25kph/1000rpm)

Suspension: Solid axles mounted on half-elliptic leaf springs

Dimensions: Wheelbase 7ft 10in (2388mm). Track, front 3ft 9in (1143mm). Overall length 11ft 7.5in (3543mm)

Unladen weight: 16.5cwt (838kg)

Cost when new: £412.10s.0d. plus £115 6s.8d. purchase tax

Performance: (From contemporary reports) Top speed 76mph (122kph)

Owner: Eric Nicholls

Right: The leather-covered bench seats are extremely comfortable and can be adjusted to accommodate drivers of widely differing heights – so long as the passenger moves as well! The "Brooklands" steering wheel and passenger's grab handle are period extras.

Left: The 8-inch (203mm) TC headlights gave good illumination although some of the later cars that were built for the American market had smaller sealed-beam units. Light glasses on early cars differed from those seen on this 1949 car.

Left: The sidescreens can be stowed in a compartment at the rear of the body when required. With the hood up the car is snug on cold days and winter journeys are no hardship. Late model TCs, like this, have fabric-covered dashboards and early cars veneered wood.

Below: The large spoked wheels were a relic from earlier models but they add considerably to the look of the car. The windscreen wiper motor is well placed to bang the passenger's head in an accident and certainly would not meet modern safety requirements.

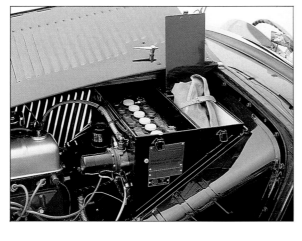

Right: When the TC was adapted from the pre-war TA/TB design, the twin batteries mounted by the back axle were replaced with a single 12-volt unit in the engine compartment. The useful tool box is accessible from either side of the engine compartment.

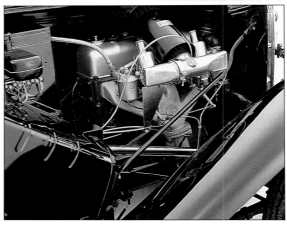

Above left and right: LXA 52 is an export model TC and owner Eric Nicholls bought it as a partly-completed restoration project. The results of the considerable effort he made to get the car exactly right can be seen in these pictures but what cannot be seen is just how well the car runs on the road. Much time and effort were spent making this TC drive just as it did when it was newly built. Well set-up TCs do steer well and are a pleasure to drive – unlike poorly-restored cars.

Above: The 1250cc XPAG engine, basically the same as that used in the TB, is capable of being tuned to give much more power than standard. A popular method was supercharging.

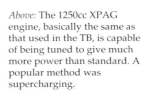

Right: When new, TCs had a single rear "D" lamp to provide a rear light, stop lamp and illumination for the number plate. Modern regulations mean that two lights are now needed and many owners fit even more.

Above: The ignition side of the engine. The dynamo has a drive through a reduction box for the mechanical tachometer, which is set on the dashboard in front of the driver. Just below the radiator tie rod can be seen the externally-mounted oil pump and the oil pipes which are a source of oil leaks from some XPAG engines, but not this one!

of the English Gentleman's Club atmosphere of leather seats and woodwork, all finished in the most tasteful of colours, about the cabin fittings. Anyone brought up in a period when leather interiors were the rule, rather than the exception, will recognize the smell inside any well used Y-type. The mixture of leather, wood varnish, warm "Bakelite" and musty carpets is very evocative and will instantly bring back memories of trips out in the family car, or the occasional lifts to school in days when it was more usual to walk or travel by bus.

In their efforts to make the new saloon identifiably an M.G., the designers produced a dashboard layout that used octagonal surrounds for standard round instruments. Although the car was not as well adorned with octagons as some later offerings, the badges on the boot lid and on the traditional radiator certainly left the observer in no doubt that this was an M.G.. The

Above: A YA chassis. Note the box-section side rails, swept under the rear axle, and the outriggers for mounting the body. The "Jack-all" unit is mounted on the bulkhead, alongside the engine, and one of the hydraulic pistons that lift the wheels off the ground can be seen beneath the suspension on the left-hand front wheel.

clad with separate steel or aluminium panels. Although not following the most modern practice of using a unitary body/chassis unit, the body was of all-steel construction and built by Nuffield Metal Products in Birmingham. As the basic structure, the main shell and the doors, was shared with the Morris Eight of the period there were obviously economies made that allowed this method of construction for what was, in normal car factory terms, a fairly low volume car. Even by the standards of 1947, the overall styling employed was still conservative when many cars appearing at that time had bulbous lines with wings, running boards and headlights all blended into the main bodywork. The Y-type, however, adhered to a more traditional body shape with only the disc wheels, instead of wires, betraying the more up-to-date thinking behind the design.

Rack And Pinion Steering

In addition to independent front suspension, the other change made for the Y-type that was to have a profound effect on both this and most subsequent M.G.s, was the adoption of rack-and-pinion steering. The improvement brought about by using this component can really only be appreciated by anyone who has driven, say, a TC and a TD in quick succession. The precision, not to mention the longer life, of the rack-and-pinion system is light years ahead of the old Bishop Cam box fitted to the earlier cars. In good condition this is just adequate for the task it performs but once it is even slightly worn, steering a straight line on any road with camber changes can be an interesting experience. Nevertheless, it is surprising how many cars, even sporting cars, were still fitting similar, inferior steering boxes right through the 1950s.

The main charm of the Y-type was the well-appointed and comfortable interior and the overall appearance of the car. There is something

separate front bucket seats, and the rear bench with its central armrest, were all trimmed with leather facings and the dashboard, as well as the wooden cappings for the doors, were finished in polished walnut. There was a choice of maroon, beige or green upholstery which featured an attractive pattern of pleated panels on the seat faces. The windscreen could be wound open on hot days and the small rear window covered by a remotely operated blind to avoid dazzle from the lights of following cars at night. Inside the car the roof was fitted with twin sun visors and a central reading light, as well as a metal sliding sun roof. Altogether a comfortably appointed small sporting car.

At Abingdon the production lines started rolling and, with streams of fully painted bodies arriving daily, batches of completed cars were soon ready for delivery around the world. The painted body shells were transported to the fac-

Left: During the war many women replaced male workers called up to fight. Although after the war many lost their jobs, some were employed to make and fit the trim to the Y-type saloons.

Above: Bodies were trimmed on the top deck and then lowered onto assembled chassis. Here, towards the end of the production line, a front wing is fitted to a two-tone painted car.

tory on lorries and hoisted up to the top deck for trimming. At that time this work was carried out mainly by women, many of whom had originally been recruited to work on armaments. Once trimmed, the bodies were lowered onto completed chassis for final finishing.

By 1947 the Nuffield Export Organization had recovered from the wartime interruptions and a dealer network was well established. This was the dawn of a real boom in British car exports with much of the industrial world, outside the U.S.A., still building up capacity after the destruction wrought by the war. It was the time when British cars were exported in greater numbers than ever before, and sold on all continents. Unfortunately, the quality of many of these was poor and not really suited to the conditions they were to encounter. This was not true of most M.G.s, although there were still the occasional problems – especially with electrical components – but the small Y-type saloon soon found friends around the world.

An Open Tourer

Although the Y-type was popular as a saloon car, the company felt there was a demand for an open version which would give rather more passenger room than was available in the strictly two-seater TC. To cater for this market, satisfied pre-war by tourer and Tickford versions of the saloon models, the Y-tourer was conceived. Handsome styling had been a hallmark of the M.G. tourers and, in particular, the Tickford drophead-coupé was an imposing car. In contrast, the Y-tourer, known by the factory as the YT, was rather more workmanlike than handsome. One motoring writer described it as "a bathtub on wheels" – which is, perhaps, a little unfair. Actually the styling grows on you and it is certainly a useful machine for the enthusiast who needs a roomy, four-seater, open car.

Although the standard saloon had to make do with a single carburettor version of the XPAG engine, the open tourer seemed to require something a bit more sporting and was fitted with a TC specification engine, complete with twin carburettors and modified camshaft. Another feature transferred from the sports car was the dashboard. Although not identical to the TC, essentially it looked the same, using a similar fabric-covered board with a large tachometer in front of the driver and matching speedometer placed in front of the passenger. The minor dials and the switches were all contained in a TC-style central panel. This dashboard made more sense for an open car with sporting pretensions than the polished, walnut-veneered wooden one used in the saloons.

Designed For Export

As the export market was to be the prime target, the car was designed to be easily built in left-hand-drive form. The coachwork design was based on that of the saloon but with just two rear-hinged doors which were constructed rather differently. At the back, the boot was virtually unchanged giving adequate luggage capacity and still making it possible to carry additional suitcases on the lowered boot lid. The doors were cut away at the top, in the current sporting fashion, and the windscreen could be lowered if required. The interior trim was similar to the saloon, as was the interior space, although rear seat passengers had their elbow room slightly reduced by the pockets needed to store the hood irons. The front seats could be tipped up to ease access to the rear seats.

The hood stowage was particularly neat. When lowered, the hood and frame were kept in a compartment which extended behind and round each side of the rear seat and could be concealed by zip-fastened flaps. The rear window in the erected hood could be lowered to provide additional ventilation. Apart from the more powerful engine, the mechanical specification remained unchanged but the bodywork modifications reduced the overall weight by nearly 90lb (41kg), which helped to improve the performance. Like the saloon, the tourer had the

Above: A rare right-hand-drive Y-tourer. Unusually, this car was paid for in overseas currency but delivered and registered in Britain. The car is now owned by John Finch, who restored it in the early 1970s.

Left: The Y-tourer is a full four-seater and very little rear-seat room has been sacrificed to accommodate the soft-top. Zipped pockets either side of the rear seat conceal the roof framework when it is lowered.

Right: A factory publicity picture of a TC, with the later style spot lamp, and a YA saloon. The badge between the twin auxiliary lamps on the Y-type is that of The Royal Automobile Club who, like the Automobile Association, still offer a range of breakdown and touring services to their members.

very useful "Jackall" jacking system which hydraulically raised the car off the ground to allow for wheel changes.

Almost 800 tourers were built for the export market but, from the point of view of sales, the YT could hardly be called a huge success. What isn't clear is whether there was not the same demand for open tourers as existed pre-war, or because there was a shortage of cars available for sale. Most of the production went abroad, and perhaps more examples would have sold had they been available on the home market.

In common with the rest of the British motor industry, overseas sales had increasingly become the focus of attention at M.G. Steel and other essential raw materials for car production were restricted by the government when Sir Stafford Cripps, the Chancellor of the Exchequer, introduced a rationing system with the majority of supplies being available for production destined for overseas markets. It was vital for the country to earn foreign currency, especially American dollars, to help pay off the crippling overseas debts accumulated during the war. Home buyers were greeted with the sight of hundreds of new British cars destined for overseas customers being transported to the docks, whilst they had either to join long waiting lists for a new car or pay an inflated price for a worn-out pre-war model.

M.G.s Overseas

At first The M.G. Car Company did little to pander to the needs of overseas customers. The TC was only ever built in right-hand-drive form with minor variations to electrical components and instrumentation to suit local conditions. However, the growing number of these being sold in America, following the establishment of The Hambro Trading Company as the sole concessionaire for that country, led to there being

calls from dealers for some changes to suit the cars better for a life on the streets of New York or Los Angeles. By 1948, to cater for this demand, there was a special version of the TC which carried the chassis plate designation EX-U (Export United States). To help ward off the attentions of people parking large American cars carelessly, these TCs were equipped with full-width bumpers, fitted with overriders, attached to the ends of the chassis rails. They were similar to, but not the same as, those later fitted to the TD. The centre of the back bumper had a plinth with a cast M.G. badge, with raised lettering, fixed to it.

Above: All the Y-tourers were built on the YA chassis, but at least one has been updated to YB specification. The windscreen folds flat, like the TC, although it is unlikely that many owners used their cars for racing! The dumpy styling has often prompted criticism, but a Y-tourer is a useful car to transport all the family to M.G. meetings.

To accommodate the sealed beam headlamps that were mandatory in the United States, smaller seven-inch (178mm) Lucas S700 type lamps were fitted and the front fog lamp deleted. To improve the lighting at the rear, the single combined brake and side light was replaced by a pair of high mounted, circular lamps fitted each side of the petrol tank on special brackets. These also doubled as flashing indicators – along with

Above: This beautiful TD is owned by Jonathan Goddard, who restored it from a "pile of bits". Unusually, as a very early car, it has solid disc wheels, unlike the later cars with pierced wheels pictured on pages 96 and 97. The luggage rack is a period accessory.

Below: The engine compartment of the early TD. Note the oil-bath air cleaner. These were fitted to many 1940s' and 1950s' cars.

Right: The dashboard and controls are well laid-out in the TD. This early car has the TC-style instruments with flat-faced dials.

the front side lights – using a pair of brake switch override relays to interrupt the brake light circuit when the indicators were needed.

As well as removing the fog lamp from the badge bar bracket, the horn was also moved. This was replaced by a pair of scuttle-mounted horns, one high and one low note. The positions of the other dials and switches on the dashboard were also modified and most of the cars fitted with a three-spoke steering wheel finished in a light tan colour, rather than in black as was more usual. Tan wheels are now a rarity.

Sales Record For The TC

The TC was the most successful sports car the company had ever manufactured and by the time production ceased in 1949 10,000 examples had been built. The TC was also the first Abingdon product to sell in large numbers abroad and it introduced a whole generation of drivers to the joys of sports car motoring, and in so doing it was partly responsible for the growth of interest in sports car racing in the United States. However, the numbers sold in that country were small when compared to those of its successor, the TD.

Having the more up-to-date Y-type built alongside the TC made it obvious that a redesign of the sports car was long overdue. The strength of overseas sales made it imperative that any new car should be able to be built in both right- and left-hand drive without too many production line difficulties. In the event it was the Y-type chassis that provided the inspiration for the new TD. Initially experiments with a shortened saloon chassis, fitted with a TC body, were

carried out at the factory before the drawings for the new car were done by Jim O'Neill in the design office at Cowley. The production TD chassis was similar to the Y-type at the front end but the rear axle was mounted on half-elliptic leaf springs below the frame at the rear; the Y-type had its axle above the chassis rails. The Panhard rod used on the YA rear suspension was omitted, and the rear axle itself was fitted with hypoid-bevel gears which promised quieter running. This axle was also later fitted to the Y saloon. As with the Y-type, the wheels were pressed steel. The braking system was an improvement over that used on the TC, with twin leading shoes on the front brakes and a "fly-off" hand brake mounted on the central tunnel operating the rear brake shoes via twin cables. The handbrake fitted to the earlier car had been mounted on a cross-shaft – a leftover from the days when M.G.s had cable-operated, rather than hydraulic, brakes.

The TD body, which was built at Morris Bodies Branch, was made roomier than the TC and its construction incorporated a pressed steel rear bulkhead behind the seats to provide far more rigid mounting for the door pillars. The rear wings were bolted to the inner wings which had captive nuts incorporated – an improvement over the wood screws used to hold the TC wings in place. Because the TD used smaller wheels, the wings themselves were deeper, giving a more solid appearance. This was further enhanced by the shorter, but deeper, fuel tank and more steeply sloping spare wheel mounting. Neat steel valances covered the front and rear of the chassis.

One of the most pleasing views of the TD is from the rear. The combination of wider wings, the strong spare wheel mounting, and the rear valance give the car an appearance of strength and solidity. For the first time on an M.G. sports car, with the exception of the special American market TCs, bumpers and overriders appeared as standard equipment and these contributed to this appearance of strength. The bumpers were carried on bumper bars bolted directly to the rear chassis rails and to extensions of the front chassis frame. This helped them protect the vulnerable flowing wings from parking knocks.

From the outset the car was designed to be built with the steering wheel on the left-hand side for some overseas markets. The rack-and-pinion steering was carried over from the Y-type, although the pinion shaft is longer than that used on the saloon. This steering gear is ideally suited to the TD and gives precise steering and secure handling. The wheels are perhaps the one feature of the TD that first attracted adverse comment from the M.G. purists at the time. Particularly abroad it seems to be accepted that sports cars should have wire wheels, and these were never an option on the TD. Later, when the TF was introduced, wire wheels were offered as an optional extra and many cars where fitted with them. At the same time kits were sold to convert TDs. After about 500 cars had been built, the appearance of the disc wheels was improved when cooling holes were punched in them.

The interior of the car was very similar to the TC but the wider cockpit provided the occupants with more comfort. As with the earlier cars, the interior trim was available in either red, green or tan leather with the dashboard trimmed to match. A useful addition was the small glove box, although if the optional valve radio was specified this was mounted in here. The area behind the seats could stow a small suitcase or a few soft bags, but for serious touring a luggage rack could be ordered. The four sidescreens were stowed in a compartment at the back of this luggage area. The hood gave adequate weather protection when fitted but headroom was later improved by the adoption of a modified hood frame with an extra supporting bow.

A Heavier Car

The penalty for all this strength and extra comfort was an increase in weight of about 160lb (73kg). As the engine was virtually unchanged, apart from the introduction of the, then, fashionable oil bath air cleaner, performance was only maintained by a reduction of the rear axle ratio. This change reduced the miles per hour per 1000 revs to 14.4 against the TC which was 15.5. The road testers of the time gave the new car high praise and one team recorded a time of 23.5 seconds to reach 60mph (97kph), which was a little slower than had been recorded for the previous model, but the ride comfort and handling received favourable comments. The testers commented on a marked feeling of increased solidity about the car, resulting from the more rigid chassis frame, but said that it had gained enormously in comfort when tackling the types of surfaces a car of this kind was likely to encounter.

The TD sold extremely well and it is this car that won most converts to the marque in the early 1950s. Its popularity, especially in the United States, led to its becoming the best-selling M.G. thus far. It outshone the TC with around 30,000 cars built, of which only 1656 stayed in the United Kingdom. The United States imported 23,488 and quite a number of these continue to give their owners a great deal of pleasure.

Around 1700 of these cars were specially tuned competition versions called the TD Mark

Right: A picture of the attractive showroom poster that depicts the TD in a "Grand Canyon" setting. This same illustration appears in one of the sales brochures for the car.

Below: The rear view of the TD is particularly attractive and certainly the standard disc wheels suit the car much better than wire wheels, which were never a factory option on this model.

II. There has been much confusion surrounding this model with many owners of standard cars fitted with engines bearing the prefix TD/2 claiming that they had one, when all they had was a later TD – all of which had these engines. The only reliable indication of a genuine car is the chassis number – which carries the prefix TD/c. The matter is further complicated as, externally, there was little to distinguish it from the standard model until late in the production run. When sales of TDs in general were slowing down, badges to identify the Mark II were fitted to both sides of the bonnet and on a plinth on the rear bumper. At the same time TF-style black and white octagons were fitted to the radiator and to the spare wheel hub cap.

The chassis for the Mark II was modified by the inclusion of brackets at the rear, and the provision of holes in the front suspension arms, for additional shock absorbers. These Andrex adjustable friction-type shock absorbers are a left-over from pre-war technology. Adjustment of the internal friction discs is achieved by screwing a bolt inwards to tighten them and out-

wards to loosen them. The front pair are mounted on the suspension arms which both increases the unsprung weight and makes adding an anti-roll bar difficult, if not impossible. Actually their use in competition seems to have been to stiffen the car against roll but at the same time they also made the ride harder.

There were many small changes to distinguish the Mark II from the standard cars. Briefly, these are; modified cylinder head with larger valves and raised compression, larger 1½ inch (38mm) H4 carburettors, twin SU fuel pumps and Lucas Sports coil, higher ratio rear axle (4.875:1) with 4.55 and 5.125 as options, plus the extra shock absorbers mentioned earlier. The engine changes raised the power output from 54 to around 60bhp. The Mark II was built throughout the production run of the TD. They can have engines prefixed TD, TD2 or TD3. However, the TD3 engine was only fitted to this model. Externally the bonnet side panel on the right-hand side has a bulge to clear the larger carburettors. These are also fitted with a larger inlet pipe and a different air cleaner. However,

some of the first Mark IIs had no air cleaner or bonnet bulge.

Inside all was standard TD. Bucket seats were not fitted except as a special order for competition use. Serious competitors could also order a higher state of tune and the XPAG engine could be modified to easily give up to 50 per cent more power – especially when supercharged. The Mark II was road tested on both sides of the Atlantic and was shown to be the fastest of the T-series cars until the TF 1500 arrived.

Time For A Facelift

By 1953 the appearance of a new breed of sports cars, like the Triumph TR2 and the Austin-Healey 100, made the TD look rather old-fashioned and sales were suffering as a result. In addition the traditional styling of the car was causing some problems. For example, the separate headlights on the TD were costly and easily damaged or knocked out of alignment when opening the bonnet, and in hot climates the lack of pressurized water cooling reduced the efficiency of the system. A change to a more modern design, however, meant modifying the radiator, header tank and filler cap.

Above: An early TD chassis without a scuttle hoop. A comparison with the YA chassis pictured on page 90 is interesting. The TD side rails sweep over the rear axle.

Right: The TD/Y-type production line. The front car is destined for the United States and Abingdon employee, Bert McIntyre, carries out the last few tasks before the bonnet is fitted.

In 1953 there was no design office at Abingdon, this was not re-established until 1954 when the urgent need for an entirely new car was realized by the BMC management. However, when the TD was redesigned to produce the TF, such developments were in the future and the "powers that be" would only sanction a facelift of the old model to be carried out at Cowley. Aesthetically, this was very successful and the lowered scuttle and sloping bonnet, allied to beautifully sculptured front wings that now incorporated the headlights, produced a very attractive car. The new, more sloping radiator shell was now topped by a dummy radiator cap with the proper filler for

the pressurized cooling system being placed under the left-hand bonnet top. This bonnet still featured a centre hinge but now only the top panels lifted while the side panels remaining fixed in place, unless they were unscrewed for major work. This arrangement looked smart but accessibility for routine maintenance was more difficult than on the previous models.

At the rear, the fuel tank was reshaped and lowered, and the rear wings made more elegant with the leading edge curving to meet the running boards. The strips on the running boards were chrome plated rather than aluminium and rubber, and were now longer and carried up onto the front wings. The circular rear lights

Left: One of the TD Mark II competition models. Externally, there is little to distinguish this car from a standard TD, although those Mark IIs built towards the end of the production run had special badging.

Above: A Mark II engine bay. Twin fuel pumps feed larger carburettors that sit under a bigger air cleaner. The cylinder head has larger valves, and a higher compression ratio, to boost power output.

fitted to later TDs were carried over to the TF, as were the front side lights.

Inside the cockpit much was new; the bench seat familiar to generations of Midget owners was replaced by a pair of leather-upholstered bucket seats which, although very comfortable, did not have quite the range of adjustment of the earlier seats. However, the TF seats could be moved individually which was a lot more convenient. Both as a styling gimmick, and also to ease production of both left- and right-hand-drive cars on the same production line, the instruments were now all grouped in the centre of the dashboard. Following the style of those fitted to the Y-type saloon, they were set in chromed, octagonal bezels with the rev counter placed nearest to the driver and the speedometer on the passenger side. In the centre a combined instrument took care of water temperature, oil pressure and ammeter.

Mechanically Unchanged

All these changes to the exterior and interior of the car could not disguise the fact that the chassis and other mechanical components were unchanged from the TD. The only mechanical improvements made were the standardization of a higher state of tune for the engine, similar to that used on the TD Mk II, and the adoption of the higher ratio rear axle from that car. The engine changes improved the power output by a modest 4bhp. In addition, because of the restricted space under the bonnet, the oil bath air cleaner was replaced by a pair of pancake filters.

Although they had a new M.G. to sell, the Publicity Department did not exactly go out of their way to promote the car in the home market. After the initial announcement in "The Motor" and "The Autocar" magazines in 1953, no cars were made available to them for road test. Perhaps M.G. feared that those journals would point out how little progress had been made in terms of comfort and performance. Even company press advertisements tended to dwell more on the new, 1½ litre Magnette saloon rather than on the virtues of the TF.

Above: A Clipper Blue TD restored by Tom Metcalf. This car had a blue grille from new, but usually the grille colour matched the upholstery. Perhaps a new blue-painted one was fitted before the car was sold.

Overseas magazines did test the car and, on the whole, liked it, particularly the styling revisions. However, although most publications were too kind to mention it, the car was beginning to look a bit dated when compared to those from other manufacturers tested in their pages. "Road and Track" in America was given one of the new cars to try and it published a test report in March 1954. The magazine found that the performance was better than the TD, but not quite as good as the TD Mk II. It felt that the higher gearing improved the car but that the larger carburettors were not an improvement. This reinforces the view that with a capacity of only 1250cc, the larger carbs are really more for appearance than effect. Summing up the report it said that the M.G. was still the greatest sports car for the money available and that it was well able to stand up to hard day-to-day driving.

The need to improve sales of the car, which was not really holding its own in competition with other marques, led to the development of the larger 1500cc engine introduced after some 6000 TF 1250s had been built. For some time a number of people had been enlarging the XPAG engine by over-boring. This process was not always successful as it reduced the wall thickness around the bores below acceptable limits. To enlarge the capacity without changing the cylinder bore centres, or the head stud positions, the factory produced a new block casting which eliminated the water jacket between 1 and 2, and 3 and 4 cylinders, and reduced the size of the jacket between the two pairs of cylinders and at the front and rear of the block. The effect of increasing the bore size from 66.5 to 72mm was to increase the capacity from 1250cc to 1466cc. A thicker cylinder head was used, but the increase in swept volume meant a corresponding rise in compression ratio to 8.3:1. The power output increased by a useful 6bhp and the torque was also improved.

To help market the new version of the TF the factory added "TF 1500" plates to the sides of the

Below: Although this car looks nothing like the others here, it is a TD. In Italy the Arnolt TD had its Abingdon chassis clothed with this elegant bodywork by Bertone. There was also a closed coupé version.

1955 TF 1500 MIDGET

The TF 1500 is considered by many to be the most desirable of all the post-war T-types. Earlier TFs had 1250cc engines, and the larger engine gave the later cars better performance, but this was insufficient to compete with the more modern sports cars available in 1955 and did little to halt the overall decline in sales. Replaced as it was by the streamlined MGA, the TF 1500 was the last M.G. to wear the traditional style of bodywork made popular some twenty-three years earlier when the J2 first appeared.

SPECIFICATION

Model: TF 1500

Engine: Four-cylinder in line, overhead valve, water cooled. 72 x 90mm, 1466cc. 63bhp

Gearbox: Four-speed with synchromesh on three higher ratios

Final drive: 4.875:1. Top gear 15.2mph/1000rpm (24kph/1000rpm)

Suspension: Front: Independent with coil springs, wishbones and rack and pinion steering. Rear: Live axle suspended on half-elliptic leaf springs

Dimensions: Wheelbase 7ft 10in (2388mm). Track, front 3ft 11.75in (1213mm), rear 4ft 2in (1270mm). Overall length 12ft 3in (3734mm)

Unladen weight: 17.25cwt (876kg)

Cost when new: £550 plus £230.5s.10d. purchase tax

Performance: (From contemporary reports): Top speed 88mph (142kph)

Owner: Margaret Andrews

Right: The main instrument panel was placed centrally to facilitate production of both right- and left-hand-drive versions. The separate bucket seats fitted to the TF are easier to adjust than the one-piece bench seat fitted to the previous models.

Below: If required, the windscreen can be folded flat once the two wing nuts have been loosened. This option was offered for those wishing to reduce wind resistance when racing.

Left: Like the earlier cars, the TF was supplied with a tool box for the comprehensive tool kit. M.G. owners were expected to work on the cars themselves, indeed it was felt to be a part of the fun of running one! Luckily, a well-maintained TF is a reliable car and capable of covering considerable mileages without trouble.

Below: Owned now by Margaret Andrews and restored for her by husband, Terry, over a five-year period following its purchase in 1989, the superb condition of this car gives no clue as to just how bad it was before work on it started. The M.G. was involved in an accident many years ago which had pushed one front corner back

RLY 209

almost to the bulkhead. To add to the damage, it was stored in a Scottish barn with the front portion of the car exposed to the weather. The story of the rebuild would fill a book and the finished car is a tribute to Terry's skill and dedication. The car is now enjoyed to the full and has been taken on a number of long trips.

Below: For the first time on an M.G. sports car, the radiator cap on the TF was actually a dummy. To allow for a pressurized cooling system the real filler cap was moved under the bonnet.

Below: The petrol tank on the TF was more steeply raked than that fitted to the TD, enhancing the sleeker appearance of the car. The petrol cap pops up when the release lever is pressed.

Above left and right: The styling changes made to the TD to produce the TF resulted in a very attractive car. The headlamps were set into the front wings and the sloping radiator and lower

bonnet line changed the appearance considerably. The twin front lamps and pair of reversing lamps fitted here were not standard equipment but are 1950s approved accessories. In spite of being

mechanically virtually identical to the previous TD model, the styling and cockpit changes make the car feel like quite a different machine when viewed from the driving seat.

Right: The XPEG engine fitted to the TF 1500 was externally identical to the 1250cc XPAG engine previously fitted to the TF and earlier models. Space for the larger bores was found in the block by eliminating the water jacket between 1 and 2 and between 3 and 4 cylinders, and by reducing the size of the water jacket between the two pairs of cylinders. The cylinder head was unchanged, and the greater swept volume of the 1500 engine increased the compression ratio, further improving power output. The side panels remove to improve accessibility.

Right: The rear mounted spare wheel is both attractive and gives useful protection for the petrol tank in an accident. Wire wheels were an optional extra for all TFs. An ingenious locating key ensures that the M.G. badge is always vertical, no matter in what position the spinner is placed.

Below: This neat rear lamp serves as both a stop/tail light and as a flashing indicator. A relay interrupts the circuit to flash the brake light when the indicator switch mounted on the right of the dashboard is turned.

bonnet. In advertisements the slogan "There's a new bee in its bonnet!" was used to emphasize the improved performance. However, good though the new engine was, sales of the now seriously outdated car did not pick up and at Abingdon the newly re-formed design team were hard at work on an up-to-date replacement – the MGA.

More Records Are Broken

Competition and record-breaking had always been seen as a cost effective way of establishing the M.G. marque and promoting sales. Following the success gained by Goldie Gardner just before the outbreak of war, his EX135 record-breaking car, had been stored at the old clothing factory in West St. Helen's Street, along with the rest of the stores and spares from the factory. Unfortunately, a severe fire in 1944 gutted a part of this building destroying much of its contents, including most of the spares for the record-breaker and the 1500cc engine, although the car itself survived. In 1946 Goldie Gardner decided to make a further record attempt using the surviving 750cc engine and arranged for it to be brought back into running order. Pressure of work at Abingdon meant that any help from that quarter would have to be unofficial, and the employees who accompanied him to Italy for the venture did so using part of their annual holi-

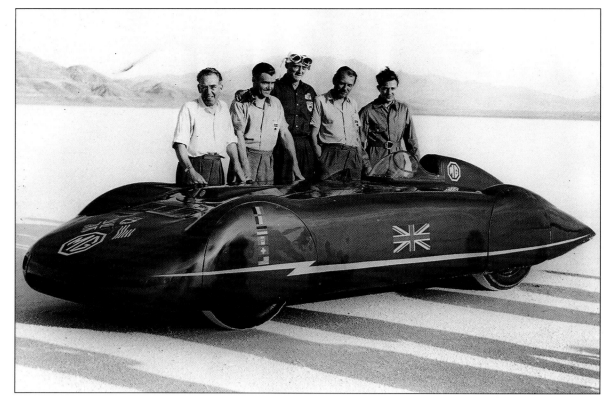

Above: The 1489cc B-series engine with twin carburettors in the ZA which is owned by Phil Jones.

Below: Although the ZA Magnette shared most of the body panels with the previously announced Wolseley 4/44, a revised mechanical specification and lowered suspension made it the better car.

Above: The old pre-war record-breaker, EX135, was taken to the Salt Lake in Utah for an attempt on National and International records. Driven by Goldie Gardner, and fitted with a tuned XPAG TD engine, new records were set at speeds up to 139.3mph (224.18kph) over distances of up to 200km. A more highly-tuned engine was then fitted, but runs at higher speeds did not bring any new records because of timing equipment problems.

Above: The dashboard in the ZA is attractive, as is the half-octagonal speedometer. There is no tachometer.

day. In the event the chosen site near Brescia was unsuitable for the high speed runs and despite their best efforts the team returned home without taking any new records

Undaunted, Goldie Garner next took the car to Belgium where he was able to use a section of dual carriageway road built in 1939 as part of an ambitious new transcontinental highway scheme that had never been completed. This road at Jabbeke proved ideal and new 750cc records were set. In 1947 he returned to Belgium and took records in the 500cc class by the expedient of removing two of the six pistons in the 750cc engine and replacing them with balance weights. The following year he lost the 500cc records to the Italian driver, Piero Taruffi, who took them in what was really a four-wheeled motorcycle which weighed only about a third of the M.G. record-breaker.

In 1949 honour was regained when Goldie Gardner once again took the car to Belgium and raised the 500cc kilometre record from the

128.85mph (207.38kph) set by Taruffi to 154.9mph (249.28kph). This time a new crankshaft had been made allowing him to use just three of the engine's six cylinders. By this time the chassis, which had started life as a K3 racing car, was nearly 16 years old and the basic engine design was even older, which makes the speeds obtained all the more remarkable. Encouraged by this success, the engine was further modified for an attempt on the 350cc records in 1950. Using just two of the six cylinders, and with the car's final drive ratio reduced to help this tiny engine propel a car weighing nearly a ton, the kilometre record was raised to an impressive 120.394mph (193.75kph).

XPAG Engine Records

Interesting though these records were, they had little relevance to the average M.G. customer for the TD Midget or Y-type saloon. To demonstrate that the engines fitted to these cars could also be tuned for record-breaking, the factory modified a couple of TD engines and took them, and the old record-breaker, to the Salt Lake at Utah in America for Goldie Gardner to attempt to set new national and international records in the 1250cc class. The less highly tuned engine set the longer distance records at speeds between 127.8mph (205.7kph) for 50 kilometres and 139.3mph (224.18kph) for 200 kilometres. The more highly tuned engine was fitted for the high speed attempts but, though runs at over 190mph (306kph) were made, unfortunately the timing equipment failed. By the time this had been mended, the rains came and flooded the salt pan, forcing the team to return home. As a bonus, however, in between the runs with the record car a standard TD Mark II from a local dealer's showroom had been used to set a number of American records for "stock" – that is standard production cars, which was to be useful in their advertising campaign. Following this expedition the old record-breaker was bought by the factory from Goldie Gardner and now forms part of the collection of historic vehicles on display in the Heritage Motor Centre museum at Gaydon, in Warwickshire.

Following the retirement of Goldie Gardner and EX135 from record attempts, that giant amongst record-breakers, George Eyston, persuaded the factory of the need to return to Utah for another record attempt so as to obtain more publicity for the marque. A new car was built, EX179, and a couple of the enlarged T-type engines – the XPEG units that were to power the TF 1500 – were prepared. The idea was to use any new records achieved as publicity for the revised TF, and the successful Californian driver Ken Miles joined George Eyston on the salt flats. The first engine installed was tuned for endurance, and records ranging from 250 kilometres to 12 hours were taken at speeds around 120mph (193kph). The more highly tuned "sprint" unit was then fitted and Ken Miles did a flying ten-mile lap at 150.69mph (242.51kph) – a tremendous feat for a car powered by an unsupercharged T-type engine and evidence to American enthusiasts of the potential of this engine.

Above: The ZB Varitone model. The two-tone paintwork and larger rear window make these cars look quite different. This car is owned by Eric Nicholls. Unlike the Varitone, ordinary ZBs had straight chrome strips above the front wheels, rather than the curved ones fitted to ZAs.

Right: A photograph of one of the most attractive showroom posters ever produced for an M.G. The slogan "Safety Fast M.G. in airsmoothed style" was also used in the advertising brochures for the ZA.

The little Y-type saloon had proved a popular model that earned new friends for the marque around the world. By 1953, however, it was looking more than a little out of date and a replacement was called for. A talented BMC designer, Gerald Palmer, had drawn up a streamlined four-door saloon which had a one-piece chassis-cum-body monocoque shell and was fitted with the old XP series 1250cc engine. This was to be the Y-type replacement but a last-minute policy change within BMC saw it being launched in 1952 as the Wolseley 4/44. An M.G. version was finally announced in October 1953, alongside the TD replacement – the TF. Initially enthusiasts saw this new car, called the Magnette, as nothing more than a badge-engineered successor to a famous name but it proved to be a worthy bearer of the octagon.

Unlike its Wolseley badged cousin which was built at Cowley, the ZA Magnette, as it was to become known, was assembled at Abingdon, and differed also in being fitted with the 1500cc B-series BMC engine. This unit was the first to emerge from the rationalization carried out after the merger between Austin and Morris in 1952

and was based on an Austin design. It proved to be a simple and reliable engine that went on to power the MGA and MGB with the capacity being progressively increased to 1800cc. Although they appeared similar, the differences between the 4/44 and Z Magnette were not confined to the power unit. The body shell was changed to give the M.G. rounded sills and modified rear wings, and a different suspension allowed the car to sit lower on the road.

The engine, gearbox and back axle were from the Austin-derived BMC designs, and the suspension was by coil spring and wishbones at the front and half-elliptic leaf springs and torque arm at the rear. As a departure from previous M.G. practice telescopic, rather than lever arm, dampers were fitted. The resulting car was modern, comfortable and handled well, and in addition the 1500cc engine gave it good performance for a 1953 saloon car of this size.

The introduction of a thoroughly modern saloon to the Abingdon production lines alongside the old T-series Midgets once again showed the need to build a more up-to-date sports car. Time, indeed, for the new MGA.

In Britain's principal export market, the United States, the demand for foreign sports cars was primarily met by the TC and TD M.G.s. These later competed with the Triumph TR range, and the Austin-Healey, with Jaguars or the more expensive offerings from Aston Martin, Mercedes-Benz and Porsche vying for the wealthier customers. The T-type M.G.s had sold well, in far greater numbers than any previous M.G., but by the time the TF was announced in 1953 it was obvious that a completely new and more modern car was called for. The arrival in the showrooms, at the same time as the new TF, of the sleek, modern Z Magnette must have made M.G. sports car enthusiasts crave something a bit more up-to-date.

The team of development engineers in the newly re-assembled department at Abingdon did not have to start with a clean sheet of paper when the new sports car was proposed. A suitable chassis for the new car had been designed by Roy Brocklehurst in the early 1950s when it was realized that the TD-based chassis used on a special Le Mans car built for George Phillips had certain limitations. Although the shape of the bodywork on that car resembles the later MGA, the chassis rails were set too close together for the driver to sit between them, and the seating position was thus higher than desirable. The Brocklehurst-designed chassis was used in EX175, built to make an attempt on some speed records. However, the body shape proved unsuitable and in the event another car, EX179, was constructed for the record attempts.

Cars For Le Mans

Once the M.G. team were given permission to develop a new car, it was to EX175 that the design office at Abingdon turned. A very tight timetable was set to get it into production as it was decided to enter a team of three cars in the 1955 Le Mans 24 Hour race to publicize the new MGA. Actually, the process of turning a development car into a production model took rather longer than anticipated and the three cars entered in the race had to be described as prototypes – EX182s – rather than production models. At Le Mans, which was marred by the worst accident in motor-racing history, two of the M.G.s finished, one in 12th place overall and the other 17th. The third car, driven by Dick Jacobs, was involved in a very bad crash; he was so seriously injured that he was lucky to survive and never raced again.

As a publicity exercise for the new car the event was something of a let-down as there was, as yet, no car ready for the public to buy. However, some motoring journalists were aware of its imminent arrival and had the chance to drive one of the Le Mans cars. In a report of this drive they commented on the interest the car drew whenever it was parked and that it was obvious that the production version was eagerly awaited.

The new car, which would be called the M.G. Series MGA, was a development of the previous models rather than completely new. As already mentioned, the chassis was a redesign of the TD

PUBLICATION No. 5555 H & E

First *of a new lin*

THE COMPLETELY NEW MG SERIES MGA

chassis with the side rails moved further apart to allow the occupants to sit between rather than on them. The front suspension and rack-and-pinion steering from the TD/TF were retained, although the detail design of the components changed, and at the rear the chassis rails still swept over the leaf-spring-suspended rear axle. This axle was similar to that used in the Z Magnette, rather than the earlier design fitted to the TD/TF. Like the ZA, the new car had the sturdy and reliable 1500cc B-series engine. For the MGA the Magnette gearbox was retained, but a remote gear lever assembly was fitted.

The most noticeable feature, its striking aerodynamic body, was evolved directly from the styling of the Le Mans TD and the later EX175. It is remarkable how closely the production car followed the shape of the experimental one. There is no doubt that had the development of the car been less rushed there may have been the temptation to go for a combined chassis/body monocoque design, like the Magnette, and at the Cowley design studio at least one mock-up of such a car had been built in the early 1950s which had been considerably lighter than the MGA proved to be.

The separate chassis and body were obviously more expensive to produce than a single unit but initial tooling costs were less, development time shorter, and production could follow the traditional Abingdon procedure without major upheavals. As with all previous M.G. sports cars, the chassis, running gear and mechanical components could be assembled first, before the completed and trimmed bodies were lowered onto the chassis from the upper deck. The bodies arrived on transporters ready painted and finished, and with the hoods and sidescreens in place. At the factory the dashboard was installed

Left: The modern shape of the MGA was a radical change from the traditional look of the T-series cars that preceded it. The advertising campaign to sell the new car stressed that it was "First of a new line" and this theme was maintained for the showroom displays mounted by dealers around the world to launch the new model. This picture is of the front cover of one of many MGA sales brochures of similar design issued between 1955 and 1958.

Safety MG fast!

Above: A showroom poster to publicize the record-breaking runs on the salt lake in Utah. EX181 has a tubular chassis, MGA-based independent front suspension with rack and pinion steering and a narrow-track De Dion rear axle fitted with a single disc brake. 14in (356mm) wheels and low-profile tyres are used. The supercharged, 1500cc, twin overhead-camshaft engine is mounted behind the driver. The shape of the streamlined body was developed in a wind tunnel using models.

Left: In August 1957 Stirling Moss in EX181 took five international 1500cc flying-start speed records for distances between 1km and 10km. The car travelled at speeds of up to 245.64mph (395.3kph) on the salt lake at Utah. The attempt very nearly had to be abandoned after a freak storm had flooded the surface of the salt. Luckily this dried enough for runs to be made in less than ideal conditions just before the end of the record-breaking session.

before they were lowered onto the rolling chassis that had been piped, wired and had even had the carpets fitted.

The name MGA was chosen for the new car to replace the term Midget, which had been used by M.G.s since 1929, to reflect just how much the car had grown up over the years. The engine size had gone up from 850cc to 1500cc and the car's length from just over 10 feet to 13 (3048 to 3963mm), hardly a small car now. Also, having reached the designation Z-type with the Magnette a year or so previously, there was not much else they could do but start again at the beginning of the alphabet.

The MGA Is Announced

On the 22nd September, 1955 the new M.G. sports car was announced to the public. Journalists had already been let loose in a production car and their road-test reports made the point that the racing and record-breaking activities of The M.G. Car Company had helped development and that the differences between the Le Mans car and the production car were small. They were impressed by the performance and recorded a best time to 70mph (113kph) of around 21 seconds, which they thought was commendable for a car with a full load on board. Interestingly the highest speed recorded, 99mph (159kph), was achieved with the hood and sidescreens in place and was some 3mph (4.8kph) faster than that reached by the same car fitted with the optional low racing screen and with a tonneau cover over the passenger side of the cockpit.

It was important that it was well received in America and luckily when the prestigious magazine "Road and Track" was given a car to test it was equally impressed, particularly when com-

1957 MGA 1500 COUPÉ

With the launch of the MGA in 1955, M.G. produced a car that was both thoroughly modern and stunningly attractive to look at. Although it was radically different visually from previous models, under the skin the separate chassis and the suspension owed much to the superseded TD and TF Midgets, while the engine, gearbox and rear axle were standard British Motor Corporation components. The even prettier closed MGA Coupés appeared some eighteen months after the open cars were announced.

Left: Although the MGA had the advantage of a separate luggage compartment, this was too small for many owners, and the makers of suitable externally-mounted luggage racks did good business. The tool kit supplied with the MGA was more comprehensive than for subsequent models.

Below: The exterior door handles on the MGA Coupé were cunningly designed not to spoil the uncluttered lines of the bodywork.

Above: The interior of the closed MGAs was more luxuriously finished than the roadsters. Right from the start, the dashboard was fabric-covered – a feature that appeared only on the Twin Cam and on 1600 Mark ll open cars. The dashboard panel itself was of a slightly different shape. The pattern of the leather seat covers was changed and all the floor and rear section was carpeted, usually in grey.

SPECIFICATION

Model: MGA 1500 coupé

Engine: Four-cylinder in line, overhead valve, water cooled. 73.025 x 89mm, 1489cc, 72bhp at 5500rpm

Gearbox: Four-speed with synchromesh on three higher ratios

Final drive: 4.3:1. Top gear 17.3mph/1000rpm (28kph/1000rpm)

Suspension: Front: Independent with coil springs, wishbones and rack and pinion steering. Rear: Live axle suspended on half-elliptic leaf springs

Dimensions: Wheelbase 7ft 10in (2388mm). Track, front 3ft 11.9in (1217mm), rear 4ft 0.9in (1242mm). Overall length 13ft 0in (3963mm)

Unladen weight: 18.5cwt (940kg)

Cost when new: £724 plus £363.7s.0d. purchase tax

Performance: (From contemporary reports): Top speed 101mph (163kph)

Owner: Chris Alderson

Right: This angle shows best the "wrap-around" rear window, and the quarter-lights and winding windows in the doors. The fixed steel roof had light-coloured headlining and neat trim panels around the door openings.

Above left and right: Chris Alderson has owned this beautiful car since 1982 when he fell in love with it while judging the MGA class in the concours d'elegance at a meeting. So taken with the car was he, that there and then he told the owner that he would like to buy it should it ever be on the market. Luckily, he was offered the car shortly afterwards and, apart from having been re-sprayed – twice – to cure micro-blistering of the paintwork, it has needed little attention since and continues to give him considerable pleasure.

Left: Lighting was modified as regulations changed. The 1500 sidelights doubled as direction indicators, but later cars had separate, orange indicators placed within a section of the sidelights.

Right: Steel disc wheels and hub caps were standard on the 1500, wire wheels were optional. On late 1500 models, the design changed slightly to give space for the planned 1600 disc brakes.

Above: The Austin-designed BMC B-series engine is a strong and reliable unit. Given that the 1500 MGA has only drum brakes, power output is sufficient for most owners and on test the Coupé just topped 100mph (161kph). The square box with eight terminals on the rear bulkhead is the relay for the flashing indicators, showing this to be a 1500. Also, the coil was not dynamo-mounted on most later cars.

Below: The carpeted area behind the seats provides a small amount of room for possessions. However the spare wheel protrudes into this a little and on the 1600 the wheel was moved back to be completely within the luggage compartment. Also, the rear shelf below the window was cut back and these changes give enough room for a small suitcase. The batteries are on each side of the rear axle, under the rear compartment.

pared with the performance of the superseded TF. The magazine was surprised by just how much the top speed had increased bearing in mind the similar weight and power output for the two cars. An increase of over 10mph (16kph) in top speed was recorded, which it attributed to the lower drag body and better overall gearing. Test equipment showed a reduction in drag of 21 per cent at 60mph (97kph) which is a considerable saving and fully justified the adoption of the radically new body style.

Public reaction to the new car was equally enthusiastic. Of course, those who ran the earlier models bemoaned the scrapping of the familiar M.G. design, but few of them would have passed up the opportunity of changing to one of the new cars had they been able to afford it. To enthusiasts the car had, indeed it still has, almost universal appeal. The attractive cockpit layout had comfortable leather-covered seats set low between the perimeter chassis rails, and a large steering wheel placed exactly right for most drivers to feel immediately at home. The short gear lever, too, was well sited and the haphazard arrangement of dials and switches soon became familiar. Even that throwback from previous M.G.s, the dashboard-mounted horn button, was conveniently placed. The self-cancelling flashing direction indicators, first introduced on some TDs and all TFs, were operated by a switch which was placed close to the steering wheel rim. Leg room was adequate for all but the tallest drivers and the high cockpit sides, with leather-covered cappings, gave a feeling of security to passenger and driver alike.

Stowing The Hood

Although not as simple to operate as later hood designs, the stowage arrangement does have the advantage of completely concealing the hood when it is packed away. The collapsed frame, complete with the hood itself and the windscreen header rail, folds down under the rear deck. This does slightly restrict the rearward seat adjustment for taller drivers and later in the production run the system was modified to move the hood frame further back, and to allow the sidescreens to be stowed above the rear bulkhead rather than between it and the back of the seats.

In September, 1956, to cater for those wanting all the comforts of a closed saloon and the appeal of a two-seater sports car, a coupé version was announced. This had an integral steel roof incorporating a wrap-around rear window and a larger and more curved windscreen. The doors were completely redesigned and featured winding windows and swivelling quarter-lights. They were lockable and, for the first time on an MGA, had exterior door handles. These handles were very neat and rested on rubbers set into the window frame when the door was closed – the designers could not bring themselves to spoil the lines of the MGA by adding conventional handles. At first only the left-hand door had an exterior door lock – even on right-hand-drive cars!

The interior was differently and more luxuriously trimmed with a covered dashboard and a

map pocket in the foot well. The roof had headlining and the entire floor area, even the rear bulkhead and shelf, were carpeted – usually in grey. The new body style was welcomed by the motoring press who found that, in spite of a slight increase in weight of about 32lb (14.5kg), the top speed was higher and the Coupé was a genuine 100mph (161kph) car. The heat in the cabin on hot days was criticized, as was the shortage of luggage space; this latter failing was usually addressed by fitting the optional luggage rack.

Sports cars are all about speed as well as style and although the MGA was sufficiently fast to satisfy the average buyer, there were always customers looking for cars with more performance. For them, the factory had been working ever

since the MGA was first launched on a higher performance model. Prototypes of two different versions of twin-overhead-camshaft B-series engines had been tested. In 1957 a brand new record-breaking car, EX181, was fitted with a twin-camshaft version of the B-series engine for an attempt on the 1500cc international records still held by Goldie Gardner and the pre-war M.G. record-breaker, EX135.

MGA Twin Cam

Driven by Stirling Moss the new car broke five records for the 1 kilometre to 10 kilometre distances at speeds of around 240mph (386kph). Following the successes gained with this engine it was no surprise when the MGA Twin Cam was announced as a production car in 1958. The modifications for the new model were mostly mechanical with the body appearing almost unchanged, although there were a number of detail changes to the metalwork not immediately apparent.

The higher performance Twin Cam could be distinguished immediately from the standard car both by the discreet "Twin Cam" badges on the boot lid and alongside the scuttle vents, and by the standard centre-lock Dunlop steel wheels. These wheels hid the other main distinguishing feature of a Twin Cam, the replacement of the standard Lockheed drum brakes by the Dunlop all-disc set up similar to that then fitted by Jaguar to their sports cars.

In addition to the mechanical changes, the cockpit received a rexine-covered dashboard and a different speedometer and rev. counter, and the option of more heavily padded "competition" seats. It is a popular misconception that all Twin Cams had these seats, whereas at first very few were so equipped. To add to the usual long list of extras on the standard cars, the Twin Cam was also available with an oil cooler and close ratio gearbox. In addition there was the option of a 4.55:1 rear axle ratio which was also available on the pushrod car.

The extra cost of the Twin Cam over the standard 1500 was just £180 but the performance model did have some drawbacks. Journalists found the car noisier and with a considerably greater thirst for oil, and there is no doubt that the car was more suited to the competition driver than for use on shopping trips. However, many were sold to ordinary buyers, especially abroad, and were used in heavy traffic and in ways for which they were not suited. Add to this a network of dealers whose expertise with this type of car was limited, and it was not surprising that problems arose.

These difficulties reached such a pitch that Nuffield Exports, who were responsible for the servicing in overseas markets, employed an engineer, R.G. (Bob) Seymour, to visit dealerships in Eire, the United States and in Canada. He had received considerable training on the engine and in the light of his findings on the visits he made, some changes to the design were carried out. When investigating a complaint from a dealer or customer he employed a standard test procedure which involved establishing

Above: An MGA 1600 roadster in Iris Blue with the standard steel wheels. With the marque facing increasing opposition in the world sports-car market, the greater power provided by the larger-capacity engine, and the fitting of disc brakes to the front wheels, helped to maintain sales.

Left and right: On the MGA 1600, and on later Twin Cam MGAs, larger front sidelights were fitted that had separate segments for the lights and the flashing indicators. At the rear, the stop/tail light and the flashing direction indicator lights were mounted on plinths on the rear wings.

"A racing car for the road" sums up the MGA Twin Cam. Standard MGA 1500s provided adequate performance for most buyers, but there were always those who wanted more. Right from the first MGA, the factory had in mind a higher powered version and, following some competition experience, the company was ready in 1958 to launch the new car as an additional model. With only 2111 Twin Cam MGAs built, today they are one of the most desirable M.G. models and worth considerably more than standard MGAs.

Above: The ideal place to enjoy open motoring! The cockpit of the MGA is comfortable and the high doors, and the driver's close proximity to the windscreen, provide more protection in cold weather than some open cars. The competition deluxe seats fitted to this car were an optional extra on the Twin Cam and also, later, on the 1600 model. All Twin Cam dashboards were fabric covered. Top speed of the car was increased with the hood and sidescreens erected. For owners who preferred not to be in too close a proximity to the elements, the Twin Cam was also available with the coupé body.

Below: This picture shows just how streamlined the MGA is, with almost nothing to mar the purity of its shape. No major changes to the basic design were carried out during its life and the last car built in 1962 is visually almost identical to the first built in 1955. The Twin Cam production run lasted from 1958 to 1960 with this car being built in 1959.

Above: The extra bulk of the Twin Cam engine makes access for routine servicing difficult but the polished camshaft covers look most impressive. Panels were provided under the wings on all but the first few cars to aid access to some items. For reliable running with lower octane fuels, on later cars the compression ratio was lowered from 9.9:1 to 8.3:1, but Geoff Barron has higher compression pistons in this car. The radiator header tank is positioned alongside the wing with a separate pressure release valve to the rear of it.

Above: The traditional slatted M.G. radiator grille had to be totally redesigned to allow it to blend with the streamlined MGA body. The badge sits on a chromed, shaped pressing similar to those used on earlier M.G.s.

Right: Luggage space was always at a premium on the MGA as the spare wheel, tools and stowed hood took most of the available space. There is no exterior boot handle, but a pull behind the seats, under the rear deck, releases the catch. The spare wheel is concealed by the cover seen lifted here.

Above left and right: When Geoff Barron bought this car in 1990 the body was split into two pieces and it had been further damaged by having the engine dropped on the front! The cost of the wreck was a very good standard MGA he had previously restored but, nevertheless, he had obtained a car which was basically sound and suitable for restoration. The result of his labours is one of the best Twin Cams in the UK.

Right: The sidescreens supplied with the open early Twin Cams had a lower lifting signalling flap but here the later sliding panel sidescreen is fitted. These stow in pockets in a hood cover that hangs from the rear deck behind the seats.

Above: The rear lights on this 1500-based Twin Cam serve both as side and brake lights and as flashing indicators. The fuel cap is released by pressing its lever.

Right: Twin Cam badges were placed alongside the vents on each side of the bonnet and below the M.G. badge on the boot lid.

SPECIFICATION

Model: MGA Twin Cam

Engine: Four-cylinder in line, twin overhead camshaft, water cooled. 75.4 x 89mm, 1588cc, 108bhp with 9.9:1 compression ratio (later reduced to 100bhp with 8.3: compression)

Gearbox: Four-speed with synchromesh on three higher ratios

Final drive: 4.3:1. Top gear 17.3mph/1000rpm (28kph/1000rpm)

Suspension: Front: Independent with coil springs, wishbones and rack and pinion steering. Rear: Live axle suspended on half-elliptic leaf springs

Dimensions: Wheelbase 7ft 10in (2388mm). Track, front 3ft 11.9in (1217mm), rear 4ft 0.9in (1242mm). Overall length 13ft 0in (3963mm)

Unladen weight: 19.4cwt (986kg)

Cost when new: £843 plus £422.17s.0d. purchase tax

Performance: (From contemporary reports): Top speed 115mph (185kph)

Owner: Geoff Barron

the conditions under which the vehicle operated, the state of tune and whether this was in accordance with factory specifications, and whether all the recommended service modifications had been carried out. Often he would strip and rebuild the engine before setting it up properly, but in spite of all this work he recalls that it was often impossible to get some cars to idle evenly. The idle was usually "lumpy" and the engines sometimes stalled after a short while at idle. Some cars continued to give trouble and where an owner complained enough they apparently were offered a free change to a pushrod engine.

Later modification to the design, which in all honesty should have been incorporated from the outset, improved matters but not before the reputation of the Twin Cam had been for ever sullied and the standing of M.G. in general tarnished by the problems.

The standard MGA received a much needed update in 1959 to enable it to meet increasing competition. The Twin Cam had featured a larger capacity, 1588cc, engine and this was achieved by increasing the bore from 73 to 75mm. This change was now carried over to the pushrod car and thus raised the power by 7.5bhp and the torque by 12 per cent. As the axle and gear ratios were unchanged, this gave a welcome boost to the performance.

By 1959 disc brakes were becoming the desirable feature that anti-lock brakes have been in recent years. Triumph had them on the TR2 and

the recently announced Sunbeam Alpine was also so equipped, as well as pointing the way to future sports cars with wind-up windows and comfortable cockpit. M.G., therefore, had to do something with the MGA brakes and they fitted discs to the front wheels. This time, unlike the Twin Cam, they chose Lockheed equipment but, as drums were retained for the rear, there were none of the hand-brake problems often associated with all-disc set ups.

MGA 1600

The appearance of the 1600 was little different to the 1500 it replaced. Changes in legislation, outlawing the previous system of interrupting the brake light circuit to flash the rear lamps as turn indicators, forced the company to fit separate amber flashers at the rear and to provide an amber segment in the front side lights. At the rear the existing brake/side lights were mounted on plinths with the new amber flashers. The bodywork had "1600" badges on the boot lid and scuttle in the same positions as those occupied by the "Twin Cam" badges.

Some new colour schemes were adopted and the previous hood colours, including black, were dropped in favour of grey, beige or light blue to

tone with the exterior colour. At the same time the side screens were changed to incorporate sliding windows in place of signalling flaps. The Twin Cam was still in production when the 1600 was announced and the later cars received the external changes to colours, trim and lighting introduced on the pushrod cars. Incidentally, when the Twin Cam was introduced the bonnet had to be modified to allow it to clear the slightly bulkier engine, and in due course all MGAs were fitted with the modified bonnet.

The changes to the coupé versions of both models also included a repositioning of the spare wheel. On the 1500 this was mounted, as on the roadster, with part of it protruding into the cabin. As a consequence the rear shelf below the window was fairly deep but with little room to store anything much behind the seats. On the 1600 the wheel was repositioned entirely within the boot and the shelf below the window was cut

Below: An MGA 1600 Mark II Coupé. On the Mark II cars the bars on the radiator grille were recessed at the bottom, a change not liked by some.

Right: The rear lights and flashing indicators of a Mark II car. Units taken from the Mini, mounted on plinths, fit on the rear panel.

Above, right and below: Trimmed MGA bodies arrived at Abingdon on trucks and were loaded onto the top deck of the assembly building. Here electrical equipment, dashboards, etc. were installed before the bodies were lowered down onto rolling chassis. On the ground floor, the body and chassis were bolted together and the final assembly completed prior to a full road test being carried out.

back far enough to provide stowage for a medium-sized suitcase.

The improvements that came with the 1600 certainly helped sales and in 1959 over 23,000 MGAs were sold, the greatest number for any single year. In the following year sales fell to just under 17,000 and it was obvious that the now aging design needed replacing. The Sunbeam Alpine, with its winding windows, was proving increasingly popular, and with Triumph poised to introduce the much improved TR4 at the 1961 Motor Show something had to be done. As a stop-gap, whilst a completely new car was designed, Abingdon introduced the final version of the MGA in June 1961. The most significant external changes were to the lights and grille. The rear light clusters were replaced by combined side/stop and indicator lights "borrowed" from the BMC Mini-Minor, and these were mounted on plinths on the rear panel rather than on the wings. The changes to the grille meant that the vertical slats were now recessed at the bottom – this in some eyes spoilt the lines of the front of the car. In the cockpit the dashboard received the same style of fabric covering previously reserved for the Twin Cam, and the top of the scuttle was covered to remove reflection from it in the windscreen on light coloured cars. Although these were small changes, the cockpit looked much better for them. To record the change of model "1600 Mk II" badges were fixed to the boot and scuttle in place of the previous "1600" badges.

A More Powerful Engine

These cosmetic changes are, however, only part of the story. The most important changes, and the ones that make the Mark II probably the best of the MGAs, were under the skin. The engine capacity was increased from 1588cc to 1622cc and it was substantially redesigned internally. Changes to the width of the main bearings allowed for a stiffer and sturdier crankshaft. The pistons and con-rods were redesigned, as was the cylinder head. Much work was carried out reshaping the combustion chambers and the valve sizes were increased. The effect of the

changes was to raise the power output to 90bhp at 5500rpm which compares favourably with the Twin Cam output of 107bhp at the higher engine speed of 6500rpm. As the later Twin Cams had their power output reduced to 100bhp by a lowering of the compression ratio then you can see that the Mark II is potentially almost as fast in normal driving, as opposed to competition driving when higher engine speeds are used as a matter of course.

However, the final change made for the Mark II, the adoption of a higher axle ratio of 4.1:1 meant that acceleration was not quite as quick as the extra power would suggest. The higher ratio does give more relaxed cruising at motorway speeds and is certainly recommended for travel-

Left: The Mark I Austin-Healey Sprite had a one-piece steel front that lifted to reveal the BMC 948cc A-series engine. Although this produced a modest power output, the combination of light weight and superb handling and roadholding make the Sprite an enjoyable car to drive, especially on winding country roads.

Below: Although many criticized the appearance of these cars when they were new, currently the Mark I is the most highly-priced of all versions of the popular Sprite/Midget range. This late Mark I Sprite is owned by Laura Peaple.

ling long distances. In may ways the last MGA was also the best – which cannot be said of most cars. Fortunately the basic design was not spoilt by external changes and, apart from the modified grille on the Mark II, a 1962 car looks almost identical to the first 1500s built in 1955.

In the 1950s M.G. faced competition in the sports car market from a number of other manufacturers, including Austin-Healeys that were also built by BMC – first at Longbridge and then alongside the M.G.s at Abingdon. The Austin-Healey 100, and later the 100/6 and 3000 models, were always fitted with larger engines than the current M.G.s, and were thus more costly, but Leonard Lord, the head of the corporation, always harboured the ambition to market an Austin-badged sports model at a lower price. In 1956 Donald and Geoffrey Healey, and the team at their premises in Warwick, started working on designs for such a small, and affordably priced, sports car. The advantages of working with a small, close-knit team immediately became apparent, with designs for the new model being drawn up and produced in a very short space of time.

The Affordable Sprite

The car, to be called the Austin-Healey Sprite, was based around the engine, gearbox and front suspension components from the popular, small Austin A35 saloon. To save both weight and cost, the chassis and body were to be produced as a single unit – a first for a British Motor Corporation sports car. The strength of the basic chassis was centred around a boxed scuttle structure, deep section, boxed sills and rigid prop-shaft tunnel. The triumph of the basic chassis design was its light weight and rigidity which gave the car good performance from engines of modest power output combined with a virtual absence of scuttle shake on bumpy roads – a failing of many an open car.

Like the chassis, the body design was kept as simple as possible. The rear section had pleasing, rounded lines but no external access to the luggage compartment was provided. The front wings and bonnet were joined as a single, rear-hinged unit which, when raised, gave excellent

access to the engine and front suspension. The headlights were set in pods on top of the bonnet and it is this unusual styling feature that has given the car the universal nickname of "Frog-eyed Sprite". The rear suspension was unusual as quarter-elliptic springs were used which gave the car a firm ride allied to a small degree of rear-end steering as the axle deflected under weight transfer on corners. The Morris Minor rack-and-pinion steering gear had been adopted and the result was a car that delighted enthusiasts with its nimble handling and quick response to the steering wheel.

The Sprite was built at Abingdon alongside the MGA and Z Magnette, and much of the final development work to get the car into production was undertaken by the Abingdon Development Department. The car was an immediate sales success but was only sold through Austin dealers – as yet there was no M.G. version. Initially the building of the new car was not without its problems. Whilst the first batch of cars was being run down the line some of the pre-production cars were being tested. It was standard procedure at Abingdon to run a 500-mile (800km) test over the rough "pavé" section of the test track and this revealed that the cars started to break up and bend at a point just behind the rear door pillar. There was nothing else to do but reverse the assembly procedure for the cars built so far so that the monocoque body tubs could have reinforcing sections welded in to strengthen the rear section. Although this modification was costly and time-consuming to do, it was infinitely preferable to having one of the cars loaned to a journalist start to come apart!

Attractive though the Sprite was, the heavy one-piece bonnet and lack of external access to the luggage compartment was not appreciated

by all, and some cars were modified to overcome these shortcomings. This was not lost on the management and an updated model was planned for introduction in 1961. At the same time it was decided that there should be an M.G. version so that dealers could have a lower-priced car to sell alongside the MGA. The changes when the Mark II Austin-Healey Sprite was announced were mainly to the bodywork and they radically changed the appearance of the car. The idiosyncratic "frog-eyed" head-lamps were changed for conventionally placed units in the front wings which were themselves now fixed, so only the bonnet panel was hinged. At the rear, the wing line was changed to incorporate small fins and with separate access to the luggage compartment.

Although the cockpit, seats and trim were virtually the same, and the engine and gearbox received only minor modifications, the changes to the body produced a much more practical car that was only slightly heavier than the model it replaced. The M.G. version when it arrived was called the Midget – reviving the name used for all the small pre-war four-cylinder sports cars. The 948cc A-series BMC engine used for the Sprite and Midget made it the first under-one-litre M.G. since 1936 but nevertheless gave the car good performance at a low price.

The Post-war Midget

The Sprite and Midget were mechanically identical – indeed they were built on the same production line – however, the Midget was more highly priced than the Sprite. The cosmetic changes made to justify the greater cost included a slatted M.G. radiator grille, side chrome strips and a better standard of interior trim. There was also a different range of colours to choose from and even, initially, a differently styled hardtop. The Healey family were still much involved with the Sprite and offered owners of these cars a number of tuning and chassis modifications from their factory and showrooms at Warwick.

Although no one was fooled into regarding it as anything other than a re-badged Sprite, the new Midget was well received by press and public. However, as the Sprite was built at Abingdon, and much of the re-design work was done there, it was really almost as much of an M.G. as any of the other cars they built. The arrival of the Midget coincided with the announcement of the revised MGA 1600 Mk ll, but that model was shortly due for replacement and work on a new sports car, which was going to be called the MGB, was speedily advancing in the Abingdon Development Department.

Developing an entirely new car is a long process and work on the MGA replacement had commenced as early as 1957. The Italian stylist, Frua, designed a new body for an MGA 1500 chassis he was given, and the result was sent to Abingdon for assessment. The car produced bore more than a passing resemblance to other Italian sports cars of the period – like the Maserati 3500GT – with an abundance of chrome trim and the "wrap-around" windscreen so popular on American cars at that time. Drawings

were produced, and both hard-top and GT versions were considered, but the car was really both too heavy and too expensive to produce to be a real contender and the one prototype built was destroyed to avoid paying the government any import duty.

There were a number of in-house proposals for replacement bodies for the existing chassis but these equally suffered from similar weight and cost shortcomings and eventually Syd Enever decided that the new car would have to be of monocoque design in spite of the inevitable

Above: The Italian stylist, Frua, designed this MGA replacement using an MGA 1500 chassis. The wrap-around windscreen and the excess of chrome at the front are in tune with the styling of many other 1950s cars. The proposal was rejected by M.G. as being too heavy and too expensive to build. The car was subsequently cut up under the watchful gaze of customs officials.

Right: To gain publicity, in the 1950s and 1960s the BMC Competition Department entered MGAs, Magnettes, Midgets and MGBs in rallies and races. At that time, the Le Mans twenty-four hour race always attracted enormous attention and any success gained could be exploited to help sell cars. Although they were never in contention for overall victory, the MGB scored a number of creditable results. In 1964 an MGB, BMO 541B, was entered. The engine was modified to stage 5 in the factory tuning booklet, using parts available to any owner, and a non-standard streamlined nose section fitted to improve aerodynamics. The drivers were Paddy Hopkirk and Andrew Hedges. The car performed reliably and was placed 19th overall at an average speed of 99.9mph (161kph). They collected the "Motor" trophy for the best performance by an all-British car and crew.

higher tooling costs. The project was now given a new experimental number, EX 214, and work on the design started with a clean sheet of paper. Released from the constraints of using the old chassis design, the wheelbase of the new car was to be shorter than that of the MGA by three inches (76mm) but was to retain the tried and tested Issigonis coil spring and wishbone independent front suspension, while on the rear he decided to try out a system using coil springs with trailing radius arms and a Panhard rod.

The initial designs for a new body on the old

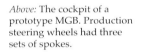

Above: The cockpit of a prototype MGB. Production steering wheels had three sets of spokes.

Above right: Early American market MGB. The large numbers sold there ensured the survival of the marque.

chassis had featured a rounded shape at the front influenced by the EX181 record car and the shape of the existing MGA. For the MGB the length of the bodywork ahead of the front wheels was reduced with the traditional slatted M.G. grille being mounted vertically and the headlamps slightly inset into the front wings. This change both reduced the overall length of the car and improved its appearance, although the inches removed were later added on again when heavy impact absorbing bumpers were fitted in 1974 to comply with American legislation.

Unfortunately, development and handling problems forced the abandonment of the coil sprung rear suspension, and the traditional half-elliptic leaf springs and live axle were adopted for production. Actually finding sufficient money to meet the huge tooling costs of the body was causing Abingdon some difficulties. Pressed Steel were asked for an estimate but when this was received it proved to be rather more than the budget would meet. Fortunately for generations of MGB owners, a deal was worked out that halved the initial tooling costs in exchange for a higher unit cost for each bodyshell. As the MGB was in production for rather longer than the five to six years originally envisaged, this must have proved more than profitable to Pressed Steel in the long run.

Although other power units were considered, once again cost restraints decreed that the MGA B-series engine in its modified 1622cc form was

Above: Steel disc wheels are fitted with whitewall tyres on this left-hand-drive MGB. Early cars like this have pull-handle door handles but these were replaced in 1965 by the push-button type.

Right: By the time this 1965 car was built, the MGB engine had been modified. Originally it closely resembled the MGA unit, with three main bearings, but in 1964 it was substantially redesigned, gaining a five-bearing crankshaft and many other minor changes.

to power the new car. At a late stage the capacity was enlarged to 1789cc, by increasing the bore size, which gave a power output of around 95bhp – sufficient to make the MGB a genuine 100mph (161kph) car. The gearbox was a standard British Motor Corporation unit but was available with the option of an overdrive, which was particularly useful now that motorways were becoming common. For some years there had been a tendency for road wheel sizes to be reduced and the MGB was fitted with 14-inch rims in place of the 15-inch fitted to the MGA. Once again wire wheels were an option which was to prove popular, especially with the customers in overseas markets.

The most attractive feature was the cockpit. The unitary construction had enabled the designers to give the occupants a lot more room

Above: The Mark III Magnette was closely related to the Morris Oxford and Austin Cambridge. The twin-carburettor, 1489cc engine produced 68bhp.

Above: The Mark IV M.G. Magnette was introduced in October 1961. The wheelbase was longer and the track wider than the Mark III; engine capacity was 1622cc.

than was available in the MGA. There was sufficient leg and head room for even the tallest although, in order to reduce drag, the windscreen height was set at the minimum allowed by United States regulations. This was retained throughout the life of the roadsters although the GT, when it arrived in 1965, was given a taller windscreen. Comfort was given a higher priority and no longer did the M.G. driver have to struggle to fit separate side screens in wet weather. The winding side windows and swivelling front windows fitted to the doors brought the MGB in

line with its competitors from rival manufacturers Triumph and Sunbeam.

The MGB made its public debut at the 1962 London Motor Show at Earls Court. Motoring journalists and general public alike were quick to praise the new M.G. The wider cockpit, larger luggage capacity and improved comfort were as much lauded as the excellent performance and safe roadholding. The space behind the front seats was particularly appreciated by owners with young children to accommodate, and a cushion for this rear shelf was an optional extra for a while. The performance was much improved with the top speed recorded by "The Autocar" being 105mph (169kph), with acceleration to 60mph (97kph) taking just over 12 seconds. The car was an immediate sales success; the order books at Abingdon quickly filled.

Left: When the M.G. 1100 was announced in October 1962 it was billed by the marketing men as the first M.G. since the R-type racing car of 1935 to have all-round independent suspension. Closely related to the Morris and Austin 1100s, the M.G. had a 55bhp, twin-carburettor engine, front disc brakes, plush interior and, of course, the prestige of the M.G. radiator grille. In all honesty, like the Marks III and IV Magnettes, the cars were just badge-engineered versions of the more mundane models but were, nevertheless, attractive and comfortable cars that possessed sporting handling and roadholding. This 1963 car is owned by Ray Shrubb.

Above: Like the Mini, the 1100 range were designed by Alec Issigonis and also had transverse engines. The gearbox and final drive were lubricated by the engine oil.

Above right: The interior of the M.G. 1100 was better finished than the Austin or Morris versions. The wood-veneered dashboard has a ribbon speedometer.

Above: A two-door M.G. 1300 Mark II. The M.G. 1300 benefited from having a 1275cc version of the A-series engine that produced a healthy 75bhp – 20bhp up on the 1100. The Mark II had better instruments, alloy steering wheel and optional reclining front seats.

So far in this chapter all the talk has been of the M.G. sports cars but the company continued to sell saloon cars to satisfy marque followers with a need to accommodate more than one passenger in any degree of comfort. The Z Magnette introduced in 1953 had proved a popular and worthy successor to the earlier saloons and this model was improved with the introduction of the ZB in 1956 when engine power output was increased, and small changes were made to the dashboard and exterior brightwork. In addition a Varitone model was introduced which featured an enlarged rear window and buyers could chose from a range of two-tone colour schemes. Production of the Z Magnettes ceased in 1959 and was to be the last M.G. saloon to be built at Abingdon.

Badge Engineering

The replacement for the Z Magnette was a re-badged Morris Oxford/Austin Cambridge that had been kitted out with an M.G. grille, two-tone paintwork, twin-carburettor engine and a more luxurious interior. All this did little to hide the fact that this car was no M.G.! The steering and roadholding were no match for its predecessor and enthusiasts who traded in their old Magnettes for the new car, styled the Magnette Mk III, were very disappointed. In 1961, in common with other BMC cars that year, the Magnette was fitted with an enlarged engine – increased to 1622cc – and in addition the steering and suspension were revised in an attempt to improve the poor handling and roadholding. The revised model was called the Magnette Mark IV and was an improvement over the Mark III. This was to soldier on selling in small numbers until it was finally dropped in 1968.

Sharing the 1962 London Motor Show stand with the new MGB was another new M.G. – this time a saloon and a car better able to wear the octagon. The brilliant engineer, Alec Issigonis,

following his success with the revolutionary Mini introduced in 1959, was in the process of changing the image of the British Motor Corporation model line-up. The previously conservatively-engineered cars were to be replaced with models that followed his philosophy of maximum space utilization and innovative technical design. To cover the market sector previously held by the Austin A40 and Morris Minor he designed the Austin/Morris 1100. This car followed the Mini in having the A-series engine transversely mounted at the front, driving the front wheels through a gearbox and final drive that were integral with the power unit and sharing the same oil. The innovation for the 1100 was the adoption of interconnected "Hydrolastic" suspension which both helped smooth out the ride and dispensed with the need for separate dampers.

Once again the designers sought to set the M.G. version of the new car apart from its humbler stablemates by endowing it with a twin-carburettor engine, two-tone paintwork and better interior. In spite of it being designed and built away from Abingdon, this little car possessed enough of the M.G. attributes of performance and roadholding to endear it to those needing a four-seater. However, the MG 1100 never really captured the market for high-per-

formance small saloons as another car from the BMC stable – the Mini-Cooper S – attracted so much publicity in the following years that it eclipsed the larger M.G. saloon and set a standard for performance versions of popular cars, a market now mostly catered for by the modern "hot hatchbacks".

Right from the outset, the Abingdon design team intended that there should be a closed version of the MGB. The MGA coupé had established a market amongst those wanting a sports car without the inevitable discomfort associated with open cars. The arrival of the much more civilized MGB which, hood up or with a hard-top fitted, could rival most saloon cars for comfort meant that any closed version built would have to offer buyers something different. John Thornley had always wanted M.G. to build a sort of "poor man's Aston Martin" and when the MGB GT was designed it was not seen as the sort of family hold-all it was later to become. On the continent the 1964 Brussels Motor Show was the debut of the Berlinette MGB by Jacques Coune. Based on the standard

roadster, the Berlinette had a fixed, full-length, fibreglass roof neatly blended into a restyled tail and the car was fitted with a different windscreen. The front wings were modified and the interior retrimmed with access to the larger luggage area being from within the car. Over fifty examples were built before the factory MGB GT arrived at a much lower price.

MGB Grand Tourer

Abingdon gave the job of designing the conversion from open sports car to closed coupé to Pininfarina and there is no doubt that they did a good job, producing a car which still looks good more than a quarter of a century later. One aspect of the design that was a vast improvement over the open car was the height of the windscreen which had always been too low. The higher windscreen certainly improved matters for taller drivers and the large glass area of the cabin gave good visibility all round. To make the car attractive to the sports car driver with a young family, the designers incorporated a rear seat and advertised it as a two-plus-two.

It was well received by both the press and the general public and before long the GT was a common sight on the roads. Many customers bought them as second cars to use for the family shopping and found that the MGB GT was a very useful and adaptable car well capable of undertaking a wide variety of tasks.

The GT shared the mechanical specification of the roadster with the exception of the rear axle, which was changed for the quieter Salisbury unit, and the rear springs which were uprated. The front anti-roll bar was also standardized. The extra weight of the closed car (about 150lb,

Above: This fixed-head MGB, one of about fifty made, was produced in Belgium by Jacques Coune for Walter Oldfield, who ran Nuffield Press. These closed MGBs were built before M.G. launched their own version – the MGB GT. The rear window was fixed but there was a luggage compartment lid that was released from inside the car.

Left: The engine bay of an early MGB GT. The electric cooling fan is a later addition and this car has been fitted with an oil cooler. The four-cylinder BMC B-series engine fitted to the MGB is easily maintained and well suited to do-it-yourself rebuilds.

68kg) reduced the performance slightly but the one tested by "Autocar" still managed to reach a maximum speed of 102mph (164kph) and accelerate to 60mph (97kph) in 13.6 seconds. This was good performance for an 1800cc car in 1965 and the road test team were also impressed by the engine's flexibility at lower revs. Overdrive was available as an extra and was much appreciated for motorway trips. The addition of the GT to the model range certainly widened the appeal of the marque and increased the overall sales of the MGB to the extent that, in 1966, an additional production line was needed to cope with annual production at record levels.

From the early design stage of the MGB the idea of building a larger engined version was considered. This stemmed from the desire to replace the aging Austin-Healey 3000 – also built at Abingdon – with a car that could be sold as both an Austin-Healey and as an M.G. without incurring the considerable cost of designing a completely new car. Bearing in mind that the company was already fully stretching its meagre development budget to find the necessary money to replace the MGA with the MGB, the scheme of basing the 3000 replacement on this new model seemed attractive. At first it was planned that the new car would use a version of the 2433cc Australian six-cylinder engine which had been developed from the four-cylinder B-series engine that was already destined to be used in the MGB.

Longbridge Development Department allocated the experimental numbers ADO 51 for the

Austin-Healey version and ADO 52 for the M.G., with the basic body design being based on the still-unannounced MGB. However, the Healey family still had considerable influence on how their name could be used by BMC and the idea of using the MGB as a Healey 3000 replacement, with only minor badge changes to distinguish it from the M.G. version, found little favour with them. Donald and Geoffrey Healey pursued the idea of updating the existing Austin-Healey 3000 by widening it and installing the 4-litre Rolls-Royce power unit already licensed for use in the large Austin Princess R saloon. In the end this idea, too, was cancelled by the BMC management and Healey 3000 production ceased at Abingdon in 1967 without any replacement model being in the offing.

Top and above left: A well-restored MGB GT owned by Gary Stafford. The attractive lines of the GT still look fresh in spite of having first appeared on the roads as long ago as 1965.

Above: The spare wheel is stored beneath the rear compartment floor. The rear seat back can be lowered to extend the length of the rear deck, making the MGB GT an ideal shopping car.

The inevitable development problems that occurred with the new MGB in early 1962 meant that little work on the six-cylinder version was carried out until the four-cylinder car was safely launched and in production. The Abingdon engineers had failed to persuade the existing 3-litre Austin-Healey engine to fit under the low bonnet of the MGB and were casting around for another suitable engine – the Australian idea had by now been abandoned. Over at Long-bridge, engineers were looking for a replacement for the large Austin saloon cars that used the same 3-litre engine fitted to the Healey 3000 and were asking the designers at Morris Engines at Coventry to produce a replacement for the new cars that was lighter, more powerful and less bulky than the old unit. At last here might be the answer to Abingdon's problems. If the engine was to be lighter and smaller it should fit in the MGB – after all, under the bonnet there was a considerable amount of room ahead of the radiator to accommodate a larger engine.

Nevertheless, the new power unit was still going to be a tight squeeze in the engine bay and a considerable amount of work on the body shell would be needed to persuade it to fit. In the end, the changes made to the structure were extensive, requiring what was virtually a brand new

It was always intended that there should be a larger-engined version of the MGB, but it was not thought that it would be five years before this appeared on the market. Difficulties in finding a suitable engine delayed the introduction of the MGC and the poor reception from journalists, who at the time viewed unfavourably any new models from the troubled BMC, hampered sales. In spite of this, the MGC is now highly regarded by a loyal band of owners who appreciate fully its virtues as a long-distance touring car.

Left: MGB and MGC cockpits are identical, save for a leather-covered steering wheel for the MGC and minor changes to instrument specification. Later both had all-black trim, with more comfortable, reclining seats, when the 1969 model-year cars arrived. There was some criticism that the MGC looked too much like the MGB inside and out, and that to justify the higher price it should have been better equipped. Similar remarks were made of the MGB GT V8 in 1973.

Above: This picture shows the size of the MGC engine. The inner wings, front suspension, front panels and much else was completely changed to accommodate it. Later MGCs had the heater valve repositioned, the anti-gulp valve for the closed circuit breathing system removed and other minor changes under the bonnet.

Left: This chromed grille covers the inlet to the fresh air heating system. For a change, the heater was now part of the basic equipment and not an extra.

Below: The MGC wheels were an inch (25mm) larger than the MGB wheels and this made the car stand higher than the smaller-engined model. Also, the bulges to clear the larger engine in the aluminium bonnet gave the car a bulkier frontal appearance.

Right: Abingdon was unjustly accused of copying this MGB/MGC headlamp styling feature from the Renault Floride, for this allegation was unfounded.

Above left and right: Although the six-cylinder MGC looks almost identical to the four-cylinder MGB, the larger wheels and bulges in the bonnet hint at its extra power and performance. With their higher price tag, they sold to a rather different sort of customer than the MGB, and the closed GT versions, in particular, were often supplied fitted with the optional automatic transmission. The superb condition of the car pictured is a tribute to the dedication of its enthusiastic owner, Frank Clemmey.

Below left and right: The slatted radiator grille carries the traditional octagon badge and there is also a three-piece, chromed M.G. badge on the boot lid. The "MGC" badge above this identifies the more powerful model to any sharp-eyed driver struggling to catch this 120mph (193kph) sports car!

Right: The workmanlike cockpit of the MGC with the large steering wheel that is needed to manoeuvre this heavy car. The speedometer and tachometer are flanked by the fuel gauge and combined water temperature and oil pressure gauge. The overdrive switch is on the extreme right.

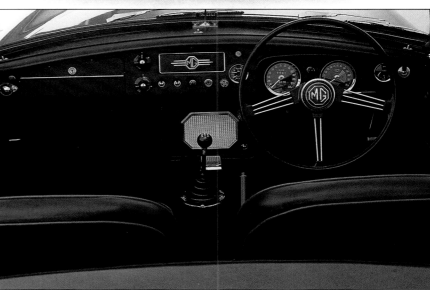

Right: Two types of soft-top were available. With the standard one the frame and fabric top were removable. For £4 extra, a soft-top that folded down behind the seats could be specified.

SPECIFICATION

Model: MGC two-seater roadster

Engine: Six-cylinder in line, overhead valve, water cooled. 83.36mm x 88.9mm, 2912cc, 150bhp

Gearbox: Four-speed synchromesh with option of overdrive or three-speed automatic

Final drive: 3.071:1. Top gear 23.8mph/1000rpm (38kph/1000rpm)(Non-overdrive cars to chassis 4235), 3.7:1 (overdrive cars from chassis 4236) and 3.307:1 (all other cars)

Suspension: Front: Independent with torsion bars, wishbones and rack and pinion steering. Rear: Live axle suspended on half-elliptic leaf springs

Dimensions: Wheelbase 7ft 7in (2311mm). Track, front 4ft 1in (1245mm), rear 4ft 1.3in (1252mm). Overall length 12ft 9in (3886mm)

Unladen weight: 21.8cwt (1108kg)

Cost when new: £895 plus £206.16s.6d. purchase tax

Performance: (From contemporary reports): Top speed 120mph (193kph)

Owner: Frank Clemmey

floor pan to accommodate the necessary revisions to the front suspension. The MGB front suspension design relied on a substantial cross member that was too bulky to fit under the sump of the larger engine, so the MGB coil springs and lever arm dampers were replaced by torsion bars for the six-cylinder car and the floor pressings under the seats were revised to accommodate the rear mountings for these.

The revised front suspension had two-piece upper and lower forged wishbones and telescopic dampers working with the torsion bars in place of the lever-arm dampers and wishbones fitted to the MGB. A new cross-member, "U" shaped to fit under the sump, provided the pivots for the wishbones as well as the mounting pads for the front of the engine. At the rear, the conventional leaf springs and hydraulic dampers used on the MGB were retained along with the Salisbury rear axle which, to take advantage of the greater power and torque of the larger engine, was fitted with a higher ratio crown wheel and pinion to reduce the engine revs at any given road speed.

The only external change made to the bodywork was the fitting of an aluminium bonnet with bulges to give clearance for the radiator and the front carburettor. Abingdon engineers would have preferred the engine to fit beneath the bonnet without the need for these, but the new six-cylinder unit had turned out to be only slightly less bulky than the old engine and certainly larger, and heavier, than they would have wished. Actually the new engine was a disappointment as it was only slightly smaller (less than 2in, 51mm, shorter), slightly lighter (around 20lb, 9kg) and less powerful (5bhp) than the Healey 3000 power unit.

Still, Abingdon had to make the best they could of an engine that was destined for use in the Austin 3-litre as well as the MGC. A larger proportion of the extra weight of this engine was carried by the front wheels, making it a little more front heavy than the MGB. To counter the extra weight lower-geared steering was fitted which made the MGC feel less nimble than the four-cylinder car on winding roads, although it did add to high-speed stability. Because of the greater weight and power, the engineers decided to fit larger diameter road wheels which made the car ride higher than the MGB. Apart from the bonnet bulge and the larger road

Below: The MGC was also available in closed form as a GT. The long-legged nature of the six-cylinder engine makes it ideally suited to the role of powering a long-distance Grand Tourer and, even by today's standards, MGC GTs make eminently comfortable motorway cruisers. This car is owned by Roger Chamberlain.

Left and below: Two aluminium-bodied, lightweight MGCs were built to compete in long-distance races. MBL 546E ran first with a two-litre four-cylinder engine in the 1967 Targa Florio, and then with a three-litre engine in the 1968 and 1969 races at Sebring, and the 1968 Marathon de la Route. Unfortunately, the Leyland take-over of BMC stopped further factory competition use of the cars which were then sold off. Today both MBL 546E and sister car, RMO 699F, survive in original condition.

Right: The interiors of both the MGB and MGC were radically modified to comply with local safety laws applying to those cars exported to the United States.

thing else, set the MGC apart from other M.G.s. It was the fastest production M.G. built until the other MGB derivative – the MGB GT V8 – arrived in 1973 and for many it is one of the best cars to come from Abingdon. Flawed as it undoubtably was when launched, it was improved by the company for the 1969 model year cars, which appeared in late 1968, when modified gear ratios and better interiors with more comfortable, reclining seats were adopted.

Sales Are Disappointing

Although nearly 9000 MGCs sold during the two years the car was in production, this was really rather fewer than the management had hoped for when the car was launched. The pity was that even a small amount of effort by tuning companies like Downton Engineering improved the engine to such an extent as to transform the car. Relatively small modifications to the suspension set-up – higher geared steering rack, wider tyres and stiffer torsion bars, for example – produced a matching improvement in the handling and roadholding. Had these changes been matched by a real effort to sell the car, the story might have been altogether different and many more cars could have been built and sold. As it was, sales flagged so badly towards the end of production that a large number of unsold cars stood in the compound at the factory. Most of these were GTs and were bought as a "job lot" by the long-time London M.G. agents, University Motors who created a number of special cars considered by many as the ultimate MGCs.

Having purchased the remaining stocks the company set about marketing them as "University Motors Specials" with the majority just being treated to a special paint finish and a different radiator grille and badging. Some had interior re-trimming with at least one being modified to include two bigger rear seats, involving changes to the floor pan and the moving of the batteries from their position in front of the axle to the boot area. One very noticeable modification made to some of the cars was the adoption of a special grille with horizontal alloy slats, but retaining the original chrome surround. The suspension was also modified on

wheels only the substitution of the letter "C" for the letter "B" in the chrome badges distinguished the larger engined car.

Delays, first whilst a suitable engine was found and then because supplies of this power unit were very slow to materialize, meant that the six-cylinder MGC was not launched until October 1967 – some five years after the MGB. The car was poorly received by the motoring press who criticized both the handling of the car and the relative lack of engine power. To be fair, the MGC was probably not exactly the type of sports car the engineers at Abingdon had set out to produce but their hands were tied by the need to use an engine that was neither as light as they would have wished or as well developed as it should have been. They were also starved of funds by the ailing parent company, as well as suffering from the poor public image of the general run of BMC cars built at that time that was prevalent.

The higher price of the new car, and the extra cost of fuel and insurance, meant that it appealed to a different sector of the market than did the

MGB. Of course, there were always going to be some MGB owners who wanted to trade up to something better but most new buyers were drawn from the ranks of those who otherwise would have looked at other large-engined sports or sporting cars. Owners of Healey 3000s, Triumphs or even Jaguars were tempted to try the car and many liked them enough to buy one. MGC owners then, as now, tended to enjoy driving them very much, and to keep them for a long time. The lack of "sports car" feel and handling on winding roads was compensated for by a surprising ability to cover long distances on motorways or autoroutes without apparent effort. This was a true Grand Tourer.

Endowed with a high top gear and the option of overdrive, the MGC was – and still is – the ideal long-distance touring car. In overdrive top the "Autocar" recorded a speed of 27mph (43.5kph) per 1000 engine revolutions which meant that the engine was only turning over at about 3700rpm at 100mph (161kph) – relaxed high-speed travel indeed. Perhaps it was this high geared touring ability that, more than any-

some of the cars, which had the effect of improving handling. No two University Motors Specials were exactly alike, and at least one was fitted with square headlights.

To improve the engine, University Motors had for some time been offering three different tuning stages by Downton. These ranged from a mild Stage 1 to the ambitious, and expensive, Stage 3. A Stage 2 conversion included a modified cylinder head, porting and valves, modified, polished and re-profiled inlet manifolds, two separate tubular exhaust manifolds, and with a dual exhaust system to match the claimed maximum power output was 149bhp at 5500rpm. Stage 3 added a triple SU carburettor installation to the features of Stage 2 and resulted in a claimed maximum power output of 174bhp at 5500rpm. Many of the specials sold had their engines converted to Stage 2 or 3 to increase their appeal further.

Improving The MGB

The development of the other cars in the M.G. range continued hand in hand with the work on the MGC. When the MGB was introduced the 1800cc engine still had the three-bearing crankshaft inherited from the earlier, smaller capacity versions of the B-series unit, but a five-bearing crankshaft was introduced in October 1964 to improve refinement. A large number of minor changes to mechanical specification, trim and colour schemes were made during the first five years of production but in 1967 enough major changes were introduced to justify the factory calling the new cars Mark II. The most noticeable change for the average owner was the adoption of a gearbox with synchromesh on all the forward gears. Previously, in common with a large number of cars of that period, first gear had not

benefited from this refinement, but its adoption meant that closer ratios with a higher second gear could be used as first could now be selected with the car moving without any need to double-declutch.

The new, and more bulky, gearbox, also fitted to the MGC, necessitated changes to the body shell. At the same time safety considerations forced the adoption of different interior door handles and switch-gear on all cars, and a more radical redesign of the cars sent to the American market. As we will see in a later chapter, the demands imposed on car manufacturers by ever more stringent American legislation was to have an increasing influence over future developments at Abingdon, with the majority of any available funds being spent merely on trying to keep the current cars in line with the requirements of National and State law makers.

The Midget, and its Sprite stablemate, continued to sell well throughout the 1960s. The

original 948cc engine and drum brakes fitted to the Mark I Midget and Mark II Sprite were replaced in 1962 by a 1098cc engine and disc front brakes (confusingly the Sprite was always one ahead of the Midget in model designation having had three years start on the M.G.). Trim was improved but the sliding side screens remained. The model designation remained but current enthusiasts now call the upgraded versions "Mark I½".

A much more comprehensive revision arrived in 1964 when the Mark II Midget was introduced. The engineers had managed to squeeze both winding side windows and front quarter-lights into the diminutive doors. This change brought the luxury of doors that could now be locked, and opened, from outside – gone were the separate sidescreens with the sliding Perspex windows that had to be opened to gain access to the door handles. A new windscreen frame and a modified, but still fully removable, hood com-

Above: The interior of the Mark II Midget and Mark III Sprite were identical, apart from the badges on the dashboard and steering wheel horn push. Note the awkward positioning of the interior door handles.

Above right: The Mark II Midget had an entirely new windscreen frame as well as quarter-lights and winding windows for the doors. The rear-view mirror can be fixed at any point on the windscreen bracing rod.

Right: A Mark IV Austin-Healey Sprite displaying the folding hood introduced for this model. Although mechanically identical to the Midget, the Sprite had less exterior chrome trim and a simpler radiator grille. They were also cheaper to buy.

Below right: By 1969, the Mark III Midget had lost the bonnet strip but gained all-black interior trim and reclining seats. This model was the last with the traditional slatted radiator grille. This car was rebuilt a few years ago by the author.

pleted the transformation. Mechanically, the 1098cc engine remained (now gaining a more robust set of bearings) but the rather quirky quarter-elliptic rear suspension was dropped in favour of a half-elliptic set up.

These changes increased the appeal enormously and performance and comfort were further enhanced when the Mark III cars came along in 1966. The 1275cc engine developed for the Cooper S and for adoption in the 1100 range of small saloons was fitted to the Sprite and Midget. This resulted in what was probably the best version of these popular cars. The fitting of a hood that could now be lowered without the need to stow hood sticks and the vinyl hood itself in the luggage compartment was much appreciated. At the time few cars could keep up with a well-driven Midget or Sprite on winding country roads where its small size, superb handling, willing engine and delightful gearbox could be exploited to the full.

The vastly increased production from Abingdon, and the popularity of the MGB all around the world, would have led the casual visitor to the factory in the late 1960s to conclude that the future of the M.G. marque was secure for some time to come. However, as has been seen with the introduction of both the highly successful MGB and the less profitable MGC, the company was always starved of sufficient money to develop the cars fully and plan ahead for replacement models. The real strength of M.G. as a marque lay in the ready availability of standard components taken from volume-produced saloon cars built elsewhere within the parent organization. Independent sports car builders had either to manufacture such components themselves, or buy them in small numbers from outside sources, either of which resulted in significantly increased costs. The price paid by M.G. management for this benefit was a fundamental lack of freedom to manage the affairs of the company in its own best interests. Time and time again plans to develop new models were thwarted by senior managers who had to consider the wider interests of the group as a whole, of which the M.G. operation was but a tiny part.

A Small Cog In A Large Wheel

The relative size of the Abingdon plant can be judged from the numbers employed there in the 1970s, 1100 in all, against nearly 200,000 in the group as a whole. Of course, there were many other workers at other British Leyland factories scattered around the country employed full time producing components to be transported to Abingdon for final assembly into complete cars. Although many components used in the MGB when it was designed in 1962 derived from those fitted to mass-produced cars, by the late 1970s the models in volume production had changed significantly and these items were now exclusively made for M.G., which was a less efficient system. Merely a small part of a large organization, and wholly reliant on the rest of the group for finance, sales policy and the majority of components required, the fate of the Abingdon factory was dependent on the health of British Leyland as a whole. At that time the group was in a parlous state.

It helps to understand how matters had become so bad to look at the recent history of the British Leyland group. In 1952 the Morris and Austin empires amalgamated under the British Motor Corporation banner, following many years when a merger between the two giants of the British motor industry had been proposed and discussed but never carried out. Negotiations between William Morris, later Lord Nuffield, and Sir Herbert Austin had actually started as long ago as 1924 – about the time the M.G. marque was born – and at that time the proposed merger would have also involved the Wolseley company – which was later bought by Morris who outbid Austin for the business. Both men were autocratic, self-made millionaires and it is not surprising that they were unable to agree merger terms that would have reduced the control they had over their individual empires.

The British Motor Corporation, as the merged company was called, inherited a large number of factories and many of the best known British car marque names. The Nuffield group, in particular, brought to the corporation widely diverse companies producing both the raw materials and the finished components needed for vehicle production. Many of these companies had been bought by William Morris in his search for greater control over prices and sources of supply, but were scattered geographically. The merger with Austin brought yet more manufacturing capacity, with much duplication of resources, but did include the benefit of Longbridge, the most up-to-date car factory in the country at that time. Under the direction of Leonard Lord the Longbridge plant had been modernized in the early post-war years with the car assembly building being fed with components from other parts of the site via a system of underground tunnels. Leonard Lord had worked for Lord Nuffield before a difference of opinion between them forced his resignation in 1936. The bitterness he harboured towards his old employers was felt by some to have influenced his actions when dealing with parts of the Nuffield Group following the merger. These actions were to have a direct effect on the Abingdon factory and on the money available for The M.G. Car Company to develop new models.

As well as inheriting the production facilities from both sides, the new British Motor

Right: The first of the Midgets to emerge after a complete re-think had this ugly, black-painted windscreen frame. Luckily, this was short-lived and polished aluminium was soon to make a comeback. A bright new range of colour schemes was on offer. The front bumper was re-shaped and the original one-piece rear bumper was replaced by a pair of neat quarter bumpers. Rubber-faced over-riders were standard.

Below: The steel wheels with separate hub caps used on the earlier Midgets and Sprites were replaced by these attractive, pressed steel Rostyle "alloy look" wheels. The chrome side mouldings on the Midget were dropped, and both models now had chrome strips and the model name on the satin-black-painted sill panels.

Corporation was now faced with a bewildering range of models, many of which were in direct competition with each other. Although billed as a merger the real control was now vested in the Austin management team and it was these men who took on the task of rationalization. The marques represented by BMC were Austin, Morris, Riley (acquired by Lord Nuffield in 1938), Wolseley (bought from receivers in 1935) and, of course, M.G. In addition there were Morris Commercials and Nuffield Tractors, and from 1952 yet another sports car marque – Austin-Healey – which was introduced by Leonard Lord although the Corporation already owned M.G. which built sports cars!

Rationalization Plans

Steps to rationalize the models on sale were taken but the requirement to support existing dealer networks, and the supposed need to maintain customer loyalties to the individual marques, led to a high degree of badge engineering with ranges of otherwise similar cars marketed under different names with but minor cosmetic variations. Something even Abingdon was unable to escape from with the Midget and Sprite. From an engineering standpoint some worthwhile changes were immediately made. The largely outdated engines used in vehicles produced within the Nuffield Group were progressively replaced by the BMC A, B and C range of Austin-designed engines and in due course similar rationalization was applied to other mechanical components.

The need to build and sell more examples of a smaller range of vehicles can be amply demonstrated by looking at the Wolseley and Riley marques. Although both companies had been brought under Nuffield control in the 1930s they continued producing their own separate range of cars even after the war. The models they produced were sold in comparatively small numbers, were usually outdated, and can have hardly made anything like the profit the parent company required for the capital invested. Unlike the position at M.G., they competed directly with other cars built within the group, something that any competent finance director must have resented. Although the position was much improved by the changes brought about under the BMC management, far too many widely scattered factories remained in operation acting as a drain on company profitability, and efficiency, right into British Leyland days.

The British Motor Corporation was, to outward appearances, successful in the market place and by the end of the 1960s was producing a wide variety of cars ranging from the innovative and popular Mini to large Austin limousines. There were still far too many different marques, albeit most were versions of popular models re-badged to appeal to small sections of the car buying public. BMC cars sold well overseas, and the company still held over 30 per cent of the home market sales, but ever growing competition from other British car makers – and increasingly from imports – was slowly eroding their market share. Of the home producers, Ford in particular, benefited from good management. In stark contrast to the scattered factories inherited from the piecemeal acquisitions Lord Nuffield had made pre-war, Ford's Dagenham plant in Essex was fully integrated and far more efficient. In addition, Ford had none of the problems associated with maintaining a number of different marque names with separate dealer networks and additional advertising and marketing costs. The net result was a more focussed overall marketing strategy, and better line-up of cars to sell, benefits which were reflected in Ford making well over twice as much profit per car as their BMC rivals.

Political Meddling

Smaller profits resulted in less money being available for re-investment, and the production facilities, particularly at Cowley and at Abingdon, were much the same in the 1960s as they had been before 1940. To add to their problems there was always the dead hand of government interference. The whole story of British car manufacture in the second half of the 20th century is inextricably bound up with the political and fiscal fortunes of the country. Ever since the introduction of special taxes during wartime austerity, governments of all parties have used the car industry as a sort of regulator for the economy as a whole, with changes in purchase tax, car licences, petrol tax and hire purchase restrictions being imposed almost without regard to the effect they may have on the industry as a whole, or on the people employed in it.

This meddling, often with the best of intentions, extended to using the car industry to try to solve unemployment problems in particular areas by persuading the companies to open up factories, even though this could create difficulties associated with a dispersal of manufacturing resources. The double burden of a "stop and go" economic policy and government interference, allied to weak management and poor labour relations, made the eventual decline of the British motor industry, and of BMC in particular, almost inevitable.

The 1960s was to be the decade of company mergers. Both "captains of industry" and government ministers had decided that the only way the industry as a whole could survive was for there to be far fewer, but larger, companies.

Above: Like the Midget, the MGBs received a new look in time for the 1969 Motor Show. Unfortunately, probably to cut costs, the seats were no longer leather-faced – so breaking a long-standing tradition.

Jaguar was one of the first to expand when they bought the ailing Daimler company, using both the production facilities and the name to expand the range of models they offered. Whether using the Daimler V8 engine in a Mark II Jaguar saloon and calling it a Daimler 250 really made economic sense only a close study of the company accounts could reveal.

The take-over, however, failed to keep the company independent for more than a few years and in 1966 they were to merge with BMC under the title of British Motor Holdings. This latest grouping was also short-lived and, at the prompting of the Labour government, the Leyland Group, which by now had control of M.G.'s great rivals, Triumph, were merged in early 1968 with British Motor Holdings as British Leyland Motor Corporation. As was later to become apparent, this was not so much a merger as a take-over of the BMC operations by the Triumph interests, which was to lead directly to decisions that finally sealed the fate of the small factory at Abingdon. Leyland had brought with them to the new operation Rover and Land-Rover and the latter company were then, and still are, a considerable asset. One result of the effective merging of M.G. and Rover within the same group was to make the highly desirable, light-alloy V8 engine available to the Abingdon designers and this was later made good use of in the MGB GT V8.

At the time, the emergence of the new British Leyland Motor Corporation was seen as a good move and one that would help the British motor industry survive in a world full of efficient car producers. In the event, the merger did not bring the efficiencies originally promised, and a failure to take the unpalatable decisions needed to rationalize production, or to produce cars of sufficient quality of design and manufacture, was to cause the eventual collapse of the company under private ownership. This forced the government to step in to try to save the hundreds of thousands of jobs at stake – both of the people directly employed and those working for dependent component industries.

The effect of the formation of British Leyland on the M.G. factory and on the range of vehicles it produced was effectively to kill any chances of an entirely new M.G. As was seen with the development of the MGC a couple of years earlier, funds for such work were extremely limited even before the merger, and the pattern for the final decade at Abingdon was for the Development Department to be allowed just enough money to enable them keep the current models sufficiently up to date to comply with amendments in legislation around the world.

A New Look

The first real changes under the new regime were to appear on the 1970 model year cars, which were first shown at the 1969 London Motor Show. These changes were announced to the press on 11th October by the Austin-Morris Division of British Leyland, which then had control of M.G. The Midget lost the chrome side strips never worn by the Austin-Healey Sprite, and both models gained a chrome strip at the top edge of the sills, which were now painted satin black, with either "Midget" or "Sprite" in chrome lettering displayed along them. In the previous model year, both these cars, as well as the MGBs and MGCs, had gained reclining seats in plain black to replace the existing non-reclining seats with contrasting piping. For that year, the MGB and MGC seats were still leather-faced but this luxury was to fall victim to the cost accountants for the 1970 model year cars and all seats were vinyl-covered, albeit with embossed, fluted central panels.

This face-lift for the cars was designed at Longbridge, not Abingdon, and one of the more controversial changes was the replacement of the traditional, slatted radiator grille by a matt black-painted, recessed grille. This change was least acceptable on the MGB where the bonnet pressing still retained the central bulge on the front edge where the M.G. badge had been fitted to the original grille. The "matt black" image popular with car designers at the time was initially extended to include the windscreen sur-

Right: MGB assembly. The body shells arrived at Abingdon partly trimmed and with the windscreens, hoods, etc., fitted. They were received on the top deck where the pipe runs, wiring, instruments and lights were installed before being lowered by a hoist onto this raised track where suspension components, engine and gearbox, and the wheels, were fitted. The crane on the right of the picture lowered the cars to ground level where they sat on their own wheels for the first time.

round and wiper arms on the Midget (possibly to comply with proposed anti-dazzle regulations in America) but luckily these changes were dropped after just a few hundred cars had been built. One reason was the difficulty there seemed to be in making the black paint adhere to the aluminium parts.

To complement the styling changes, both the Sprite/Midget and the MGB were fitted with steel Rostyle wheels instead of the ventilated disc wheels. The option of wire wheels was still offered and a large number of exported cars were equipped with these. Bright colours for sports cars were popular then, with even

Porsche 911s available in brilliant orange and lime green, so it is not surprising that M.G. followed suit with the bolder Flame Red replacing the sober Tartan Red and the then fashionable Bronze Yellow taking over from Pale Primrose. Traditionalists could still choose British Racing Green! All models now carried British Leyland badges on the front wings.

The MGC was quietly dropped from the price lists. The Magnette Mk IV saloon had been discontinued in 1968 so it was left to the MG 1300 to carry on the M.G. saloon car tradition, although neither this model nor the Magnette were built at Abingdon but were assembled in other factories.

In spite of the changes, not all of which endeared themselves to enthusiasts, the cars continued to sell well, and the motoring magazines carried favourable road test reports of the revised models. "Motor" magazine tested an open MGB towards the end of 1969 and recorded an acceleration time from 0-60mph (97kph) of 11 seconds, an improvement over the earlier model, and a top speed of 105mph (169kph). It was particularly pleased that it found the car less outclassed by more modern designs than it had expected but did criticize some of the minor fit-

Left: A 1972 MGB GT photographed at the factory in 1977. Replacing the traditional radiator grille did little to help its looks.

Below: May 1971. The 250,000th MGB built is pictured with George Turnbull, the Managing Director of Austin-Morris.

tings. Rival motoring magazine "Autocar" tested one of the automatic-gearbox-equipped MGB roadsters a few months later and once again gave the car a good report. It found that the optional gearbox did not reduce the performance vastly – recording a top speed of 104mph (167kph) – and that it suited a more leisurely style of driving than did the manual car. In spite of this good report, automatic MGBs sold in small numbers with most of them being GTs for the home market. The option was dropped from the price lists in 1973.

With cash always in short supply, every chance to save money had to be taken, and in December 1970 the factory dropped "Healey" from the name of the Austin-Healey Sprite because using it had meant paying royalties to Donald Healey. The cars now sold were badged as Austin Sprites but few were built before the model was dropped altogether in July 1971, leaving the Midget to soldier on alone. In view of the wide-ranging changes later made to that model, many Austin-Healey fans were probably not too sorry to see the name dropped. In actual fact since the changes made to the car for the 1970 model year removed all distinction between the variants, save for the badges, there was little point continuing with both models. Another reason was the removal of a distinction between Austin and Morris dealerships under the new Leyland regime.

Muddled Sales Efforts

As with much done to the British motor industry in this period, the matter of the relationship between the company and the dealers was not well handled. Prior to the mergers, there had been dealers selling Austins and Austin-Healeys, others franchised to sell Morris and M.G. cars with Wolseley and Riley added in for good measure. In addition there were Triumph dealers, Rover and Land-Rover specialists and those trying to sell enough Jaguars to make a living. The company needed to sort out the mess and in the process it removed many franchises and forced some who were purely M.G. orientated to sell a certain number of ordinary saloon cars for every sports car they were allocated. The resultant upheaval left many smaller garages, who had each sold a few cars every year, without any new cars to display resulting in them welcoming with open arms the increasing number of overseas car manufacturers trying to gain a foothold in the British market. What British Leyland failed to appreciate was that many people buy their cars on impulse from their neighbourhood garages and that to service this market one must be represented locally. Many a long-time Morris or Austin driver was persuaded to change to a Fiat or Honda just because they were more easily purchased in their area.

M.G.s continued to sell well, however, and in May 1971 the company announced that production of the MGB had reached 250,000. This figure made it Britain's biggest-selling sports car ever. Over 200,000 had been exported worldwide, with North America the largest overseas market.

inclined to invest large sums of money to develop an M.G. that would directly compete with other cars produced within the organization. Various exercises were carried out to examine the feasibility of fitting other engines to increase power, but most of these transplants would have needed considerable re-engineering of the MGB engine bay and front suspension, much as had been necessary for the MGC, and this was ruled out on cost grounds. The engine that would have fitted, the lightweight, Buick-derived V8 fitted to the Rover P6 saloons and later to the Range-Rover, was initially ruled out because of supply problems but was later used to produce one of the best cars built at Abingdon – the MGB GT V8.

The Costello Influence

The credit for prompting the eventual production of the V8 version of the MGB by Abingdon can really be given to one man – Ken Costello. Ken had made a name for himself as a racer of Mini saloons in the 1960s when he made these small cars fly. However, craving ever more power, in 1969 he fitted an American Oldsmobile V8 engine in an MGB roadster and the resulting hybrid was so successful that he started building replicas for customers. The design work for the Oldsmobile engine, and the

The factory continued to make small changes to the cars with the Midget gaining modified rear wheel arches in 1972 – this was the short-lived "round wheel arch" model. At the same time the Rostyle wheels were changed to a pattern similar to those fitted to the MGB from October 1969. Other detail changes included an enlarged petrol tank, rocker switches for the dashboard and minor trim modifications.

Facelift For The MGB

In October 1972 the MGB was also revised with that controversial grille being changed to something closer to the original design. The money men vetoed a complicated slatted grille but at least the surround returned to its original shape and the badge was located to line up with the bulge on the front of the bonnet. The central area of the grille was filled with a matt black injection-moulded mesh. The specification of both open and closed versions was improved with the GTs gaining brushed nylon panels on the seats, the tourers had tonneau covers as standard, and the closed cars heated rear windows. The colour range was changed from time to time and a number of rather unusual colours appeared for short periods.

Ever since the MGB was first announced in 1962 there had been a consistent demand for a higher-performance version. The first attempt to provide this was the MGC which, as we have seen, was not an unqualified success; the car produced ended up appealing to a different type of owner than those looking for out-and-out performance. To try to satisfy the demand, various tuning firms had made money over the years hotting up MGBs for both competition and road use. The M.G. Car Company themselves had

Above: In January 1972 further revisions were made to the design of the Midget. The rear wheel arches were rounded off and a different pattern of Rostyle wheels fitted. Mechanically the cars were unchanged, but they did gain a larger, seven-gallon (31.8 litre) fuel tank.

always been aware of the need to be in this market and were happy to supply tuning parts developed by their Competition Department for the factory competition cars. Tuning booklets were issued by the company giving details of the various states of engine tuning possible and at one time a Special Tuning Department was established that would both sell parts and modify cars for customers.

However, to supply tuning parts to upgrade the performance of the MGB was not going to satisfy the general demand for a higher performance M.G. There will always be a suspicion amongst customers, often with some justification, that modified cars are less reliable than standard production models. Another factor the marketing men at British Leyland had to face was that the competition pitted against the MGB was a lot stronger in the early 1970s than it had been when the car was launched in 1962. Ford were taking a lot of potential customers with their successful Capri, which was available with a large range of engines sizes including a powerful three-litre unit, and in America the Ford Mustang was very popular, as was the Datsun 240Z, which was introduced following success with the Fairlady that had been designed specifically for that market.

One of the difficulties faced by the designers at Abingdon was the ongoing one of cost constraints. Following the mergers and takeovers, the management of British Leyland were not well disposed towards Abingdon and were dis-

130

similar Buick V8, was started by General Motors in the 1950s when it had been decided to adopt aluminium alloy for the block and head castings to save weight. The resulting engine emerged in 1961 with a capacity of 3531cc, cast-iron cylinder liners, hardened valve seats and hydraulic tappets. The new engine was used to power the medium-sized Buick and Oldsmobile models and was also quickly adopted by the racing fraternity who appreciated its light weight and tuning potential. However, it was to have a short production life, being replaced by a new generation of cast-iron engines in 1964.

The story of that engine would have ended there had it not been for the need at Rover for a larger capacity engine to power the P5 and P6 models. It had been suggested that they seek to acquire an American V8 engine rather than develop their own unit, and General Motors were approached to see if they would consider allowing the company to use their now-obsolete aluminium V8. An agreement was reached that also allowed Rover access to the works draw-

Right: The Rover V8 engine installed in an MGB by Ken Costello. The success of this conversion was one of the factors that spurred British Leyland into authorizing M.G. to build their own version – the MGB GT V8. The Costello V8 used a more powerful version of the engine than did the factory cars, but this required a bulge in the bonnet to clear the carburettors.

Below right: The Costello V8 was expensive, with a new GT costing £2,392 in 1972. However, quite a number of new cars were sold, as well as some conversions of second-hand cars.

ings, details of modifications made in production, and the service records. The British engineers set about changing the engine to allow it to be used in their cars and built at the British engine plant. The castings were modified to allow them to be gravity, rather than die-cast. Changes were made to pistons, valve gear and carburettors and Lucas ignition equipment was fitted resulting in an engine producing around 150bhp – quite sufficient to transform the performance of the P5 saloon and coupé, the first Rovers to receive the new unit.

Below and below right: The round-wheel-arch Midget was the last of the A-series engined cars and the most popular of these models with today's enthusiasts. In addition to the exterior changes, the cockpit had received some thought. There were now rocker switches on the dashboard, the door pulls and gear lever knob were changed, and the quality of the carpeting improved.

It was this Rover engine that was adopted by Ken Costello for his conversions and eventually for the MGB GT V8. The Costello V8 was fitted with the engine in its standard 150bhp form, mated to the MGB gearbox via a larger, 9.5in (241mm) diameter clutch. The standard MGB rear axle was retained but the MGC ratio of 3.07:1 was used. The carburettors fitted to the Rover engine would not fit under the standard MGB bonnet so glass-fibre substitutes, incorporating a bulge to give additional room for the carburettors, were fitted to the Costello V8s. To further distinguish the cars, an inelegant "egg-crate" grille was fitted together with special "V-eight Costello" badges. The suspension, brakes and steering were unchanged, save for some modification made to the steering column to allow the wider engine sufficient room in the engine bay, and harder brake pads to cope with the higher speeds. The overall weight of the car was actually slightly less than the standard car and the reduction was all at the front end which improved weight distribution.

Of course, all this work was not cheap and the complete car cost a substantial £975 more than a standard MGB or MGB GT, which made it a lot more expensive than other cars of similar performance. In spite of this, it was successful and road tests and articles generated sufficient interest for the small workshops at Farnborough in Kent to be kept quite busy. All this activity did not go unnoticed at British Leyland, who had been quite happy to supply Costello with engines in spite of their apparent shortage, and Ken was asked to convert a LHD GT for them to assess. This car was tested by the engineers at Abingdon who were eventually asked to design a V8 MGB themselves.

There was no doubt that, in spite of having limited testing facilities, Ken Costello had built a good, well-engineered car. The press found few faults with the modified cars and most of their criticisms centred around design and equipment shortcomings in the original MGB – nothing that Ken Costello could do anything about without further increasing the price he would have to charge. The effectiveness of substituting an engine twice the size, but weighing less, on the performance can be judged from the "Autocar" report which recorded a reduction of the time taken to reach 60mph (97kph) from 13 seconds to just 7.8 seconds. The maximum speed recorded rose from 102mph (164kph) to 128mph (206kph). The increased torque of the larger engine, up by no less than 82 per cent, made the car easy to drive in a leisurely fashion, with adequate performance being available from low engine speeds in any gear. Altogether a great improvement on the four-cylinder car.

Enter The MGB GT V8

Given the green light to develop their own V8, the factory development engineers had a prototype running in a very short space of time and this was passed to go into production. Unlike Costello, the car Abingdon eventually built used the lower compression Range-Rover unit, which produced 137bhp at 5000rpm, and this was installed in the MGB after being fitted with a carburettor manifold and air cleaner arrangement that eliminated the need for a bulge in the bonnet. Some changes were made to the inner wheel arches in the engine compartment and these were subsequently incorporated on all MGBs. The weight of the M.G. version of the Rover V8 was slightly greater than that of the B-series engine it replaced but its far greater power and torque dramatically improved the power to weight ratio of the car, lifting its performance into an entirely different league.

The Abingdon engineers decided to make changes to the gearbox, suspension and brakes of the V8 considered unnecessary by Costello. The gearbox was mated to a different clutch and bell-housing (with a modified clutch withdrawal bearing) and was altered to restrict the use of overdrive just to top gear. The road springs were changed for the stiffer police specification versions and the brakes uprated by fitting thicker front discs and different front brake callipers. Both for strength, and to distinguish the car from its lower-powered stablemates, Dunlop D4 wheels shod with wider section tyres were specified. These wheels had alloy centres fitted to steel rims and, together with the wider section tyres chosen, made the car look quite distinctive.

The new car was launched on 15th August 1973, unfortunately at what was to prove a difficult time to sell a large-engined, high performance car. Quite outside the control of the company, or even the government of this country, the world was to experience a major fuel crisis. In October that year Egypt and Syria attacked Israel and this resulted in a five week conflict – the Yom Kippur War. As a consequence, the Arab oil producers stopped supplies

Right: The MGB GT V8 was announced in August 1973 and the Land-Rover version of the V8 engine proved sufficient to give it a top speed of over 120mph (193kph). Unfortunately, many expected that the higher-priced V8 would have had better trim and equipment, but this was not the case.

Below: The 1975-model-year V8s received impact-absorbing bumpers. All V8s were fitted with these smart wheels which had alloy centres riveted to chromed steel rims. Wire wheels were not available on this model.

to the West. The following shortages and price rises were to frighten people off buying cars perceived to be "gas guzzlers" and this was to affect the sales of the MGB GT V8 even though the car was to prove no heavier on fuel than the four-cylinder version when driven at similar speeds.

The performance of the car was praised by the motoring press but the lack of any real change in its appearance, or the comfort offered to the occupants, did cause a lot of adverse comment. The MGB GT V8 was fitted with tinted windows and overdrive as standard, and the dashboard contained slightly changed instruments, but to all outward appearances it shared all the virtues and drawbacks of the standard car. In particular the wind noise coming from the top and rear edges of the frameless door windows was especially annoying – perhaps because of the greater refinement of the V8 engine and the higher cruising speeds of which the car was capable. Once again the cause was largely the lack of development funds to make the changes to both the interior trim and exterior appearance that the higher price of the new car would have seemed to have justified.

The real tragedy of the whole exercise was not that a bad car resulted – the V8 was a very good car – but that it could have been much better,

and would have sold in larger numbers had it been exported. There is no doubt that Abingdon wanted to export the car – indeed the early press releases and brochures speak of the car being able to pass safety regulations abroad and being available in LHD form. A number of prototypes were built to overseas specification and American dealers were confident that they would be able to sell sufficient quantities to make it well worthwhile to export the car. However it was not to be, and the Triumph-orientated management once again had their way, with cars being built purely for the home market so as not to compete with the Triumph TR6 and Stag models. Because the car was not to be exported there was no effort made to develop a roadster version, which further restricted sales. To be fair, the forthcoming changes in US legislation meant that the 1975 model year cars were going to need drastic modification and the effort of working towards these must have been absorbing a considerable proportion of the restricted funds available.

The oil price rises imposed by OPEC, the Arab-led organization of oil producers, in the early 1970s were dramatic. In 1973 alone the price of crude oil rose 70 per cent, with consequent rises in the cost of petrol at the pumps. The

Above left: The MGB GT V8 shared with the four-cylinder car the practical advantages of this elegant body style. Ample luggage space for two occupants made it an ideal touring machine.

Above: The installation of the engine on the MGB GT V8 was an example of good packaging. A modified inlet manifold, and different air cleaners, enabled the standard bonnet to be used.

effort – the perseverance by Triumph engineers with their own V8 for the Stag is a case in point. Failure to rationalize production facilities or deal with the poor labour relations satisfactorily meant that the day of reckoning would eventually come.

Government Help

In December 1974 the company finally ran out of money, and credit with their bankers, and the board was forced to turn to the Labour government for assistance. The government reaction was to appoint Sir Don Ryder both as Industrial Advisor to the Prime Minister and as Chairman designate of the National Enterprise Board. This board was, in effect, to run British Leyland with powers to appoint directors and channel funds from the exchequer to the company, after the government had taken it over by buying up the majority of the publicly quoted shares. In his role as advisor, Ryder was to report to the government, assessing how British Leyland could be saved and returned to prosperity. Remembering

effect of the "oil shock" was to spark off a deep world recession that was to have far-reaching consequences within the British Leyland group. Since its formation in 1968 there had been many changes of policy within the company and attempts had been made to try to develop models that could compete with rival manufacturers from Britain and Europe (Britain had joined the EEC in 1973), and also the growing number of imports from Japan. Ford had enjoyed considerable success with the Cortina, which was conventionally engineered but highly profitable, whereas BMC had concentrated on technically innovative but poorly developed cars such as the Mini, Maxi, 1800 and, later, the Allegro. These had proved less profitable, partly because of their more complicated design, but largely because of the scattered factories, poor management and abysmal marketing that characterized the company.

To try to emulate Ford, British Leyland rushed into production the uninspiring Morris Marina which used the conventional front-engine, rear-drive layout Ford had retained during the time BMC had travelled the Issigonis front-wheel-drive route for their new cars. The new Marina, however, did little to improve profitability or reduce the many duplications of engineering

Above: Larger-section tyres and stronger springs raised the ride height of the V8 by about an inch (25mm) over the four-cylinder MGBs. Small "V8" badges, and special wheels, distinguish the more powerful car.

Below: The 1975-model-year M.G. range. Although many felt that the rubber bumpers spoilt the appearance of the cars, they still sold in large numbers. Many preferred the extra protection they afforded in everyday use.

the huge number of jobs at stake, and the commitment of a Labour government to saving jobs by intervention, the prospects for a complete closure of the company could not be contemplated.

The Ryder report setting out the future of British Leyland was proved in the long run to be wildly over-optimistic in its forecast of available growth potential, and naive in the extreme when dealing with the labour relations problems. The management struggled for the next few years under the double burden of bureaucratic control from the National Enterprise Board and a poorly conceived plan for dealing with the future of the company. One result of decisions taken earlier, and reinforced during this period, was to affect M.G. enormously – indeed it was one of the reasons Abingdon had to close down in 1980, but we will look at that later.

A New Look

Just before the company finally ran out of money, the M.G. range had undergone a massive face-lift – literally! Those US changes to safety regulations, brought on directly by the efforts of Ralph Nader with his campaign against unsafe cars, meant that if the United States market was still to be open for M.G. exports a vast number of changes had to be made to both the MGB and the Midget. One of the problems faced when working to meet the new regulations was finding out exactly what the legislators intended when they drew up the rules! Each country and, in the case of America, each state had their own ideas on legislating for cars. All over the world an army of pressure groups were trying to force governments to impose restrictions on car manufacturers for a variety of reasons. However, within every manufacturing country the car companies were lobbying to try to limit the effects that any proposed changes would have on their products. The net result of this was a requirement to produce cars with many variations to suit each market, a tremendous imposition for a comparatively small manufacturer like M.G.

As has already been seen, the budget available for research and development was tiny when compared to other rival manufacturers and any changes made to the basic design of the cars necessarily had to apply to all cars produced, rather than just to those built for one country. To some extent the position was eased by a withdrawal from all but the UK and US markets for the bulk of production – possibly so as to eliminate competition for the forthcoming Triumph TR7 which was due for launch in 1975. Since the passing of various Clean Air Acts all cars destined for the American market had been modified to reduce harmful emissions and the requirements were being progressively tightened year by year. As a result, even before the drastic changes introduced for the 1975 model year cars, the vehicles exported to that market differed from those sold elsewhere in the world.

Legislation designed to protect the occupants from injury in the event of an accident had meant that US market M.G.s were fitted with rocker switches, padded dashboards and seat-

Above: The much larger rubber bumpers seemed to affect the looks of the Midget rather more than they did the MGB. Somehow, they blended less well with the shape of the bodywork, although they were equally valuable in resisting minor car park damage.

Left: The rear MGB bumpers were designed to protect the rear lights from receiving any damage in 5mph (8kph) accidents. Later cars had black-painted covers for the number-plate lights.

Right: A particularly smart rubber-bumper MGB GT fitted with a non-standard front air dam. Buying one of these models is the cheapest route into MGB ownership as they now cost much less than the open cars.

mounted head restraints from 1968. Minor accident damage resulting from low speed collisions and careless parking was costing insurance companies a lot of money and legislators decided that it should be possible to design cars to be able to withstand these impacts without sustaining any damage. For the 1974 model year cars the regulations called for there to be only minor damage resulting from such impacts and the Midget and MGB had to suffer the indignity of being fitted with large, energy-absorbing overriders to meet these requirements. However, for the following year the legislation called for there to be absolutely no damage – not even to a side-light lens – from 5mph (8kph) collisions and this was a lot more difficult for the engineers to achieve.

Added Weight

Faced with such a task, which was worsened by the need for the bumpers to meet a standard height requirement that meant raising the MGB ride height by 1.5in (38mm), the engineers had to do a lot of work. The design of the then 12-year-old MGB and 16-year-old Sprite/Midget bodyshells had to to be considerably changed to strengthen them to take the additional loads. Large and heavy "rubber" faced bumpers were

mounted front and rear on extensions to the "chassis" rails and the front bumpers had the flashing indicator lamps recessed within them. In an attempt to blend these large, and deep, bumpers into the overall design they were shaped to align with the existing bonnet and wings. The result for the MGB was reasonably acceptable, especially on dark-coloured cars, but those fitted to the Midget blended less happily.

The chassis modifications and heavy bumpers increased the weight considerably, reducing performance at a time when many ordinary saloons were getting ever quicker, but from the driver's point of view it was the increase in ride height that had the worst effect. Both suspension mounting points and spring heights were changed to give the required 1.5in (38mm) increase in ride height, with the result that the cars rolled more when cornering, and the handling was less predictable. In addition, the emission requirement for US markets had further reduced power outputs for cars sold there, especially those destined for California where the regulations were more stringent than for the other states. To help offset the penalty of the greater weight, and also to simplify the spares position for the company and their dealers, the A-series engine and gearbox used in all versions

Above and below: Cars built for the North American market had different lights. These side marker lamps and reflectors were fitted to both the Midget and the MGB. Additionally, the rear indicator lens covers differed from those fitted to home market cars.

of the Sprite/Midget since it was first launched was replaced by the same 1500cc engine and gearbox used in the Triumph Spitfire.

So it was with heavier and less attractive cars, that had lost the fine handling qualities they had previously possessed, that the company faced the difficult economic conditions of 1975. Worse still, these cars had not been developed quite as well as they might have been, not withstanding the difficulties the engineers faced. To launch cars with the basic handling defects that the 1975/76 MGBs possessed was poor, even by the British Leyland standards of the day. The situation was much improved with the introduction of a rear anti-roll bar, and revised front bar, in August 1976. In truth, these changes should have been made by the factory when the ride height was first altered.

Although the handling of the Midget was also compromised, no changes were ever made, but one problem apparent from the start of 1500 production was eventually remedied as late as August 1977. The Triumph engine was not as strong as the original A-series unit and in particular it seemed to object to being run at high engine speeds for long periods – on a motorway for example. The Spitfire 1500, which used the same engine, could be fitted with an overdrive to

reduce engine revolutions at higher speeds, but the Midget never enjoyed this luxury with the consequence that total engine failure was not uncommon. A higher differential gear ratio was finally fitted in 1977 and this certainly helped, but it should have been introduced right from the start of 1500 production and it is hard to understand the reason why it was not.

The whole attitude to M.G. car building was just a symptom of the malaise affecting both British Leyland and much of the rest of British industry then. It had already been decided that there were to be no entirely new M.G.s built at Abingdon and that the Group sports car efforts were to be centred on the TR7 to be built at Speke, near Liverpool; a factory with poor labour relations and no experience of building such a car. As a result the large amounts of money invested were wasted in producing a poor product, badly designed and assembled, and one for which there really was not a market for it to sell in the numbers originally planned.

Proposed vehicle safety legislation in America in the early 1970s had threatened the very existence of open cars in that market and this had meant that the TR7 was initially only available as a closed car. The majority of M.G. sales in that country had been of open cars, although quite a number of MGB GTs were sold there until they were withdrawn in advance of the announcement of the new Triumph, so it is hardly surprising that a purely closed car was not the hoped-for success. With so much being spent on one project from a limited budget, it was no surprise that Abingdon failed to receive any more finance than just the minimum required to keep on building the old models.

In spite of the poor position of British Leyland (or perhaps because of it), 1975 was chosen as the year to celebrate the M.G. Golden Jubilee. As a part of these celebrations it was decided that a special version of the MGB GT would be built. The major revisions to the MGB having already taken place, it was this rather flawed car that the company used to provide the basis of the Jubilee GT. Changes made for the short production run of 750 cars were few, but significant enough for the car to look different from the standard GT and for there to be an enthusiastic following for the model now. The paintwork was Racing Green, BLVC 25, the chrome waistline strips were painted over and the external mirrors black painted, to avoid a clash with the gold side stripes. These stripes incorporated the jubilee logo, and to complement these all the badges were gold and black rather than silver. Incidentally, all the 1975 MGBs and Midgets were fitted with gold badges to commemorate the anniversary. Instead of the standard steel or optional wire wheels, these special cars were fitted with V8 alloy/steel wheels, the same as those used for the MGB GT V8 but painted in gold and black to complement the dark green paintwork. The extra price for all the equipment, and the rarity value, was a modest £130, making the total cost £2,668.77.

Golden Jubilee Cars

To improve the specification, all the Jubilee cars were fitted with head rests, tinted glass, carpets in place of rubber mats and overdrive gearboxes. All of these were later to become standard items on the GT. In addition to the external badging, there was a dashboard plaque which was supplied to the dealer for him to engrave with the car's limited edition number and the owner's name. Although there were originally to be 750 cars, an extra one had to be built to replace one damaged whilst making an advertisement, and one Brooklands Green open car was finished with the same side stripes and wheels to celebrate the production of the millionth car from the Abingdon works. This car was offered as a prize for a rally in the United States and today is in an M.G. collection. One MGB GT V8 was also finished in the "Jubilee" colour scheme, as was a Midget which was the prize in a local raffle.

August 1976 saw the handling improvements for the MGB which were introduced as part of a package of changes designed to address, at last, some of the long-standing criticisms. Many of the changes were aimed at improving comfort, and most were welcomed, but there were also detail mechanical modifications. There were the improved anti-roll bars, an electric cooling fan

Left: The new car park at Abingdon in May 1975 was home to this batch of the special Limited Edition MGB GTs produced to celebrate 50 years of the M.G. car. 750 examples were built and all had the MGB V8-style wheels painted gold to match the gold side stripes. Racing Green was used for the paintwork, which also covered the usual chromed side mouldings. More luxurious carpeting, and tinted windows helped to set the model apart.

Right: Just one MGB roadster carried the Golden Jubilee colour scheme and this was used as a rally prize in the United States.

with the radiator mounted further forward in a position previously adopted for the V8, lower-geared steering rack and halogen headlamps. Inside the car there were bright "deck chair fabric" striped seats with head rests, a new fascia and central console with a glove box that could at long last be opened without a key, changes to switch gear and steering wheel, and a number of other detail modifications and the addition of previously extra items as standard. The prices of all cars had risen sharply over the preceding years and customers were looking for more items to be included as standard equipment. No longer could the old BMC trick of charging extra for basic accessories such as heaters work with a more discriminating buying public!

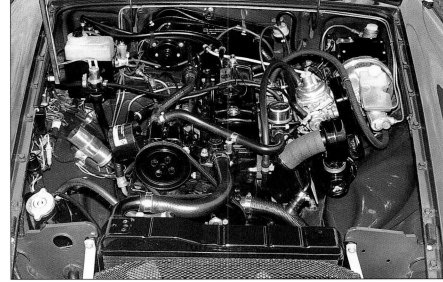

These changes certainly improved the cars but could not disguise the fact that they were now too heavy, too slow and generally outclassed by the modern saloons and hot-hatchbacks that were starting to appear. A road test of the new version of the GT appeared in 1977 giving the price as £3,576, the maximum speed as 99mph (159kph), and the acceleration to 60mph (97kph)

Below: Quite a novelty at an M.G. Car Club race meeting at Brands Hatch in Kent in 1975. The Royal Air Force Red Arrows aerobatic team gave this demonstration of extremely low-level "formation flying" – using brand new, red-painted Midget 1500s. A range of manoeuvres were shown.

Above: The complex equipment required to meet strict emission regulations can be judged from this picture of a late-model MGB engine bay. All this extra equipment, and the use of a single carburettor and smaller valves in the cylinder head, reduced the power output considerably.

from rest taking 14 seconds. In the same year a test of the new VW Golf GTi gave the cost as £3,372, top speed 108mph (174kph) and the acceleration from 0 to 60mph as 9.6 seconds. A new breed of sports car had arrived and, like it or not, the days of the traditional Abingdon product were numbered.

Disaster Strikes

1977 was a low point in the affairs of British Leyland as a whole and a series of disastrous strikes reduced the total output by nearly a quarter of a million vehicles. M.G. did not escape the chaos. The production of many cars was lost because of shortages of components made by other factories in the group. This, allied to a change in the way employees worked and were paid, must have further reduced profitability and brought the day of reckoning nearer still. In October 1977 the Labour government took a hand in the affair by supporting the appointment of a member of the National Enterprise Board, Michael Edwardes of Chloride, to the post of Chief Executive of British Leyland. At last there was to be a determined effort made to try to resolve the long-standing difficulties of the company and initially it looked as if things might also improve at Abingdon. In a move to try to re-establish the old marque loyalties after a decade of British Leyland corporate identity, the M.G. name was once again painted on the signs outside the factory. M.G. was to come under the wing of the Specialist Car Division and employees were now given copies of the magazine devoted to affairs of this division – not that there was ever much about M.G. to be read within its covers.

The reorganization by Michael Edwardes saw The M.G. Car Company grouped with Jaguar, Rover and Triumph, rather than with Austin and Morris – now considered as the volume car section of the Group. In order to give the marque names more prominence, the Group title was changed from British Leyland to just BL Ltd. There was also a wholesale shake-up of management with sackings and recruitment from outside the company as Edwardes considered that there were far too many people within the group who were in positions they were unsuited to hold. A start was made on rationalizing the

manufacturing capacity when the strike-ridden Speke plant was closed and production of the TR7 transferred to Canley.

In the Development Department at Abingdon work on replacing the aged B-series engine in the MGB with the new O-series OHC unit fitted to other British Leyland vehicles offered the promise of the continuation of that model into the 1980s. The feeling around the factory was that at long last things were improving and that maybe there was a long-term future for M.G.s at Abingdon. However, this proved not to be the case and the closure of the factory was announced to a stunned work force, and shocked M.G. enthusiasts worldwide, on 10th September 1979. The fact that the announcement of the closure came just after the company and work force had celebrated 50 years of car production in Abingdon with open days, a carnival and other celebrations, just added to the misery of the workers and their families. Initially the blow was softened by a statement that the factory would continue to be used to prepare for export cars built at Cowley, but this was never to happen and the last car built, an MGB, rolled off the production lines in October 1980, and the factory closed.

Production of the 1500 Midget had ceased almost a year earlier, in November 1979. The last 500 examples built for the home market were all painted black, and were supplied with a commemorative plaque inscribed "1929-1979 – Fifty years of the M.G. Midget". These last cars are much cherished with many surviving in enthusiasts' hands – some having covered purely nominal mileages. In addition to MGB and Midget production, for a period the Vanden Plas version of the Austin Allegro was completed and trimmed at Abingdon to utilize spare production capacity – a job well suited to the adaptable work force employed there.

An Overvalued Pound

The reason given for the closure was the unprofitability of the M.G. operation. Just how the accountants separated the M.G. losses from the huge deficit being run up by the group as a whole remains a mystery, but they came up with a much-publicized figure of a loss of £900 on every car built at Abingdon. Whether this figure is right or not, there is no doubt that the decision to concentrate sales effort on the home market and the United States that had been taken a few years earlier was much to blame for the closure. After the election in 1979 of a Conservative government under the leadership of Margaret Thatcher, the Foreign Exchange Market decided that the combination of a right-wing administration and an oil-rich economy made sterling a strong currency. The value of the pound against other currencies, and especially against the American dollar, rose sharply. At home inflation was rampant with frequent pay and price rises the norm. As a consequence the prices BL needed to charge for the cars they exported rose inexorably but those of their competitors did

Above: This 1976 MGB has just been lowered down onto its wheels at the factory so that the last few assembly tasks can be carried out. Once fully assembled, oil, water and a little petrol were added so that it could be driven onto a rolling road for a full test routine.

not. In 1979, to remain competitive in a weak American market, the prices charged there for M.G.s could not be raised to cover the increases in both home market prices and in the value of the pound, leading to losses – a situation also faced by other marques exported by the group. The company accounts for that period show that they were making, on average, a loss of at least £500 on each and every vehicle they sold – both on cars destined for export and those sold in the home market.

BL were not alone in suffering from the higher value of the pound in the world market. Successive administrations have struggled with the need to protect the value of the currency and to hold down inflation, and often it has been British industry and British workers who have paid the price. In the late 1970s and early 1980s a large section of British manufacturing industry lost their markets with devastating effects in some parts of the country. Pleas from industrialists, Michael Edwardes of BL amongst these, fell on deaf ears and the damage done then by government policy and the Foreign Exchange Market will probably never be repaired.

Even beyond the workers directly involved, the news of the closure of M.G. provoked a storm of protest which extended to support from

Above: Inevitably, a few cars received minor paintwork damage during assembly. Repairs were carried out in B block, where there were paint booths and drying ovens.

Left: Cars for export were loaded onto special trains at Abingdon and taken to the docks. These Midgets await shipment at Southampton.

Below: The end of the line for Abingdon. After over 50 years as a sports car producer, the factory closed and parts of it were completely demolished.

a large group of Members of Parliament, headed by Robert Adley, MP for Christchurch, and Tom Benyon, MP for Abingdon, who wanted the company to reverse the closure decision. There were campaigns to save the marque run by both the M.G. Car Club and the M.G. Owners Club, with a convoy of cars being driven to London to protest at the company's headquarters and to deliver a petition. The amount of publicity given to the campaign by the newspapers, television and radio did much to raise public awareness of the marque, and boosted membership of the M.G. clubs, and there was tremendous popular support at home and abroad for the efforts to save the Abingdon factory

A proposal was considered for production to be taken over by a consortium headed by Aston Martin Lagonda Limited and on 31st March, 1980 a statement from BL Ltd. confirmed that discussions for the sale of the Abingdon factory, and a licence to use the M.G. name, were taking place based on an offer made by the company on 7th March. However, all this effort was to no avail and the factory finally closed with the production of that last MGB. The plans to keep the work force employed there on export packing were abandoned, and the site, plant and equipment and all the other assets were offered for sale by auction in March 1981 – a sad occasion. The catalogue for that auction makes interesting reading, listing everything from a dynamometer to a spray gun, office furniture to sets of motoring magazines – everything had to go! Wandering round the factory to examine the lots allowed access to sections that had previously been closed on open days and works tours, but it was sad to think that 50 years of sports car production had ended.

The Final MGBs

As with the last Midgets, there was a final run of Limited Edition MGBs for the home market. This was not the first such run of special MGBs as, in addition to those produced in 1975 to celebrate the Golden Jubilee, in 1979 there had been a Limited Edition MGB roadster built especially for the American market. Again, black was the chosen colour and the model was launched at the 1979 Auto Expo in New York. Down each side of the cars were distinctive silver side stripes featuring the British flag The cars left Abingdon fitted with attractive alloy wheels and stainless steel luggage racks were mounted on the boot lids in America. However, as with all MGBs exported there, they had to suffer the indignity of an engine with smaller valves, single carburettor and emission control equipment, all of which reduced the power output drastically. California specification cars had also to carry catalytic converters.

The final home market Limited Edition took the form of 1000 cars which were advertised and sold after the factory had closed. Much was made in advertisements of their status as "instant collector's items" and some were bought and stored unused, to emerge at auctions and in dealer's showrooms many years later. There were 420 roadsters and 580 GTs with one example of each going directly into the Heritage Trust Museum (now displayed in the museum at Gaydon in Warwickshire alongside one of the last, black-painted Midgets). Mechanically the cars were identical to the standard production vehicles but the GTs were all painted Pewter Metallic, with silver side stripes of the same design as those fitted to the American Limited Edition cars, and the roadsters were painted Bronze Metallic with gold coloured side stripes of the same design.

Like the standard cars, the last 1000 Limited Edition cars had the striped seats – grey for the GTs and orange for the roadsters. The grey trim blended well with the silver paint on the GTs but the orange was not as successful at harmonizing with the Bronze of the roadsters. It is a pity that black-covered seats were not used. These final versions of the MGB remain as examples of the last M.G.s to be built at the historic Abingdon factory.

There were just one thousand Limited Edition MGBs built. The 420 roadsters and 580 GTs were amongst the last cars to be assembled at Abingdon, and thus are an important part of M.G. history. The cars were sold only on the home market, after the factory finally closed, and company advertising made much of their status as future classics. Quite a number of them were bought by collectors who hoped that they would appreciate in value. Occasionally examples are offered for sale that have covered very few miles.

Left: In August 1976 revisions to the MGB were announced. Mechanically the car gained a rear anti-roll bar to improve the handling and an electric cooling fan. However, it was comfort for the driver and passenger that received most attention. High rates of inflation in the 1970s were inexorably raising the prices of all British cars, so prompting the company to improve the specification.

Below: Although the heavy impact-absorbing bumpers introduced in 1974 meant the demise of the radiator grille, space naturally had to be found for the traditional octagonal M.G. badge.

Below: Amongst the 1976 package of improvements were seat head restraints of a new pattern as standard, and sunvisors with a mirror for passengers. Unfortunately, with the low windscreen, these tend to restrict vision for taller drivers.

Above: The most controversial change made was the introduction of striped fabric seat covers for some markets. Two patterns were offered, the orange and brown seen here and two-tone grey. More appreciated were the dashboard changes. A new moulding contained revised instruments and, at last, the glovebox could be opened without a key. The overdrive switch moved to the gear lever knob.

Below: All the open Limited Edition cars were finished in Bronze Metallic paint and had gold side stripes. The GTs were painted Pewter Metallic with silver side stripes and had two-tone grey seat covers. All the closed cars, and 212 of the open tourers, had these distinctive alloy wheels, which carried 185/70 tyres. All had black rubberized spoilers mounted beneath the front bumpers.

SPECIFICATION

Model: MGB LE two-seater roadster

Engine: Four-cylinder in line, overhead valve, water cooled. 80.26mm x 88.9mm, 1789cc, 90bhp

Gearbox: Four-speed synchromesh with overdrive

Final drive: 3.909:1. Overdrive top 22.1mph/1000rpm (36kph/1000rpm)

Suspension: Front: Independent with coil springs, wishbones and rack and pinion steering. Rear: Live axle suspended on half-elliptic leaf springs

Dimensions: Wheelbase 7ft 7in (2311mm). Track, front 4ft 1.5in (1257mm), rear 4ft 1.75in (1264mm). Overall length 13ft 2.25in (4019mm)

Unladen weight: 20.9cwt (1062kg)

Cost when new: £6445

Performance: (From contemporary reports): Top speed 105mph (169kph)

Owner: Eric Nicholls

Right and far right: Although mechanically the LEs were identical to standard MGBs, it is interesting to see how much the cars had changed over the years. By 1980 the radiator had moved forward and the fan was electrically powered, not belt-driven. There was a servo for dual-circuit brakes and a closed circuit engine breathing system that fed the crankcase gases directly into the carburettors.

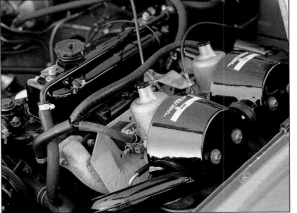

Above left and right: Eric Nicholls bought this MGB LE from a work colleague some years ago and it is in original condition apart from having received some attention to the paintwork. He also owns a Limited Edition GT and number of other M.G.s, including the TC featured earlier. All his cars are kept in superb condition in spite of being used all the year round. These late model MGBs are popular and there are usually quite a few to be found entered in any club competition.

Above: Although this car has alloy wheels, wire wheels were fitted to 202 of the roadster LEs. The alloy wheels were first used for the United States market Limited Edition cars which were introduced there in 1979. The American cars were all painted black and had the silver version of the stripes along each side.

Left: One of the stipulations in the legislation that forced the introduction of impact-absorbing bumpers was that lamp glasses must not to be damaged by minor accidents, hence the protection given them seen here.

THE STORY CONTINUES

The final closure and sale of the factory at Abingdon following the failure of frantic last-ditch attempts by workers, M.G. dealers and enthusiasts from all around the world to save M.G. production was thought by many to signal the end of the M.G. marque. Recent history had recorded the end of other well-known sporting cars, Riley and Austin-Healey, which had previously been marketed by first the British Motor Corporation and then British Leyland, only to disappear into obscurity once production had ceased. There was no reason to suppose that M.G. would not suffer a similar fate.

However, the vociferous campaign to save the marque must have done more than anything else to convince the British Leyland management of the priceless asset they possessed in the M.G. name and it is to their credit that they took note of this and used it – even if only for purely marketing reasons – as the badge to identify performance versions of the range of family cars they built in the 1980s. The "Save M.G." campaign certainly raised the profile of the marque and re-awakened public interest in the cars. It seems no coincidence that membership of the M.G. clubs increased dramatically around that time, with many people either joining the ranks of M.G. enthusiasts for the first time or returning to the fold, perhaps prompted by nostalgic memories of cars they owned in earlier years.

Looked at dispassionately, the closure of the M.G. factory at Abingdon now seems to have been inevitable bearing in mind the parlous state of the British Leyland Group and the lack of any investment in new M.G. models over the previous decade. Yes, the MGB could have been revitalized by giving it the O-series OHC engine,

Right: One of the most serious proposals to save the M.G. factory from closure came from a consortium headed by Aston Martin. Under the direction of the designer William Towns, a plan to develop the cars was drawn up. This envisaged initially giving the MGB some cosmetic changes and fitting the O-series engine already used in other models in the BL range. An ordinary MGB was modified to show to the press and while this car did not have the new engine, it did have most of the styling changes he had proposed for the first year of production.

Below: A frequent criticism made of the MGB roadster was that the screen was too low for taller drivers. William Towns proposed using the MGB GT-height screen and side windows, together with a modified hood. Front and rear bumpers were re-styled and the sides of the body painted to link them visually.

and perhaps some minor facelift, much as was tried by William Towns for Aston Martin when they proposed taking over the company, but this would have done little to increase the number of cars sold each year. The high value of the pound against other currencies had made selling the cars abroad unprofitable and there was little scope for either raising the price or reducing production costs. The only answer would have been a completely new M.G. and neither the time nor the money existed then to develop one.

Because no new M.G. sports cars were being produced, there was an ever increasing interest in keeping the existing cars on the road, or restoring to good health cars that had previously been pushed into sheds or garages after suffering some mechanical or body ailment. The "classic car movement" generally was growing strongly in the early 1980s with a proliferation of magazines, car shows and even training courses on car restoration to stimulate interest. Many small businesses sprung up around this time

both to supply the parts requirements of home restorers and to provide maintenance and rebuilding services for owners unable, or unwilling, to get their own hands dirty. Many of these small firms have since expanded to become multi-million pound businesses with worldwide interests. As a result, the parts supply situation for MGBs, in particular, is as good now as it was when production of those cars ceased in 1980, and many thousands of them still provide their owners with reliable, everyday transport.

A New M.G. Saloon

For years BMC, and later British Leyland, had been thinking about a replacement for the successful Mini and many projects were considered. In 1977 when the new management team, under the leadership of Michael Edwardes, looked at their overall model line-up they decided to scrap the plans to replace the Mini. The work done on this project was to be transferred into efforts to introduce a slightly larger small car as an additional model. This car was coded LC8 but eventually launched as the Metro following a naming competition amongst the employees. It was dimensionally larger than the originally intended Mini replacement because, after looking at the opposition in the marketplace such as the VW Polo and Ford Fiesta, it was thought that a Mini-sized car would have not been suitable.

To assemble the Metro, upon which rested the hopes of the company's future, a new 725,000 square foot (67,350m^2) factory at Longbridge, Birmingham was built and equipped. A first for BL was the installation of computer-controlled robots to assemble the body – a far cry from the largely hand-assembly practices used for earlier models – and the tooling and equipment to build the engines and gearboxes was updated to improve the refinement of what were, basically, the same units as those used in the Mini since its launch in 1959. Announced to the public at the Birmingham Motor Show in 1980, the new car was an immediate success and helped in no small measure to restore the fortunes of both the BL company in particular, and the British motor industry in general.

In May 1982 the first realignment of the Metro range was carried out with an M.G. 1300 version. As befitted this inheritor of the M.G. badge, the power was increased by 12bhp over other 1.3 litre Metros and the interior trim was upgraded. Alloy wheels, lower profile tyres, and a rear spoiler added to the sporting image. Inside and out, prolific use of the M.G. logo left no one in any doubt about its identity, although many purists muttered darkly about "badge engineering" and "desecration of the sacred name"! Of course, all this was nothing new and, as some historians were quick to point out, the first M.G.s were only hotted-up Morris products.

Above: Owners of the turbo version of the M.G. Metro certainly could not get lost in a crowd! These large logos on the sides of the body left onlookers in no doubt that this car was something out of the ordinary.

Above right: The 1275cc engine was based on the old A-series unit used in the Midget and many other BMC and BL cars. For the Metro, it was substantially re-designed and when turbocharged gave 93bhp.

The new M.G. Metro performed well, with a top speed of around 100mph (161kph) and brisk acceleration allied to surprisingly good fuel economy – a feature of the Metro range as a whole. The car sold well and encouraged British Leyland to introduce an even higher performance version, the M.G. Metro 1300 Turbo, a few months later. This car featured an engine that was extensively modified to cope with a power output of 93bhp - 30 per cent more than the ordinary M.G. Metro. The water cooling in the cylinder head was improved, the crankshaft strengthened, solid-skirt pistons fitted and the

compression ratio was lowered to 9.4:1. The Garrett AiResearch T3 turbocharger was sited between the transverse-mounted engine and the bulkhead. To stop this projectile – billed then as the fasted M.G. saloon – ventilated front disc brakes were used. Alloy wheels fitted with lower profile tyres than those on the non-turbocharged car were specified, and the oil and water cooling was upgraded by the use of larger capacity radiators. Handling was improved by fitting stiffer anti-roll bars and uprated Hydragas suspension units. Improved creature comforts included side window de-misting, opening rear windows, remote-control door mirrors and stereo radio/cassette. These were later also fitted to the standard M.G. Metro 1300.

Although the arrival of the Metro heralded the start of an improvement in company fortunes it was certainly not enough on its own to ensure their long-term survival. The ageing model line-

Right: There can be no overstating the importance of the Metro to the company in the early 1980s. Had the car failed in the marketplace then the already difficult position of this British volume car producer would have been considerably worsened. Luckily, the car was good, and it sold in large numbers. The M.G. version, with better trim and performance, was popular and introduced a new group of drivers to the marque.

up was boosted for a while by the introduction of a Triumph-badged, and UK built, version of the Honda Accord. This was really a stop-gap until the BL-designed replacement medium-sized car, the Maestro, appeared in 1983. As with the Metro, there was an M.G. version in the model line-up – the M.G. Maestro 1600. The company's move into high technology continued with this model, which was drawn up using new computer-aided design techniques, the same system being used to control the manufacture of body panels and many other components. The car was assembled on an automated production line with much of the work being carried out by computer-controlled robots. Neither was the technology confined to design and production. Customers for these smart new cars were faced with electronic instruments and a synthesized voice intoning warning messages, a feature not everyone liked. One advantage of the electronic instruments particularly liked by travellers to mainland Europe was the ability to change the reading from miles-per-hour to kilometres at the flick of a switch.

Improvements To The Maestro

As with the other M.G. saloons, the Maestro in M.G. trim featured an uprated engine and both cosmetic and mechanical changes. Initially the engine was a 1600cc unit from the standard Maestro, fitted with different carburettors and manifolds boosting the power output by over 20bhp to 102bhp, but this was later replaced by the 1600 S-series engine giving a slightly greater power output. In this form the car was capable of around 110mph (177kph) with the rest to 60mph (97kph) in under 10 seconds. Good though it was, this performance was considered by the motoring press to be inferior to that possessed by some rivals and from October 1985 the two-litre O-series engine, capable of producing 115bhp at 5500rpm, was fitted. In this form the car was much quicker and was capable of 115mph (185kph) and reached 60mph (97kph) from rest in 8.7 seconds. In addition, the VW-produced gearbox fitted to the earlier cars was changed for a better, Honda-designed, unit and later the suspension was modified to improve the handling.

This two-litre version of the Maestro proved a popular choice for motorists looking for a car with good performance, excellent interior accommodation and with the added appeal of the M.G. badge. During the time the car was in production there were a number of minor specification changes including the provision of better-looking alloy wheels and a new range of exterior colours, with "colour-coded" bumper inserts, side rubbing strips and revised interior trim. Quite a number of these cars are being actively restored and preserved by M.G. club members to appear at meetings alongside the earlier "Abingdon" cars.

In February 1984 the M.G. name was given a boost by the announcement of the M.G. Metro 6R4 rally car. This four-wheel-drive, two-seater competition car was powered by a V6, all-aluminium engine that was mounted behind the

driver. Development work on the prototype cars was done jointly by Austin Rover Motorsport and Williams Grand Prix Engineering of Didcot under their chief Formula One car designer, Patrick Head. After initial tests were successfully carried out, the requisite 200 cars were built to qualify for international competition with some being sold to the public at £35,000 each. In basic "Clubman" form the engine was tuned to give around 250bhp but this was increased to as much as 400bhp in cars built to full international rally specification.

Above: The mid-sized Maestro had the popular and useful "hatchback" design so suited to family use. The 1598cc single overhead-camshaft engine produced 103bhp, giving the car good performance. Later versions had larger engines.

Below: To compete adequately with overseas manufacturers BL had to completely re-equip their factories. Here Maestro body shells enter an automatic welder during assembly.

Right: The M.G. Metro 6R4 rally car was eventually built in sufficient quantities to qualify for international rallying. 200 examples were assembled and were on sale in two states of tune. The Clubman version with 250bhp cost nearly £35,000, and the "full house" International specification car was priced at £47,000. Unfortunately, all the cars built to this formula were banned from international rallies by the governing body as they were just too fast.

Although based on the standard Metro, almost all the body and mechanical parts were specially made for the 6R4. To accommodate the wider wheels the wheel arches were extended and at the rear the lifting engine cover incorporated a huge spoiler to increase downforce on the rear wheels. When this cover was fully opened the engine was exposed for ease of maintenance. Unfortunately, specially developed cars, like the 6R4, were deemed to be just too quick and were banned by FISA, the body that governs motor-sport, before their full potential could be realized. However, the limited use they had before being banned did return the M.G. name to front-line motor sport. Even ten years after the ban, Metro 6R4s were still competitive in specialist fields of motor sport, like rallycross, where the huge acceleration available could be used to greatest advantage.

Following on from the success in the market of the Maestro, a slightly larger car, with a separate luggage compartment rather than a hatchback, was announced by Austin Rover in March 1985. Called the Montego, this car was aimed at the lucrative "fleet" market that was dominated by Ford and Vauxhall. Once again, an M.G. version was included in the range with the usual trim and engine modifications to justify its higher price tag. The two-litre O-series engine that was later to also be fitted to the Maestro gave the car good performance which was further enhanced when a turbo-charged version was announced

Above: The specially-built V6, 2991cc engine in the four-wheel-drive M.G. Metro 6R4 is rear-mounted, unlike the road car.

Below: Door trims and dashboard might lead one to think that the 6R4 was closely-related to the standard car – not really!

in April 1985. This car boasted an engine producing 150bhp making it, according to press releases issued at the time, "the fastest production M.G. saloon ever".

The turbo-charged car featured suspension and braking modifications to control the extra power, different wheels with lower profile tyres and front and rear spoilers to help keep the car on the road. The Montego turbo-charged engine was fitted to a limited-edition version of the Maestro in 1988 to produce a real high-performance M.G. The exterior appearance of this model was transformed by Tickford coach-builders who added side skirts and deeper spoilers painted to match the body colour. The Maestro Turbo was advertised as "Faster than a Ferrari, a Porsche, a Lamborghini, a Lotus, an Aston". With a claimed acceleration to 60mph (97kph) of just 6.7 seconds, this £12,999 saloon was not for the faint-hearted – nor was it the car to drive if you didn't want to attract attention as the word "Turbo" was written in large letters down both flanks! The Maestro Turbo was built in small numbers but many remain as the final, and fastest, testament to the M.G. of the 1980s.

Although the M.G. variants of the Metro, Maestro and Montego saloons had been very successful in marketing terms, and had served to keep the marque alive when it could have died with the closure of Abingdon in 1980, they were in the enthusiasts' eyes not really what M.G.s were all about. Ever since the last MGB rolled off

Above: The two-litre Montego Turbo was a fast sports saloon. The Garrett AiResearch T3 turbocharger boosted the power of the 1994cc engine to 150bhp, giving the car a top speed of around 125mph (201kph).

Left: The engine fitted to the two-litre fuel-injected version of the Montego produced 115bhp. Although not as fast as the Turbo, it was still good for 116mph (187kph). These roomy saloons proved capable of giving good service with many examples clocking up high mileages without trouble.

the production line there had been speculation in the motoring press about possible successors. In 1985 Austin Rover themselves fuelled speculation by showing off a beautiful "concept car" – The M.G. EX-E – at various motor shows.

A Stunning Show Car

The EX-E was a closed coupé built with an adhesive-bonded aluminium alloy frame clad with plastic panels. The Metro 6R4 V6 engine developing 250bhp was rear mounted and the car had independent, coil-sprung suspension with double wishbones on all four wheels. The ride height could be adjusted by the driver and an anti-lock, all-disc braking system was fitted. In line with its advanced specification were such features as automatic rain-sensitive windscreen wipers, head-up instrument display on the windscreen, and credit-card magnetic keys that also set seat position and mirrors to suit each driver. It is a pity it never went into production.

As already mentioned, the growth in interest in the older M.G.s fostered by the publicity surrounding the closure of the factory in 1980 prompted the foundation of a large number of spares businesses to cater for these cars. As the original builders of M.G.s, and as suppliers of spare parts for the cars they had built, Austin Rover were already in the business of servicing the needs of owners of older M.G.s. However, in 1983 a separate company, British Motor Heritage, was formed specifically to supply parts for those obsolete vehicles originally built by the Austin Rover Group and their predeces-

sors – M.G.s, Austin-Healeys, Minis and Triumphs. At first this was limited to mechanical components and body panels etc., but the obvious need for replacement complete body shells for the more badly rusted cars led the enthusiastic team at British Motor Heritage to look at the feasibility of satisfying this need. Luckily a large proportion of the hugely expensive press tools needed to produce the 240 separate parts contained in an M.G. body shell were still in existence. These tools and a huge press machine were collected together at a new factory at Faringdon where they were refurbished. In addition some of the assembly jigs, used originally at the body plant at Swindon to build the MGB bodies, were also acquired, and some new jigs constructed, so that the pressed parts could

be assembled into complete body shells. The welding used so much power that the local electric supply was unable to cope and a generator was installed to power the spot-welding machines.

Complete new body shells were available for the MGB roadster in 1988 and to publicize the advantages of re-shelling otherwise scrap cars a rusty MGB was stripped and rebuilt into one of the new shells at a Classic Car Show by a team of mechanics drawn from some of the M.G. specialists. The large amount of press coverage given to this event ensured that a great deal of public interest was aroused in the project and a healthy order book developed for the new shells. These were initially only available without doors, front wings, boot lid and bonnet but were

later supplied complete after Heritage received complaints from home restorers over difficulties experienced when fitting these panels.

The MGB shell successfully launched, Heritage went on to build a very small batch of MGB GT bodies followed by ones for the later Midgets and Sprites. Leaving aside the ethics of creating what were, to all intents and purposes, brand new cars using the identities of cars beyond repair, there is no doubt that the Heritage body shells have enabled people to rebuild a number of cars that would have otherwise been lost. However, perhaps the most important outcome of this project was the building of a new version of the MGB for the 1990s – the RV8 – which arguably put the M.G. name back on the sports car map and paved the way for the MGF.

The idea of building brand new MGBs using a Heritage shell as a basis was considered by the Heritage team, under their Managing Director David Bishop, almost as soon as the new bodies were being produced. The idea seems to have been to build virtually new MGB V8 roadsters to much the same specification as the MGB GT V8s produced in the 1970s – in other words to build the car many people felt the company should have produced at that time. Research was carried out as to the feasibility of building a small number of new MGB V8s at Heritage's own plant but in the end the project was taken over by Rover Cars as it was felt that Faringdon did not have sufficient resources to tackle the whole task in its own right.

Back To V8 Power

It is not surprising that, when considering building new MGBs, the only serious contender as an engine should be the Rover V8. The Buick-derived, light alloy, eight-cylinder engine is a tremendous unit that is both compact and powerful. Since the 1970s, when it was fitted in de-tuned form to the MGB GT V8, considerable development work had kept this power unit thoroughly up-to-date and eminently suited for fitment to a sports car of the 1990s. Indeed, the manufacturer TVR had been fitting tuned Rover V8s to their powerful sports cars for many years with much success.

With the task handed over to the Rover Group, the responsibility for development was given to Rover Special Projects, which was a small division of the company specially created in 1990 to work on low-volume product lines and specialist development work outside that done by the main Rover design teams. Once work on the RV8 design was started in earnest, and some prototypes were built and tested, it became clear that quite a number of modified components would be needed. Parts used on the original MGBs were either no longer made or were deemed not good enough for a 1990s high performance car.

Externally, although the basic MGB structure remains, the wings, bonnet and front and rear bumpers have been extensively remodelled to produce a more up-to-date design. When the MGB was first built it was considered a very

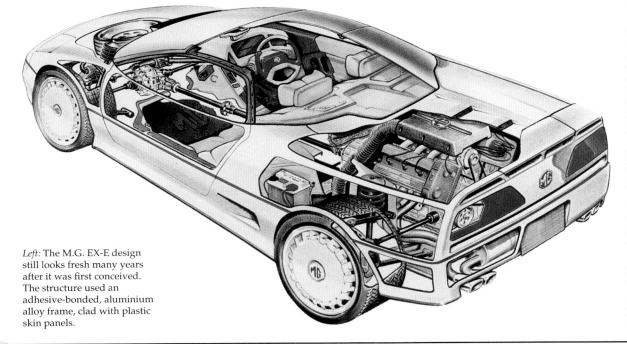

Above: The M.G. EX-E concept car bristled with new ideas. A full electronic dashboard faced the driver and an aircraft-style head-up display of information, like engine speed, was projected onto the windscreen.

Below: The power for this attractive car came from a rear-mounted M.G. Metro 6R4 engine which produced 250bhp in road trim. An exciting M.G. would have resulted had the EX-E ever gone into production.

Left: The M.G. EX-E design still looks fresh many years after it was first conceived. The structure used an adhesive-bonded, aluminium alloy frame, clad with plastic skin panels.

good-looking car, indeed, even now there are few 1960s cars that look as attractive. However, the 1974 changes that introduced heavy, impact-absorbing bumpers and raised the ride height produced a car that was by no means as pleasing to look at – especially when finished in lighter colours where the black bumpers appear more evident to the eye.

Radical Re-Design

Modern cars are routinely fitted with knock-resistant bumpers finished with flexible paints that match the colours used on the steel body shell, so it was easy for the Rover team to achieve a more integrated design by utilizing this technology. The decision to fit the car with wider 15-inch wheels shod with low profile tyres meant that the wings would need widening to cover these. The result is a vehicle that is slightly broader than the original MGB and looks much more "muscular". Having the front and rear bumpers finished in body colour gives the whole car a more integrated look whilst retaining the essential design elements of the earlier vehicle.

Under the skin much was new. In fact, almost all the smaller components were either specially made for the RV8, or were taken from other models in the Rover range – very few were taken from the MGB. The car was built to appeal to an affluent sector of the market so was much better finished, trimmed and equipped than were the Abingdon-built cars.

Mechanically the engine was a tuned 3.9-litre unit mated to a five-speed gearbox, no overdrive now. The power available from the larger capacity engine – 3.5 litres in the old MGB GT V8 – was increased by nearly 40 per cent to 190bhp. To cope with this extra power the rear axle featured a limited-slip differential and the new rear springs were assisted to resist axle tramp on

Above: The re-introduction of complete bodies for both the MGB and the Midget, built by Heritage on the original tooling, has revolutionized the restoration of badly-rusted cars. Many M.G.s previously considered as being beyond economic repair have been brought back to life.

Below: Rebuilds at Classic Car Shows have become popular in recent years. Sometimes they are just a demonstration of assembly techniques, but here the donor car was driven onto the stand at the start of the show and all the parts were then transferred to the new shell over a three-day period.

hard acceleration by the fitment of torque control arms between the axle and the front spring mounts. Front and rear, the old lever-arm dampers were replaced by modern telescopic units and the front suspension cross-member from the MGB was modified to accept the revised suspension. Ventilated front disc brakes boosted brake performance although drums were retained for the rear.

The RV8 body shells were assembled by British Motor Heritage at Faringdon, who built about 15 each week. They had to be rather better finished that the MGB shells they had been used to building as the priming and painting procedure at Cowley did not allow for any of the rectification of blemishes normally done by the average MGB restorer as a matter of course. To ensure high quality, Rover had their own inspectors look at the completed shells before they were transported to Cowley for painting.

A Hand-Crafted Car

A separate assembly facility was established in a former body and panel storage area at Cowley – something of a return to its roots for the M.G. marque as you will remember that the first M.G.s were built in Oxford before the company moved to Abingdon! Because the RV8 was to be hand-assembled – no robots here – the assembly area was arranged so that the small team could build up the cars by traditional methods. Each worker spent as long as two and a half hours to complete their tasks on each RV8, compared to the average in most factories of just a few minutes per car. This lengthy involvement ensured that the jobs were carried out to a very high standard and to reinforce this, each car was fully road-tested and any faults rectified before being prepared for delivery in closed transporters to the dealers. Before a rolling road was installed at Abingdon in the 1970s, all M.G.s had been road-tested in this manner before delivery.

The standard of finish and trim on the RV8 was high. Seats covered in stone-coloured leather, polished wood veneered dashboard, Tickford-designed and built Mohair hood – plus all the modern conveniences one could wish for. The suspension revisions and the wide, low profile tyres gave the car good handling and roadholding, even if the basically 30-year-old design did not allow it to compete on level terms with more modern rivals. The motoring press, on the whole, liked driving the car whilst adding the caveat that on purely value-for-money grounds the high price tag, of around £25,000 on the road, would leave all but diehard M.G. enthusiasts looking elsewhere. This, though, was really missing the point of the exercise which was to sell an updated MGB in small numbers to people who were looking for a car in the same mould as the original, but with the extra power and convenience of a 1990s-built machine. As the company reached their target of selling over 2000 cars – many of which were exported to Japan where British specialist cars are in demand - the project must be deemed a success. It certainly raised the profile of the marque in the eyes of the public and, with the new,

Right: RV8 assembly was carried out at Cowley, Oxford. As with previous M.G. sports cars, the work was largely performed by hand, with each worker spending as long as two and a half hours on a car.

Below: An M.G. sports car at a Motor Show once again. Thirty years earlier, in 1962, the London Motor Show had launched the MGB, so the Rover stand at the 1992 Birmingham Motor Show was a fitting venue for the RV8 launch.

Bottom: The very last M.G. RV8, car number 02223, is driven off the Cowley assembly line surrounded by the M.G. workers.

Although the RV8 was launched at the Birmingham Motor Show in 1992, it was in no way a brand new M.G. but was really more of a modernized old one. It owed its existence to the availability of new MGB body shells built from original tooling by British Motor Heritage. Ever since the first of these appeared, there had been speculation about the possibility of the MGB coming back into production. In the event, a thorough redesign saw the RV8 sharing just some parts with the old MGB, while following its basic design.

SPECIFICATION

Model: RV8 two-seater roadster

Engine: Eight-cylinders in a vee, overhead valve, water cooled. 94mm x 71.12mm, 3946cc, 190bhp

Gearbox: Five-speed synchromesh

Final drive: 3.31:1. Top gear 28.97mph/1000rpm (47kph/1000rpm)

Suspension: Front: Independent with coil springs, double wishbones and rack and pinion steering. Rear: Live axle suspended on half-elliptic leaf springs, twin torque-control arms

Dimensions: Wheelbase 7ft 7.7in (2330mm). Track, front 4ft 1.6in (1260mm), rear 4ft 4.4in (1330mm). Overall length 13ft 2in (4010mm)

Unladen weight: 21.7cwt (1101kg)

Cost when new: £26,030

Performance: (From contemporary reports): Top speed 136mph (219kph)

Owner: Frank Clemmey

Right: The dashboard, instruments and controls were all updated and owed more to parts available from other Rover products than to the original MGB items. The speedometer and tachometer sit behind the thick-rimmed steering wheel, with the fuel gauge placed between them. Above the central tunnel there is a voltmeter, an analogue clock and a water temperature gauge. In front of the lever for the five-speed gearbox are the heating and ventilation controls and sound system.

Left: The cockpit of the RV8 is a far cry from that of the MGB. The comfortable, deeply-upholstered seats are covered in soft leather and the dashboard and door cappings are veneered in polished elm. Although all this luxury seems at odds with the original concept of the MGB, it suited the 1990s buyers who paid over £25,000 for this hand-built sports car. A comprehensive alarm system protects their investment.

Left: The front and rear of the car were completely redesigned. The front fog lamps and indicator lights are recessed into the bumper mouldings and the sloping headlights are similar to those used by Porsche for their popular 911 model.

Right: The rear fog lamps are recessed into the bumper while the side, brake and reversing lights are fitted, along with the orange, flashing indicator lights, in enlarged MGB-style units in the rear wings.

Right and far right: The beautiful, light-alloy V8 engine, like that used in the MGB GT V8 in 1973, comes from the Land Rover. It has Lucas multi-point fuel injection which boosts the power output from the 3946cc engine to 190bhp. Although possessing tremendous acceleration, the main impression one gains when driving the RV8 is of prodigious amounts of torque produced at all speeds by this engine. In any gear the car is eager to accelerate.

Above left and right: Bearing his own personal registration number, this White Gold painted RV8 is maintained in immaculate condition by owner, Frank Clemmey. The RV8 is an imposing car on the road and with only around 2000 built, and fewer than 500 sold in their home country, they will continue to be something of a rarity. While not the completely new M.G. that the market craved, the RV8 helped re-establish the marque and paved the way for the arrival of the MGF.

Below: Although the hood and windscreen were MGB based, they underwent redesign. The previous windscreen frame was built up from large numbers of aluminium castings and extrusions but the RV8 frame is a one-piece steel unit. Unfortunately, it is still rather too shallow for tall drivers. The soft-top and frame were adapted by Tickford and the cover is no longer secured by chromed external clips.

Right: The wide alloy wheels fitted with 205/65 tyres would not fit within the MGB wheel arches. The solution was reshaped front and rear wings linked by a modified sill section. At the front, braking was enhanced by the adoption of ventilated discs but anti-lock brakes were not available.

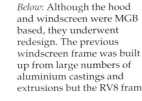

Left: The compact, light and powerful K-series engine that gives the MGF such good performance is of thoroughly modern design. Even in basic form it delivers 118bhp, and the VVC version produces a staggering 143bhp.

Below: A couple of the original drawings penned by Rover Group designer Gerry McGovern. Since the launch of the MGF, Gerry has attended many M.G. meetings and spoken both to people who have bought one of the cars, and to those who just want to know what exciting new cars he is working on – without them learning much!

previously served by the M.G. marque and who now switched allegiance to the Japanese newcomer. With hindsight, the Rover Group would have done better to have had the new car on sale some four or five years earlier than late 1995, when it was eventually made available to the public, but the funds to develop it earlier were just not forthcoming.

Competing Designs

Styling proposals for the new car were commissioned from three different design establishments and each was given the basic layout to work with and the brief that the new car had to be unmistakably an M.G. The eventual style chosen was one proposed by MGA Developments and it was their basic model that was refined and prepared for production by the Rover Group Canley Design Studio under in-house designer Gerry McGovern. The most obvious change that the Rover team made was to introduce styling that echoed the frontal design of both the later MGBs and the RV8. This distinctive M.G. "nose" was a very prominent feature of the design and helped give the new car a visual link with previous models that reached far beyond the superficial addition of a number of octagonal badges.

The final go-ahead from Rover management for the new M.G. really only came in 1992, although the design team had already completed much of the preliminary work and built a number of prototypes. With no previous experience of building cars with this configuration, much testing was needed to achieve the right balance between roadholding, handling and a comfortable ride. The excellent compromise eventually adopted gives the MGF a very smooth ride – even over rough roads – without losing the handling and balance a sports car requires. The engineering solution adopted was to use the "Hydragas" units for the suspension as fitted to the Metro.

The "Hydragas" system employs a fluid to interconnect the front and rear suspension units on each side of the car. The gas-filled units take the place of conventional springs and when a front wheel hits a bump the fluid both compresses the gas within the unit to provide springing and is forced down the interconnecting tube to stiffen the rear unit thus reducing the tendency for the car to pitch on a bumpy surface. Unlike the earlier cars fitted with this system, on the MGF the hydrolastic units are assisted by separate front and rear shock absorbers. To reduce costs modified Metro/Rover 100 subframes are used front and rear to mount the double-wishbone, all-independent suspension. The advantage of the "Hydragas" suspension units over conventional springs lies in the fact that they are particularly useful on a small sports car where providing a stiff suspension can give an uncomfortable ride on poorly-surfaced roads. The refinement of adding separate shock absorbers on the MGF allowed the engineers to tune the handling, and fitting front and rear roll bars reduced body roll when cornering. The result is a comfortable and predictable car that

volume-produced MGF waiting in the wings, this was just what was needed.

Around the time that the idea of a revived MGB with a V8 engine was mooted, the Rover Group were already seriously working on a completely new M.G. sports car. By 1989 the M.G. programme was called the "Phoenix Revival" and the code letters given to the various prototypes were "PR" – presumably they wanted something different from the old Abingdon "EX" codes. One of the prototypes, PR3, was mid-engined and rear drive, and it was

eventually this formula the company adopted for the new car. Traditionally enthusiasts have always felt that sports cars should be rear-wheel drive and the Toyota MR2, said to be one of the rivals looked at by the Rover design team, had successfully adopted the mid-engine layout. The Mazda MX5 design team, ironically, had looked at two popular British sports cars, the MGB and Lotus Elan, and opted for their traditional front-engine, rear-drive layout for the car they were to launch in 1990. This car was an instant success with many customers from precisely the market

Right: A cutaway drawing of the MGF reveals just how the engine is sited behind the seats and the way the vertically-mounted spare wheel sits in the front compartment. Luggage can only be carried in the compartment behind the engine as putting anything extra in the front could compromise the crash protection that the deformable front structure affords the occupants.

Below: The official United Kingdom launch of the MGF was carried out at the Heritage Museum at Gaydon. Stirling Moss and Cecil Kimber's daughter, Jean Cook, remove the cover under the watchful eye of the museum archivist and motoring author, Anders Ditlev Clausager.

was well ahead of its rivals, the Mazda MX5 and Toyota MR2.

The distinctive design, with the low bonnet line and MGB and RV8 styling cues, together with the high tail that houses both the engine and luggage compartments, gave the car a solid, chunky appearance. From some angles the wheels look a little small, but on the road, with the hood up or down, there is no doubting the appeal of the new M.G. When it was launched at the Geneva Motor Show in early 1995 it was an immediate hit and the large amount of press and television coverage it received ensured that the order books soon filled up. Some journalists complained that it was so good it lacked the excitement they expected from a sports car, but the average buyer found the car safe and easy to drive fast – truly a worthy inheritor of the M.G. slogan "Safety Fast!"

Sports cars are as much about image and appearance as they are about performance and

Enthusiasts the world over eagerly awaited a completely new M.G. sports car and the arrival of the RV8 had done little to satisfy those craving a thoroughly up-to-date alternative to the ubiquitous "hot hatchback" that had served many of them as sporting transport. When it was unveiled to the press and the public at the 1995 Geneva Motor Show, the MGF created a great deal of interest and orders poured in, although the first cars were not due to be delivered to customers until September that year.

Right: Interior design and styling for all cars had been transformed since the MGB was announced in 1962 and any new M.G. had to look as good as the best on the market. The MGF met most expectations, although some buyers opted to have additional polished wood dashboard inserts and other embellishments. The VVC seats already had part-leather seat facings but, as an option on both models, full leather trim could be fitted after the cars were built.

SPECIFICATION

Model: MGF two-seater roadster

Engine: Four-cylinders, double overhead camshaft 16 valve, water cooled. 80mm x 89mm, 1796cc, 118bhp (1.8i) 143bhp (VVC).

Gearbox: Five-speed synchromesh

Final drive: (1.8i) 3.94:1. Top gear 22.1mph/1000rpm (36kph/1000rpm). (VVC) 4.2:1. Top gear 20.7mph/1000rpm (33kph/1000rpm)

Suspension: Independent with hydragas springs, double wishbones and rack and pinion steering. (Electric power steering optional on 1.8i and standard on VVC)

Dimensions: Wheelbase 7ft 9.5in (2375mm). Track, front 4ft 7in (1400mm), rear 4ft 7.5in (1410mm). Overall length 12ft 10.1in (3914mm).

Unladen weight: (1.8i) 21cwt (1073kg), (VVC) 22cwt (1121kg)

Cost when new: (1.8i) £15,995, (VVC) £17,995

Performance: (From contemporary reports): Top speed (1.8i) 123mph (198kph), (VVC) 131mph (211kph)

Left: The mid-engined layout of the MGF makes access difficult. Routine servicing and checking oil, coolant and other fluids is fairly easy. Long-life spark plugs are specified. To gain access for major work, the rear panel by the hood can be removed. Alternatively, it is possible to remove the engine, transmission and suspension as a unit without too much difficulty.

Left: The instrument panel is one of the most attractive features of the interior of the MGF. The cream-painted faces of the dials contrast well with the black markings and red pointers. The red M.G. logos are a nice touch although there is no shortage of octagonal badges elsewhere on the MGF. However, influenced by Cecil Kimber, this is an M.G. tradition that reached a peak in pre-war days.

Above: The distinctive design, with the low bonnet line and MGB and RV8 styling cues, together with the high tail that houses both the engine and luggage compartments, give the car a solid, chunky appearance. Cleverly, the Rover designers chose to echo the frontal appearance of the earlier cars and this makes them instantly identifiable on the road to other M.G. enthusiasts. With many owners of the MGF having previously run the earlier cars, this latest addition to the marque was quickly accepted as a "true M.G." and they started appearing in numbers at M.G. club events. Here the cars and owners have been warmly welcomed as evidence of the continuation of the marque as the enthusiast's sports car.

Above: The modest overall dimensions of the MGF, as well as the superb ride and handling, make it equally at home on winding country roads or in crowded city centres. This all-round ability is the key to its success in the marketplace.

Below: The side elevation is not the most pleasing aspect of an MGF. The high waist line makes the car look a bit overweight, and the wheels appear too small. However, from other angles the design looks much better and attracts admiring glances.

Above and above right: Outwardly, very little distinguishes the less powerful MGF from the 143bhp VVC, but the faster car gains five-spoke alloy wheels to replace the six-spoke ones fitted to the 1.8i.

Above: The body shell for the MGF is built by Motor Panels at Coventry, a firm well-used to making parts for specialist cars. Another project which they undertook was that of building bodies for the Aston Martin DB7.

handling. Many are bought as second cars for family use and as an alternative to an ordinary small saloon or hatchback, so it is important to have a sports car that is easy to live with and one that can be used as much for shopping trips as for runs in the country on sunny days. M.G.s have usually fulfilled this role admirably and the adaptable MGB provided, indeed still provides, many families with all-year-round transport. The lack of any spare cockpit space in the MGF, a feature shared with its rivals, limits the car's use as family transport, but in its favour are low running costs and depreciation.

Unlike the Oxford-built RV8, the MGF was to be assembled at Longbridge in Birmingham with the body shells produced by Motor Panels at Coventry, who were partners in the MGF project. In an unusual collaboration between a motor manufacturer and a component supplier, the long-established company Motor Panels agreed to find the necessary finance to fund the engineering and tooling costs of the MGF body rather than this investment falling on the hard-pressed finances of the Rover development team. In a deal reminiscent of that struck between John Thornley and Pressed Steel when the MGB was developed over 30 years earlier, the development costs of the MGF body would be recovered from Rover in the final price of the completed bodies. There is no doubt that this arrangement was crucial in ensuring the go-ahead for the new car. In a similar fashion, the soft-top and folding frame engineering was carried out by Pininfarina who went on to supply these parts for the production cars.

A Car Built To Order

In many ways the assembly line for the MGF is less automated than one would expect for such a modern car and, although each assembly operation takes just three minutes, these are all carried out by hand rather than by the use of robots. After being received from Motor Panels, the body shells are cleaned, dipped and seam-sealed before being painted and lacquered. Once allocated a specification – all cars are built to order – the bodies are first fitted with wiring loom, petrol tank, brake pipes, etc. before moving on to the trim track where the interior and the engine compartment are fitted out. With all trim in place and bumpers, lights, etc. installed, the cars are moved on to final assembly where they are united with the front and rear sub-frames that carry the suspension, engine and other mechanical components. Once the brakes, exhaust system and other under-body work is finished, and the wheels are fitted, the few final assembly stages are completed and the car is fuelled up and started so that a computer-controlled final check can be done.

The heart of any sports car is its engine and the 1.8 litre K-series installed in the MGF is a really superb power unit. Rover engineers broke new ground in 1990 when they introduced a new small engine for the Metro and Rover 200 which utilized light alloy castings and the revolutionary technique of bolting the cylinder head, block and sump together with a single set of bolts. For the MGF the capacity of the original 1.4 litre engine has been enlarged to 1.8 litres without increasing its overall size by using "wet liners" for the cylinder bores and a longer-stroke crankshaft. The larger-capacity engine is as smooth as the smaller unit, due largely to the use of much lighter pistons and a stiffer crankshaft. Power output for the 1.8 engine is 118bhp and this is the engine used in the standard MGF. However, the VVC model uses the same basic engine but fitted with variable valve timing to increase maximum power to a massive 143bhp.

The system used by Rover for their variable valve timing differs from that adopted by rivals like Honda and BMW. On the MGF there is a mechanical link that controls the cam lobes that open and close the inlet valves. An eccentric rotating disc controlled by the engine management system adjusts the length of time each inlet valve is open or closed, keeping the valves open longer for maximum power and closed longer for maximum torque. The advantages of obtaining extra power by varying the valve timing is that it comes as a result of greater efficiency; thus the VVC-engined car is as economical on fuel and as easy to drive as the lower powered car –

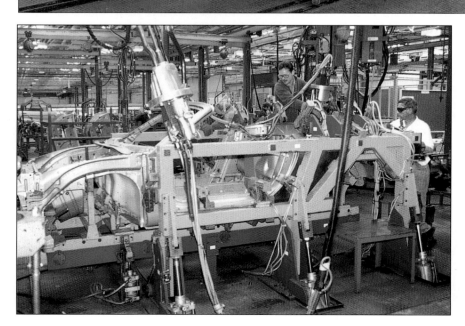

Above: A finished shell being inspected. With modern paint processes it is essential that the panels be as near perfect as possible before painting, as any blemishes are expensive and time-consuming to eradicate later.

Left: One of the framing jigs used to position critical parts of the sub-structure of the MGF before they are welded together. Accuracy is essential and the panels must be positioned to within a tolerance of 0.2mm. Misalignment here could affect not just the fit of the exterior panels, but also the handling of the finished car.

not always the case with performance models. As a bonus the more powerful car is fitted with power steering and anti-lock brakes as standard. The power steering – also available on the ordinary MGF at extra cost – is electric powered as the mid-engined layout precludes the use of one of the more usual hydraulic systems.

The tremendous interest the arrival of the MGF created meant that all the motoring magazines were anxious to get hold of cars to test. Although the MGF was first presented to the public at the Geneva Motor Show in March 1995, the company did not immediately release cars to journalists and it was September before "Autocar" printed their first road-test. Apart from making a few adverse comments about the materials used in the cabin and saying that the car was not quite as exciting to drive as the rival Mazda MX5, the report it published was full of praise for the new M.G. The performance figures recorded by the test team using a standard 1.8i were 0-60mph (97kph) in 8.7 seconds and a top speed of 123mph (198kph). When the more powerful VVC model was made available to them in February 1996, the same magazine recorded a top speed of 131mph (211kph) and an acceleration time to 60mph (97kph) of 7.6 seconds – quick for an 1800cc car.

September 1995 was also the time that the first customers took delivery of their cars – many of which had been ordered well before a finished car had even been seen. The price of the standard 1.8i MGF was set at £15,995, with the VVC costing £17,995. However, as the more powerful car came with power steering and anti-lock brakes as standard, and these cost £1200 extra if ordered for the 1.8i, the additional cost of greater performance and better interior trim was small. In the first year of production over 12,000 cars were built with the company having the capacity to increase this to more than 20,000 per year. Initial demand was strong, especially for the VVC, resulting in long waiting lists at dealers. Export demand from Japan and for left-hand-drive cars for Europe has seen quite a number of cars going to those markets.

The arrival of the MGF re-launched the M.G. marque as providers of modern and affordable sports cars and it is hoped that there will be many more such new models in the future. However, even if by some disaster no more M.G.s were to be produced, we can be certain that the many thousands of current and future owners of all the cars built thus far will continue to write M.G. history by their use of these charismatic vehicles, and that the proud letters "M.G." will still be recognized in countries across the world many years from now.

Below: Rows of brand new MGFs wait at the docks before being loaded on a boat for shipment to Japan. One of the greatest achievements of M.G. cars has been their acceptance overseas.

Right: The MGF is assembled at Longbridge, Birmingham. Here, near the end of the assembly line, an MGF 1.8i is fitted with wheels before undertaking a computer-controlled test.